Palgrave Studies in Financial Services Technology

Series Editor
Bernardo Nicoletti
Rome, Italy

The Palgrave Studies in Financial Services Technology series features original research from leading and emerging scholars on contemporary issues and developments in financial services technology. Falling into 4 broad categories: channels, payments, credit, and governance; topics covered include payments, mobile payments, trading and foreign transactions, big data, risk, compliance, and business intelligence to support consumer and commercial financial services. Covering all topics within the life cycle of financial services, from channels to risk management, from security to advanced applications, from information systems to automation, the series also covers the full range of sectors: retail banking, private banking, corporate banking, custody and brokerage, wholesale banking, and insurance companies. Titles within the series will be of value to both academics and those working in the management of financial services.

More information about this series at
http://www.palgrave.com/gp/series/14627

Rosario Girasa

Regulation of Cryptocurrencies and Blockchain Technologies

National and International Perspectives

palgrave
macmillan

Rosario Girasa
Lubin School of Business
Pace University
Pleasantville, NY, USA

Other publications by the author writing under the name of Roy J. Girasa
Cyberlaw: National and International Perspectives
Corporate Governance and Finance Law
Laws and Regulations in Global Financial Markets
Shadow Banking: Rise, Risks, and Rewards of Non-Bank Financial Services

Palgrave Studies in Financial Services Technology
ISBN 978-3-319-78508-0   ISBN 978-3-319-78509-7   (eBook)
https://doi.org/10.1007/978-3-319-78509-7

Library of Congress Control Number: 2018942528

Printed on acid-free paper

This Palgrave Macmillan imprint is published by the registered company Springer International Publishing AG part of Springer Nature.
The registered company address is: Gewerbestrasse 11, 6330 Cham, Switzerland

To a most remarkable family
Giorgio, Concetta, Rita, and Giuseppe Alescio

Preface

Most people who have read about Bitcoin and numerous other imitators have noted the incredible rise in monetary value of these offerings, leading to questions such as "What in the world is Bitcoin?", "Why is there such madness among individuals purchasing and engaging in not only Bitcoin but also in the technology underlying it?", "What is the identity of its creator?", and many other related questions. Having written several volumes on finance law topics, it was bewildering to come across an entirely new mode of financial transactions that contradicts almost all of the established norms of safety provided by governmental backing of currencies, rules and regulations that essentially keep wrongdoers at bay in their attempts to take advantage of fault lines in the system, and other safety nets.

This author's interest was sparked in part when his undergraduate students spoke about Bitcoin but he was also alerted to the many types of digital coins and tokens, their investment, and the immediate sizeable profits gained through their purchase. It was the first time in decades of teaching when students not only expressed interest in the subject matter of cryptocurrencies but were also investing in them. Thus, this author believes there was little choice but to learn about the new phenomenon and hopefully aid others interested in the subject matter.

Inasmuch as there are innumerable articles that assist the reader in understanding both the nature and how to invest in Bitcoin and other cryptocurrencies, there is little need for a volume repeating what is already widely known. This author, in each of his prior books, was interested in the government's role in safeguarding investors and consumers. Thus, the focus of this volume is the protection of purchasers of the new currencies from the inevitable fraud and other malfeasance that accompanies the world of finance. Although the concentration is on regulations that have and will arise in the United States (U.S.), the actions of other nations are also examined in an attempt to comprehend how nations grapple with Bitcoin, and its offspring. We will review governmental efforts to ban, significantly control, or simply tolerate the inevitable use of cryptocurrencies that cannot be prevented any more than government endeavors to control the use of the Internet. Regardless of how Bitcoin and other coins and tokens fare in the marketplace, it is beyond any reasonable doubt that the underlying technology will profoundly affect how the manifold types of business transactions and social activities transpire.

Having researched alone all of the materials indicated herein, any errors are mine alone. The ideas expressed are not unique but are based on hundreds of articles and sources downloaded from numerous websites globally. It is hoped that this volume brings together the collective undertakings in a manner that both the experienced entrepreneur and average reader will comprehend.

Thanks to all at Palgrave Macmillan who assisted in the publication of this work especially Alison Neuberger for her input, Tula Weis for numerous correspondence and seeing this through, and Ruth Noble for final completion of the administrative details of the text. Thanks also to D. Pavithra Muralikrishna at SPi Global for supervising the production process.

Please note. This volume is not intended to offer legal advice but rather is the author's analysis and opinions based on the numerous articles, commentaries, speeches, regulations, and other material read and downloaded in an attempt to understand the new technologies and provide a text in readable form for students and all others interested in the subject matter. Personal legal questions should be referred to knowledgeable counsel.

Pleasantville, NY, USA   Rosario Girasa

Contents

Acronyms

AICPA	American Institute of Certified Public Accountants
AIFMD	Alternative Investment Fund Managers Directive
AML	Anti-Money Laundering
API	Application Programming Interface
ASIC	Specific Integrated Circuit
ATM	Automated Teller Machine
B2B	Business-to-business
BSA	Bank Secrecy Act
BIS	Bank for International Settlements
BRIC	Brazil, Russia, India, and China
BTC	Unit of Currency or Amount
CBOE	Chicago Board Options Exchange
CEA	Commodity Exchange Act
CFD	Contract for Difference
CFE	CBOE Futures Exchange
CFPB	Consumer Financial Protection Bureau
CFTC	Commodity Futures Trading Commission
CIS	Collective Investment Scheme
CME	Chicago Mercantile Exchange
CPU	Central Processing Unit
CSA	Canadian Securities Administrators
CSBS	Conference of State Bank Supervisors
CSDR	Central Securities Depositories Regulation

DAO	Decentralized Autonomous Organization
d.b.a.	doing business as
DCM	Designated Contract Market
DCO	Digital Clearing Organization
DLT	Distributed Ledger Technology
ECB	European Central Bank
EEU	Eurasian Economic Union
EMIR	European Market Infrastructure Regulation
ENISA	European Union Agency Network and Information Security
ESMA	European Securities and Markets Authority
EU	European Union
FATCA	Foreign Account Tax Compliance Act
FATF	Financial Action Task Force
FBI	Federal Bureau of Investigation
FDIC	Federal Deposit Insurance Corporation
Fed	Federal Reserve Board
FIA	Futures Industries Association
FinCEN	Financial Crimes Enforcement Network
FINRA	Financial Industry Regulatory Authority
FMP	Financial Market Participant
FOREX	Foreign Exchange
FPGA	Field-Programmable Gate Array
FSOC	Financial Stability Oversight Council
FTC	Federal Trade Commission
GPU	Graphics Processing Unit
GSA	Government Services Administration
HSI	Homeland Security Investigations
ICE	Immigration and Customs Enforcement
ICO	Initial Coin Offering
IFPCU	Illicit Finance and Proceeds of Crime Unit
IMF	International Monetary Fund
IOSCO	International Organization of Securities Commissions
IP	Intellectual Property
IPO	Initial Public Offering
IT	Information Technology
ITO	Initial Token Offering
KYC	Know Your Customer
MiFID	Markets in Financial Instruments Directive

MiFIR	Markets in Financial Instruments Regulation
MSB	Money Services Business
NAFTA	North American Free Trade Agreement
NASAA	North American Securities Administrators Association
NDF	Non Deliverable Forward
NFA	National Futures Association
NYSE	New York Stock Exchange
OCC	Office of the Comptroller of the Currency
OECD	Organisation for Economic Co-operation and Development
OM	Offering Memorandum
P2P	Peer-to-Peer
PCAST	President's Council of Advisers on Science and Technology
PCS	Payment, Clearing, and Settlement
SDRs	Special Drawing Rights
SEC	Securities and Exchange Commission
SEF	Swap Execution Facility
SFD	Social Fund for Development
SQL	Structured Query Language
TITANIUM	Tools for the Investigation of Transactions in Underground Markets
UCITs	Undertakings for Collective Investments Securities
UN	United Nations
U.S.	United States
VAT	Value Added Tax
WEF	World Economic Forum

Table of Cases

The Digital Transformation

Introduction

The advent of the Internet and its related technological advancements have inaugurated a transformation in how we think and act that exceed any previous historical inventions and discoveries. We "speak" to each other instantaneously, spend endless quanta of time on cell phones and computers, and have created a totally new way of communicating with one another. Industries, often reluctantly, have undergone digital transformation and disruption in an endeavor to modernize, upgrade and innovate to prevent business failure. They have learned from the oft-cited lessons of Kodak and Polaroid, both which failed to update their technology, resulting in bankruptcy owing to lack of innovation.[1] Digital transformation is occurring at an unparalleled pace in human history causing new innovations to rise rapidly, fed by venture capital and other monetary investments. These enhancements are creating entirely new workforces but also causing displacements of workers unable to adapt to the new technologies. Valuations of new enterprises above $1 billion are literally generated almost overnight, rivaling the entire economies of many nations, for example, Apple ($798 billion), Google's parent company Alphabet ($667 billion), and Microsoft ($571 billion).[2]

© The Author(s) 2018
R. Girasa, *Regulation of Cryptocurrencies and Blockchain Technologies*, Palgrave Studies in Financial Services Technology, https://doi.org/10.1007/978-3-319-78509-7_1

Successful companies have or are adopting new business models to meet the technological revolution. IBM has transformed its mainframe business into technology and business consultancy services; Microsoft has gone from PC royalties to advertising and subscription-based models; and even LEGO has restructured from its near bankruptcy to new digital businesses such as Lego Digital Designer and Lego Mindstorms.[3] The "Big 4" accounting firms are experimenting with blockchain technology for auditing and related services, especially Deloitte with its launch of Rubix, a blockchain that provides advisory services and builds distributed applications for clients worldwide.[4] Legal services are entering the digital arena with firms such as Ross Intelligence leveraging and partnering with Vanderbilt Law and certain law firms to provide legal information from case citations to legal briefs.[5] For example, the uses of blockchain may include the provision of a time-stamped, secured, and scalable record to document when a trademark was first used, manage client transactions through a digital wallet, and render advice to clients in the financial sector on issues arising from the new technology.[6]

Banks are aware of the digital transformation which may make cash obsolete particularly as millennials become the mainstay of personal banking.[7] The Royal Bank of Canada is intensifying its mission by incorporating artificial intelligence and data analytics thereby lessening the need for bricks-and-mortar branches in favor of much more efficient banking online, using its personnel in the remaining branches to focus on complex problem-solving and financial advice.[8] The Federal Reserve Board (FED), has become acutely interested in distributed ledger technology (DLT) as it applies to payments, and clearing and settlement procedures, noting that its systems process some 600 million transactions daily valued at over $12.6 trillion. DLT has the potential to create news ways of immutably and securing stored information, offers identity management, provides for cross-border payments, and other essential uses.[9] While recognizing the challenges of interoperability, ubiquity, and accessibility, nevertheless, it is anticipated that the use of digital currency and DLT will deliver faster payment solutions and enhance the timeliness, cost effectiveness, and convenience of cross-border payments.[10]

The latest innovation generically that seeks to replace historical modes of behavior is that of a new format for currencies. Although banks and other financial institutions have for decades sought to replace checks and related financial instruments with the use of the then current technologies, it appears that money itself will likely diminish in its current form to be replaced or added to by a virtual currency in a form known as "cryptocurrency." In this study, we will discuss the nature of digital currencies, specifically cryptocurrencies such as Bitcoin, the technology underlying the currencies, and the regulatory enactments either proposed or already enacted by federal and state governing authorities.

Definitions and Types of Non-fiat Currencies

Money

Back to Basics. What Is Money?

On this author's office desk is a government issued "One Hundred Trillion Dollars" banknote disseminated by the Reserve Bank of Zimbabwe in 2008 that occurred during the period of hyperinflation from the late 1990s through 2011, emanating from government policies of seizures of private land and the country's participation in the Congo Wars. The sole value of these banknotes is the cost to purchase them as souvenirs or as curios to illustrate the government's failings and the total lack of trust by possessors of such currency.[11] Human beings have used money as a substitute for goods and services for thousands of years. Although one may barter, for example, one's services such as plumbing, legal, or even medical in exchange for another's goods or services, one of the difficulties is matching the needs of both parties and the valuation thereof. The commencement of substitutes led to a variety of means that was acceptable to a broader population allowing individualsto use them as desired rather than by barter, a system that was often unacceptable or inconvenient.

Early exchanges in primitive societies included the use of shells in African cultures, particularly cowrie shells around 1200 B.C., as well as salt, seeds, cattle, and other valued assets. Gradually, metal objects, especially gold bars, were used in Egypt and Mesopotamia about 3000 B.C., which were later transformed into metallic money. Other forms of metallic assets also came into existence including gold rings and other valuable metals. Metallic-like money appeared in China by 1000 B.C., bronze coins from the seventh to the third century B.C., and even leather money was used in the second century B.C. Metallic coins were introduced in Ephesus, Turkey in the seventh century B.C. and used extensively in Greece and Rome soon after.[12] Barter has never been completely banished to history's dustbin but has continued in some form, even among nations, to date.

A form of barter used extensively in the twentieth century was countertrade. At various times, countries or entities within nations have engaged in countertrade whereby large quantities of products or services have been exchanged, particularly when a nation's currency has lost credibility. During World War II and after, nations found countertrade to be beneficial due to the decimation of industrial plants during the war. Companies and individuals in countries that have a trustworthy currency at times chose countertrade in order to avoid imposition of taxes on goods or services exchanged. Nations also participated in countertrade to offset trade imbalances and protect local industries. Usually such trade concerned a seller who desired to convey goods to a country that lacked or had severe limits on the use of hard currency, such as some nations in sub-Sahara Africa and also on the Indian continent.

There are many types of countertrade exemplified by *barter* (exchange of goods or services): *counter purchase* (where a party selling goods or services to another party agrees to buy back a specific product in exchange in the future); *compensation* (where part of the payment is in hard currency); *buyback* (generally, where a company invests in the construction of a plant or other facility and agrees to purchase products manufactured from that facility); *clearing arrangement* (exemplified by the trade between West and East Germany before unification whereby companies in both nations sold goods and services and registered the sales in clearing banks in their respective countries which were then settled at the end of a designated timeframe, any balances becoming the obligation of the obligor country); *switch trade* (where one party provides goods and/or services in exchange for an arrangement to purchase goods from the buying nation); and *offsets* (where a company may construct plants or provide services in another country in order to diminish costs due and owing to the supplier).[13]

Money, in its many emanations, became a substitute for the exchange or barter of goods and services. It is based on the perception of those using the currency that it has an equivalent value for such items. The International Monetary Fund (IMF) defines "money" as anything that may act: (a) as a *store of value* that persons in possession may keep and use at a later time; (b) as a *unit of account* providing a common base for prices; or (c) as a *medium of exchange* that people use and exchange with one another.[14] Historically, the IMF has used a form of digital currency by its creation and distribution of "special drawing rights" (SDRs) commencing in 1969 as an international reserve asset which supplements a member state's official reserves and may be used in exchange for usable currencies. Although the IMF states that SDRs are not a form of currency, nevertheless, they may be used by member states as a voluntary exchange for existing currencies and as a unit of account of the IMF and other international organizations. SDRs are issued in accordance with a member state's *quota*, i.e., a required depository amount is assigned by the IMF to a nation dependent on its financial status. Interest is paid or charged for borrowing on such holdings.[15]

Reasons for the Rise of Virtual Currencies

There are a number of factors that gave rise to virtual currencies in the form of cryptocurrencies, as follows:

- *Costs of third-party servicing.* A revolution in the mode of the types of currencies used for payment, clearing, settlement, and other services is inevitable. As noted in *The Economist*, the technological revolution in digital technology has brought about significant progress in bringing financial services to previously underserved areas, particularly in sub-Sahara Africa.[16] In developed countries, the cost of such services is staggeringly high with Americans paying some $141 billion in fees and interest in 2015, much of which went to service loans, credit cards, and other services.
- *Lack of security.* There are a multitude of problems in connection with the current system of payments by cash, credit cards, automated teller

machines (Atms), and other current modes of payment for goods and services. As witnessed on numerous occasions in the past years, hacking of credit cards and even ATMs is an ongoing problem inasmuch as cybersecurity systems in place are subject to major tampering, as witnessed by cybercriminals' access to some 143 million Americans highly personal information including names, social security numbers, birth dates, addresses, and even drivers' licenses.[17] There were many other reported breaches which raise the specter of the oft-quoted comment by Scott McNealy of Sun Microsystems who said: "You have zero privacy. Get over it."[18]

- *Lack of convertibility or unavailability of funds in poor countries.* Other problems that affect those with less than excellent credit, particularly those in poorer third-world type economies, include the cost of access and interest charges for credit cards; lack of convertibility of the national currency (e.g., Venezuela in recent times); illiteracy, which affects one's ability to engage in financial transactions; inconvenience of cash wherein merchants accept cash in small denominations only; lack of transnational exchanges of currency except by payment often at poor exchange rates coupled with sizeable fees; the sums banks and related institutions charge for certain credit and debit card use as well as for an abundance of other services; and even the refusal of cash by some merchants. Thus, Bitcoin and subsequent digital currency facilities with their blockchain foundation provide a partial response to the negative aspects of the current financial system. Inasmuch as traditional banking services may be unavailable and a large percentage of the world's poor lack bank accounts, the forthcoming digital technologies offer them possible alternatives.
- *Anonymity or pseudonymity.* This covers the many users who distrust governments' alleged invasion of privacy but also includes wrongdoers who commit criminal acts, engage in terrorism, or want to avoid tax payments.
- *Universality of particular cryptocurrencies.* Cryptocurrencies like Bitcoin are exchangeable anywhere they are accepted and not forbidden, without the need for currency exchangers or other third-party intervention.
- *Inevitable modernization of payments.* It clearly appears in hindsight that millennials, who live by the use of smart phones and other computer

technology, would view fiat currencies (see below) derogatorily due to their inconvenience, cost, and other annoyances.

- *Profit motivation.* The run-up in value of cryptocurrencies has persuaded many, even those of modest means, of the possibility of substantial returns on money invested in the new technologies.
- *The trust factor.* The key to money, as illustrated above, is the trust that its possessors have in the value and use of the currency. If a large percentage of the population does not have faith in the currency, then its value declines. There is trust in fiat money in the United States and the European Union (EU) because of the central banks' guarantees of payment. Although Bitcoin (and other cryptocurrencies) has no such backing, the technology underlying it does assure a high degree of trust by its near-guarantee of immunity from hacking, transactional transparency, reliability, simplicity and speed, and security against fraud and cybercrime.[19]

Digital services are a response and means to greatly lowering costs both to financial institutions and their customers. Digital technology has extended to the use of smart phones and computers to engage in deposits, transactions in securities and other transactions, and, when coupled with ATMs, has lessened the need for tellers and other banking personnel.[20] The next innovation is the substitution of greatly enhanced digital technology that will be transformative in almost unimaginable ways. In the near future, cash will be viewed just as primitive as the Underwood typewriter of old is to students preparing research papers for class today. Credit cards have already served comparable needs for consumers and may be on the descent, thereby deeply discounting the costs to merchants and consumers. The latest modernization and its regulatory issues are the focus of this book.

Types of Currencies

Currency (*real currency* or *fiat currency*) is defined as "the coin and paper money of the United States or of any other country that is designated as legal tender and that circulates and is customarily used and accepted as a medium of exchange in the country of issuance."[21] It includes U.S. notes and silver certificates, Federal Reserve notes, and official foreign bank notes. *Electronic money* (e-money) may be defined as "electronically, including magnetically, stored monetary value as represented by a claim on the issuer which is issued on receipt of funds for the purpose of making payment transactions and which is accepted by a natural or legal person other than the electronic money issuer."[22] Examples of e-money include money stored on a chip card or on a hard drive in a personal computer. E-money is generally denominated in the same currency as central bank or commercial bank money and is usually redeemable at par value or in cash.[23] *Digital currency* is a medium of exchange and may act as a currency where accepted, but lacks the attributes of real currency. Digital currency is denominated in its own units of value rather than being directly connected to the national currency. Distinguishing between digital currencies, virtual currencies, and cryptocurrencies often leads to differing interpretations. The authors of an IMF study appear to present the most logical explanation of the generic and specific sequential taxonomy of the three modes of currencies, in descending order as follows:

- *Digital currencies* represent value denominated in legal tender such as PayPal, e-money, or may have their own value based not on the national or other governmental currency but on the law of supply and demand, i.e., the value a person possessing them and attributing to them from actual usage or based on current posted values.
- *Virtual currencies* represent a new asset class that competes and may eventually overtake fiat currencies. They are currencies not denominated as legal tender and may be either:

  – *convertible (open)*—can be exchanged for real-world goods, services, money (e.g., Bitcoin), and which may be:

    • *centralized*—with a central authority or trusted third-party, convertible to fiat money, such as WebMoney;[24] or
    • *decentralized*—peer-to-peer, without a central authority or trusted third party ledger; or

– *non-convertible* (*closed)*—such as their use as game coins; not exchangeable for fiat currencies.

• *Cryptocurrencies* make up a subset of virtual currencies that uses technology from cryptography to validate the transfer of transactions as exemplified by hundreds of such currencies such as Bitcoin, Ethereum and numerous other formats using blockchain as the underlying technology.[25]

Digital Currencies

A *digital currency* is an intangible mode of currency in electronic form whereby payments may be transferred between parties through the use of current technologies (computers, the Internet, and smart phones). It is used for payments made person-to-person or with entities for common purchases of goods and services both domestically and internationally, or may be confined to gaming or social networks.[26] It may be either a *fiat* (real) currency (e.g., e-money) or a *non-fiat* currency (e.g. a virtual currency). It is borderless and occurs instantaneously just as speedily as communication by email but may be dependent on governmental restrictions and access. The term "digital currency" is often used synonymously with virtual currency but encompasses all types of currencies that have an electronic format.

Virtual Currencies

A *virtual currency* is a digital representation of value that is not government or central bank issued which can be digitally traded and functions as a: (1) medium of exchange; (2) unit of account; or (3) store of value.[27] Rather than possessing status like the legal tender of a fiat currency, such as physical coins or bills, it is generally not widely used or circulated and has no government backing. It is distinct from *e-money* which is a fiat currency that transfers value by electronic means but possesses the characteristic of legal tender. A virtual currency may operate like a so-called "real" currency but lacks legal status in the United States. Its value is what users or traders ascribed to it.[28]

A *convertible (or opened) virtual currency* refers to unofficial convertibility or exchangeability as proposed and accepted by the participants, which may include exchange for fiat currency, property, or other forms of value. The primary example is Bitcoin which can be used to purchase goods, real property, or services from parties accepting the exchange as equivalent value with the understanding that it is not government backed. A *nonconvertible virtual currency* is a form of centralized currency issued by a central authority or administrator limited almost exclusively to particular uses and parties, mostly for gaming purposes or sites such as Amazon. Other examples include Q coins, Project Entropia Dollars and the like.[29]

A convertible virtual currency may be either *centralized* or *decentralized*. A *centralized virtual currency* is one that has a central authority or administrator that sets the rules, issues the currency, maintains a central payment ledger, and may redeem or withdraw the currency. It may have a "floating" exchange rate or be "pegged" with the former based on market supply and demand and the latter determined by the central administrator, usually based on gold, a basket of currencies, or other real-world values. Examples include WebMoney, World of Warcraft gold, and PerfectMoney. A *decentralized virtual currency*, exemplified by Bitcoin, is without a central administrator or oversight but is peer-to-peer (person-to-person) and its value is determined by the parties entering into such transactions.[30]

Non-convertible (or closed) virtual currencies are decentralized, i.e., they require a central authority to act as an administrator. They operate in a closed environment specific to a virtual domain such as game playing whereby the user must conform to the rules set forth by the administrator, usually from an online store. Any attempt to evade the rules of the game may result in termination of the user's access or other penalties. They are used for online games where the holder may trade for other in-game online tools or currency. Other examples may include credit cards or gift cards that are only redeemable at the store; frequent flyer air miles; video arcade tokens; and other restricted uses. Store gift cards and other restricted use currencies are theoretically able to be given freely (as most gifts are) or may even be sold to other persons willing to accept the currency with its restrictive use. Unlike convertible currencies, they are restricted in number, are not liquid, and easily lost through misuse or theft.

Cryptocurrencies

The word *crypto* has many meanings depending on its use as a noun, adjective, or in connection with particular modes of study. When applied in connection to currencies, we call it a *cryptocurrency*, defined as "a digital decentralized convertible currency or medium of exchange using encryption technology to verify its exchange and hinder counterfeiting."[31] It is *mined* at a mathematically controlled rate, is anonymous, is reliant on public and private keys to exchange value on a peer-to-peer basis, and its supply is based on free-market demand.[32] The term is often used interchangeably with convertible, decentralized virtual currency. Bitcoin and Ethereum are leading examples of cryptocurrencies. In the context of most commentaries, cryptocurrency is synonymous with virtual currency although, theoretically, a distinction should be drawn between the two types of currencies.

The discussion below will focus on the generic terms of virtual currencies and cryptocurrencies and their regulation.

Key Actors in Digital Technology[33]

Although digital and non-fiat forms of currencies have been utilized for decades, nevertheless, the current emanation is substantively far superior and complex. The players in the latest innovative financial evolution are as follows:

- *Inventors* (creators). The major figure who initially created the revolution of DLT is the mysterious figure(s) of Satoshi Nakamoto, who is or are responsible for the creation of Bitcoin which used as its basis a form of blockchain technology, discussed in greater detail hereinafter. Alternative versions of blockchain then evolved separate from Bitcoin so that an almost infinite multitude of players could utilize the positive benefits of DLT (e.g., government agencies, financial institutions, private businesses, professional firms, and individuals) due to its alleged total imperviousness from hacking and thus affording total privacy.

Among the emanations evolving from blockchain are: smart contracts; security by "proof of stake" (groups called "miners" are able to use computing power for decision-making and have "proof of work"); and "blockchain scaling" (acceleration of blockchain transactions).[34] Another major inventor is Vitalik Buterin, who created the Ethereum blockchain, which differs from Bitcoin (discussed at greater length below) in transaction time, the amount of Ether distributed, the method of costing transactions and other differences. The Walt Disney Company created Dragonchain which is another form of blockchain and is also a further evolution of Disney's prior animatronics and digital animation creations.[35]

- *Issuers or administrators.* Following the dizzying success of Bitcoin, there are a multitude of individuals and companies creating and sponsoring a large variety of virtual currencies and other innovations, maintaining ledgers, and redeeming virtual currency. Their activities will inevitably transform how the financial and social world operates.
- *Miners.* Miners generate new virtual currency by utilizing special computer hardware, usually with ASIC-centric machines that solve cryptographic (mathematical) problems in return for which bitcoin, Ether, or other forms of cryptocurrency tokens or awards may be issued in return.[36] The word "miners" is derived from traditional miners who dug mines in search of valuable minerals such as diamonds. Modern "miners" validate, often as a group, a set of transactions called a "block."
- *Processing service providers.* These are firms that provide the means of transferring virtual currencies from one user to another. There are numerous companies formed and are being created to provide these services (e.g., DC POS, Coinfy, CoinCorner, Coinbase).[37]
- *Users.* There are an almost infinite number of users of the technology with applications being added daily and exponentially as the technology takes hold. Among the major areas of uses are financial services including international payments; securities trades; improvement of capital markets; use of smart contracts; improvement of online identity management; regulatory compliance; protection against money laundering and theft of assets; healthcare services given the need for

privacy protection of patients' data and records; real estate transactions; record management; cybersecurity; accounting; and numerous other uses. In addition, there are the people connected to these areas.[38]

- *Wallet.* A virtual currency "wallet" is a secure medium that is used to store, send, and receive digital currencies such as Bitcoin. Almost all coins issued require the use of the particular wallet to store the designated cryptocurrency. The wallet is actually a private key containing a secure digital code known only by the person possessing the cryptocurrency together with the public key used to send and receive coins.[39] Individuals and firms engaged in mining are not completely risk free as evidenced by the theft of some 4736.42 BTC (bitcoins) on December 6, 2017 valued at $78.3 million from the cryptocurrency mining marketplace, NiceHash, that was founded in 2014. The methodology used to accomplish the theft has not been revealed and was being investigated by the company and governmental authorities.[40]

- *Wallet provider.* A wallet provider is an entity that uses software applications or other means to enable the user to store, hold, and transfer virtual currencies as well as provide the means of maintaining a customer's balance online or offline, and security.

- *Exchanges.* Exchanges are individuals or companies, almost always businesses, who operate analogously to stock exchanges by exchanging convertible virtual currency for fiat money or for other virtual currencies, precious metals, and other comparable assets and vice versa. Bitcoin has become mainstream with the announcement that Chicago's two largest financial exchanges, the Chicago Mercantile Exchange (CME) and the Chicago Board Options Exchange (CBOE) have made available Bitcoin futures that investors can engage in by shorting or otherwise, thereby giving legitimacy to these cryptocurrency trades.[41] On December 10, 2017, trading on Bitcoin was inaugurated by CBOE and trading had to be shut down due to the frenzy which caused the price of Bitcoin to surge by 26 percent. The CME launch was to take place on December 18, 2017 and proceeded to do so only to witness the extreme volatility of the futures.[42]

- *Trading platforms.* A trading platform is the means whereby currencies are exchanged. The most well-known exchange platform for the exchange of foreign currencies is FOREX, which enables parties to exchange currencies of different countries often coupled with a short-term gain for a fee. The ascendance of virtual currencies added a new wrinkle to the conversion inasmuch as trading may involve a closed virtual currency between two parties without the intervention of a third party. Nevertheless, there are numerous platforms that have arisen to engage in electronic trading of virtual currencies, particularly by parties who wish or may only be able to afford a percentage ownership of the cryptocurrencies made available for purchase. They permit the exchange of fiat currencies for digital currencies. The exchanges may be private or open to the public. The exchanges vary in fees, verification requirements, exchange rates, and other features. Among the exchanges are Coinbase, Binance, CoinMama, Bittrex, CEX.IO, and Bitfinex.[43] Investors are cautioned to be wary about platform trading especially, according to the Federal Bureau of Investigation (FBI), with respect to schemes operated by those who falsely represent that their platforms afford above-average market returns at below-market risk through the trading of bank instruments.[44]
- *Numerous other actors.* These may include merchants, brokers and dealers, software developers, and various other potential actors engaged in the latest innovative advances in virtual currencies.

Benefits and Risks of Digital Currencies

Benefits of Digital Currencies

As with almost all technological innovations, there are benefits and risks associated with the latest advances. Benefits include:

- Verification of identity;
- Significant reduction in costs due to the removal of intermediaries such as banks in the payment processes;

- Speed of money transfers by the elimination of clearing houses;
- Facilitation of micro-payments for low-cost online goods and services;
- Reduction of exposure risks that may occur when transacting bearer instruments;
- Use by those unable to use banking and credit facilities owing to lack of credit (e.g. having refugee status or lacking a credit history)[45]; and
- Recording of transactions including deeds and other indicia of property ownership.

The uses which may have both positive and negative outcomes are:

- A store of value—they are comparable to precious metals in that they do not ordinarily pay dividends or interest but unlike metals are assets that may be divisible and portable;
- Trading—virtual currencies may be purchased, sold, and act as security. As with other assets they may result in capital gains or losses but, at least at this juncture, they are much more volatile causing heightened speculation;
- Payments and transactions—may be used where accepted as payment for real and personal property or fees; and
- Transfer of money—may be utilized at a lower cost internationally to transfer remittances or for similar purposes.[46]

Risks of Digital Currencies

The negative aspects of digital currencies include:

- Lack of acceptance by banks and the protection afforded by them and by merchants;
- Loss of interest on deposits;
- Security concerns such as use by terrorists, drug dealers, money launderers, and other criminal elements;
- Currency volatility;[47]

- Payment beneficiary identification—loss of identity, for example, through death or mental incompetence may cause loss of holdings and transactions;
- Limited user base;
- Uncertainty concerning future regulation and tax treatment;
- Cyber-threats such as hacking, theft, and loss;[48]
- Cross-national nature makes prosecutions very difficult;
- Lack of governmental backstops;
- Lack of backing by other secure assets; and
- Lack of intrinsic value.

U.S. Government Agencies' Risks Advisories

Commodity Futures Trading Commission (CFTC)

The Commodity Futures Trading Commission (CFTC) categorized risks of virtual currencies as:

- *Operational risks*—virtual currencies, having many different platforms, are not subject to supervision that otherwise applies to regulated exchanges; these platforms may be missing critical safeguards and customer protection;
- *Cybersecurity risks*—some platforms may commingle customer assets which may affect whether or how one can withdraw the currency; and some may be vulnerable to hacks resulting in theft of virtual currency or loss of customer assets;
- *Speculative risks*—virtual currency is subject to substantial volatility and price swings often due to inadequate trading volume; promises of guaranteed returns may be part of fraudulent schemes; and
- *Fraud and manipulation risk*—depending on the platforms, they may be vulnerable to hacks resulting in theft of virtual currency and loss of assets, Ponzi schemes, and fraudulent "bucket shop" schemes.[49]

An example of the risks is the theft of $30, 950, 010 USDT (a cryptocurrency pegged to the U.S. dollar)[50] that was removed from the Tether

Treasury wallet on November 19, 2017 and transferred to an unknown Bitcoin address. The company, in announcing the theft, stated that it was in the process of recovering the stolen funds and further warned potential purchasers of the funds that none would be honored.[51]

Consumer Financial Protection Bureau (CFPB)

The Consumer Financial Protection Bureau (CFPB) has also posted consumer advisories noting risks as stated above by the CFTC and adding problems associated with bitcoins. Among the added risks were: (1) persons alleging they were exchange representatives to whose accounts moneys were transferred to purchase bitcoins but the exchanges never transpired; and (2) Bitcoin kiosks that are connected to the Internet to permit the exchange of cash for bitcoins appear to be ATMs but do not function as traditional ATMs in that they are not connected to a bank, lack the safeguards of bank ATMs, often charge large transaction fees as high as 7 percent, may well have high exchange rates, and when the insertion of a wrong 64-character public key can result in funds being sent to another person; and that the loss of the private key may cause a total loss of the bitcoins.[52] Initially, the Bureau had few complaints pertaining to virtual currency transactions (six in 2016) but in 2017 and after there have been hundreds of complaints from the inability to access funds within the time period promised, transaction or service problems, to fraud.[53]

Although Bitcoin and other forms of digital currencies have been associated with money laundering and unlawful drug transactions owing to the anonymity provided by bitcoins, nevertheless, it has been suggested that these risks are overestimated. The ownership of virtual currency is public thereby permitting substantial analysis of the transactions. Bitcoins have come out from undercover to be used by large companies internationally.[54] A possible contrary view was voiced by the new chairman of the Federal Reserve, Jerome Powell,[55] who warned that central banks engaging in issuing digital currencies are vulnerable to cyberattacks, criminal activities, and privacy concerns. He stated further that there are tradeoffs between strengthening security and enabling illegal activity. Advance cryptography, while reducing vulnerability to cyberattacks, also facilitates unlawful activity.[56]

Government Services Administration (GSA)

The GSA and other federal agencies are exploring the use of DLTs like blockchain for financial management, procurement, IT asset and supply chain management, smart contracts, intellectual property, etc. through its Emerging Citizen Technology program. The program launched the U.S. Federal Blockchain platform for federal agencies and U.S. businesses interested in exploring DLT and its implementation within government. It hosted the first U.S. Federal Blockchain Forum on July 18, 2017, uniting more than 100 federal managers from dozens of unique agencies to discuss use cases, limitations, and solutions.[57]

Securities and Exchange Commission (SEC)

The Securities and Exchange Commission (SEC) has issued a series of investor bulletins warning of the risks associated with initial coin offerings (ICOs) and other digital related offerings. Its Office of Investor Education and Advocacy issued a report on July 25, 2017 cautioning issuers and investors that virtual coins or tokens offered may be securities depending on the facts and circumstances of each ICO and may have to comply with registration requirements under the securities laws. It also cautioned investors to be wary of claims that an offering is exempt from registration, particularly if investors are not accredited or are described as crowdfunders. Investors are advised to ask what the moneys invested will be used for and the rights the virtual coin or token provide. Investors are particularly warned about persons using innovative technology to commit fraud or theft. The lack of a central authority and the international scope of offerings may preclude governmental intervention and assistance. Issuers are cautioned about compliance with applicable federal and state registration requirements.[58]

In a follow-up alert, the SEC's Office of Investor Education and Advocacy repeated earlier warnings to investors due to the increasing use of ICOs by developers, businesses, and individuals who may use the offerings for publicity purposes to enhance the price of a company's stock.

The SEC advises it may suspend trading under circumstances where there is a lack of current accurate information about the company; when questions arise about the accuracy of publicly available information; and when there are concerns about the trading in the stock, particularly by insiders who may engage in market manipulation such as by "pump-and-dump" schemes. Investors additionally were given tips before making investments including: research about the company; caution regarding stock promotions; possible microcap fraud; online blogs; promotional and press releases; frequent changes in a company's name, management, and type of business; and other cautionary guidelines.[59]

Immigration and Customs Enforcement (ICE)

Immigration and Customs Enforcement (ICE) is particularly concerned with the unlawful use of virtual currency at an international level. Its HSI (Homeland Security Investigations) Illicit Finance and Proceeds of Crime Unit (IFPCU) operates in conjunction with members of the compliant virtual exchange industry and with the financial industry to combat the movement of illicit funds through the financial services industry. Among its activities is the expansion of its knowledge base by overcoming technological obstacles its agents encounter involving the emerging technologies such as blockchain; investigator training and procurement of equipment to enable investigators to combat illicit online activity; and collaboration with industry leaders to acquire the latest innovative forensic tools to analyze and identify information through the blockchain.

Federal Reserve Board (FED)

The FED does have an interest in the digital economy inasmuch as the payment, clearing, and settlement (PCS) processes involve some 600 million transactions per day. Accordingly, as stated in a study of DLT, it has expressed a keen interest in the development of innovations that affect the structural design and functioning of the financial markets.

European Union Agency for Network and Information Security (ENISA)

The European Union Agency Network and Information Security (ENISA), which is the center for cybersecurity in Europe headquartered in Greece, repeated many of the concerns stated above and added or modified them, as follows: (1) *key and wallet management*—the need to protect one's private key which a malicious user may attempt to discover or reproduce; (2) *cryptography risks*—the need to follow stringent key management policies and procedures to avoid software programs used to generate keys that are weak and vulnerable to attack; (3) *attacks on consensus protocol*—the concern about being vulnerable to a "consensus hijack" or a "51 percent attack" where a malicious party may try to obtain more than 50 percent of the computing power of the entire network and possibly trigger double-spending attacks; (4) *distributed denial of service*—the use of large numbers of spam transactions in the cryptocurrency network by multiple users that may cause denial of services (this actually occurred in March 2016); (5) *smart contract management*—the substitution of code for legal language increases the complexity of the contract and requires skill usage or else is open to human error; (6) *illegal use*—terrorist and/or criminal usage; (7) *privacy*—the E.U. General Data Protection Regulation[60] may be violated by the public nature and permanency of the ledger because it requires deletion of personal data when no longer necessary; and (8) *future challenges*—the technology, especially that of quantum computing, may impede the security of algorithms and protocols.[61]

Nobel Laureates' Concerns

Two Nobel Laureates in Economics expressed their apprehensions concerning virtual currencies, particularly, Bitcoin. Professor Robert J. Shiller of Yale University noted at the World Economic Forum (WEF) that while Bitcoin is a clever idea it will not be a permanent part of our lives. Its underlying technology, blockchain, will have other applications. At the WEF there appeared to be a consensus that fiat money (cash) is going out of style.[62] Shiller said at another conference in Vilnius, Lithuania in December, 2017, "Bitcoin, it's just absolutely exciting," He noted that the concept of Bitcoin as anti-government and anti-regulation is a wonderful story, "if it were only true." Another Nobel Laureate, Joseph Stiglitz, of Columbia University, expressed the view that Bitcoin should be outlawed inasmuch as it does not serve any socially useful function.[63]

In the chapter entitled "Technology Underlying Cryptocurrencies and Types of Cryptocurrencies," we examine the technology underlying Bitcoin and other cryptocurrencies and examine some that have created a revolution in the way in which virtual currencies are currently exchanged and their increasing use in the near future.

Notes

1. Chunka Mui, *How Kodak Failed*, Forbes, Jan. 18, 2012, https://www. forbes.com/sites/chunkamui/2012/01/18/how-kodak-failed/#6550 abbc6f27, and Ankush Chopra, *How Kodak and Polaroid fell victim to the dark side of innovation*, Betanews, (2009), https://betanews. com/2013/12/12/how-kodak-and-polaroid-fell-victim-to-the-dark-side-of-innovation/
2. Matt Egan, *Facebook and Amazon hit $500 billion milestone*, CNN Money, Jul. 27, 2017, http://money.cnn.com/2017/07/27/investing/ facebook-amazon-500-billion-bezos-zuckerberg/index.html
3. World Economic Forum, *Digital Transformation of Industries: In collaboration with Accenture,* White Paper, (Jan. 2016), http://reports.weforum. org/digital-transformation/wp-content/blogs.dir/94/mp/files/pages/ files/digital-enterprise-narrative-final-january-2016.pdf
4. Prableen Bajpai, *Big 4 Accounting Firms Are Experimenting With Blockchain And Bitcoin*, NASDAQ, Jul. 27, 2017, http://www.nasdaq. com/article/big-4-accounting-firms-are-experimenting-with-block-chain-and-Bitcoin-cm812018
5. *Ross Intelligence*, Forbes Profile (2018), https://www.forbes.com/profile/ ross-intelligence/
6. Peter Chawaga, *Legal Field Embraces Promising Use Cases for Blockchain Tech*, Bitcoin Magazine, Apr. 11, 2017, http://www.ozy.com/acumen/ will-millennials-make-cash-obsolete/81212

7. Millennials consist of over 83 million persons in the U.S. as of 2015, substantially growing in number each year, and who prefer banking through smartphones. Their usage far exceeds that of baby boomers (post-World War II population), Poornima Apte, *Will Millennials Make Cash Obsolete?*, The Daily Dose, Oct. 5, 2017, http://www.ozy.com/acumen/will-millennials-make-cash-obsolete/81212

8. Joy Macknight, *RBC CEO Dave McKay looks to stay ahead of technology*, The Banker: Transactions and Technology, Feb. 10, 2017, http://www.thebanker.com/Transactions-Technology/RBC-CEO-Dave-McKay-looks-to-stay-ahead-of-technology

9. David Mills, Kathy Wang, Brendan Malone, Anjana Ravi, Jeff Marquardt, Clinton Chen, Anton Badev, Timothy Brezinski, Linda Fahy, Kimberley Liao, Vanessa Kargenian, Max Ellithorpe, Wendy Ng, and Maria Baird (2016). *Distributed ledger technology in payments, clearing, and settlement*, Finance and Economics Discussion Series 2016-095. Washington: Board of Governors of the Federal Reserve System, https://doi.org/10.17016/FEDS.2016.095

10. U.S. Federal Reserve System, *Strategies for Improving the U.S. Payment System: Federal Reserve Next Steps in the Payments Improvement Journey*, Sept. 6, 2017, https://www.federalreserve.gov/newsevents/pressreleases/files/other20170906a1.pdf

11. Steve H. Hanke, *Zimbabwe's Hyperinflation the Correct Number is 89 Sextillion Percent*, (undated), The World Post, https://www.huffingtonpost.com/steve-h-hanke/zimbabwes-hyperinflation_b_10283382.html. The country indicated would be converting its currency to that of the U.S. dollar.

12. For brief histories of money see History World, *History of Money*, http://www.historyworld.net/wrldhis/PlainTextHistories.asp?historyid=ab14 and Mary Bellis, *The History of Money*, THOUGHTCO, Mar. 26, 2017, https://www.thoughtco.com/history-of-money-1992150

13. Tyler, *What is Counter Trade?* Barter News Weekly, Mar. 11, 2010, https://www.barternewsweekly.com/2010/03/what-is-counter-trade/

14. Irena Asmundson and Ceyda Oner, *What is Money?*, 49 Finance and Development No. 3, Sept., 2012, International Monetary Fund, http://www.imf.org/external/pubs/ft/fandd/2012/09/basics.htm

15. The value of an SDR is based on a basket of five currencies (U.S. dollar, euro, Chinese renminbi, Japanese yen, and British pound), International Monetary Fund, *Special Drawing Rights*, Apr. 21, 2017, http://www.imf.

org/en/About/Factsheets/Sheets/2016/08/01/14/51/Special-Drawing-Right-SDR

16. *The third great wave*, The Economist, Oct. 3, 2014, https://www.economist.com/news/special-report/21621156-first-two-industrial-revolutions-inflicted-plenty-pain-ultimately-benefited

17. Sara Ashley O'Brien, *Giant Equifax data breach: 143 million could be affected*, CNN Tech, Sept. 8, 2017, http://money.cnn.com/2017/09/07/technology/business/equifax-data-breach/index.html

18. Steve Tobak, *You Have No Privacy-Get Over It*, Fox Business, Jul. 31, 2013, http://www.foxbusiness.com/features/2013/07/31/have-no-privacy-get-over-it.html

19. IBM, *Forward Together: Three ways blockchain Explorers chart a new direction*, https://www-935.ibm.com/services/studies/csuite/pdf/GBE03835USEN-00.pdf

20. *Underserved and overlooked*, The Economist, at 57–58, Sept. 9, 2017.

21. Internal Revenue Service, *IRS Virtual Currency Guidance: Virtual Currency Is Treated as Property for U.S. Federal Tax Purposes; General Rules for Property Transactions Apply*, https://www.irs.gov/newsroom/irs-virtual-currency-guidance

22. Directive 2009/110/EC of the European Parliament and of the Council of 16 September 2009, *On the taking up, pursuit and prudential supervision of the business of electronic money institutions amending Directives 2005/60/EC and 2006/48/EC and repealing Directive 2000/46/EC* (Text with EEA relevance, http://eur-lex.europa.eu/legal-content/en/ALL/?uri=CELEX:32009L0110)

23. Bank For International Settlements, *Digital Currencies,* Nov. 2015, at 4, https://www.bis.org/cpmi/publ/d137.htm

24. WebMoney, according to its website, is a universal money transfer system used by some 34 million people to keep track of one's funds, attract funding, resolve disputes, and make secure transactions, https://www.wmtransfer.com/eng/information/short/index.shtml

25. Dong He, Karl Habermeier, Ross Leckow, Vikram Kyriakos-Saad, Hiroko Oura, Tahsin Saadi Sedik, Natalia Stetsenko, Concepcion Verdugo-Yepes, *Virtual Currencies and Beyond: Initial Considerations,* IMF Discussion Note SDN/16/03, Jan. 2016, https://www.researchgate.net/publication/298915094_Virtual_Currencies_and_Beyond_Initial_Considerations

26. Techopedia, *What is Digital Currency?*, https://www.techopedia.com/definition/6702/digital-currency
27. For definitions and lengthy discussions, see U.S. Gov't Accountability Off., GAO-14-496, Virtual Currencies: Emerging Regulatory, Law Ernforcement, and Consumer Protection Challenges, May 29, 2014, http://www.gao.gov/assets/670/663678.pdf
28. New York Title 23, Ch. I, Part 200.2 defines "virtual currency" as follows:

> (p) *Virtual Currency* means any type of digital unit that is used as a medium of exchange or a form of digitally stored value. Virtual Currency shall be broadly construed to include digital units of exchange that (i) have a centralized repository or administrator; (ii) are decentralized and have no centralized repository or administrator; or (iii) may be created or obtained by computing or manufacturing effort. Virtual Currency shall not be construed to include any of the following:

> (1) digital units that (i) are used solely within online gaming platforms, (ii) have no market or application outside of those gaming platforms, (iii) cannot be converted into, or redeemed for, Fiat Currency or Virtual Currency, and (iv) may or may not be redeemable for real-world goods, services, discounts, or purchases.

29. There are numerous definitional sources. A primary one relied upon herein is The Financial Action Task Force (FATF), *Virtual Currencies: Key Definitions and Potential AML/CFT Risks,* Jun. 2014, http://www.fatf-gafi.org/media/fatf/documents/reports/Virtual-currency-key-definitions-and-potential-aml-cft.pdf
30. *Id.*
31. Investopedia defines *cryptocurrency* as "a digital or virtual currency that uses cryptography for security." http://www.investopedia.com/terms/c/cryptocurrency.asp. The European Union Agency for Network and Information Security (ENISA) defines *cryptocurrency* as "a math-based, decentralised convertible virtual currency that is protected by cryptography, i.e., it incorporates principles of cryptography to implement a distributed, decentralised, secure information economy." *ENISA Opinion Paper on Cryptocurrencies in the EU*, Sept. 2017, www.enisa.europa.eu
32. Andrew Wagner, *Digital* vs. *Virtual Currencies*, Bitcoin Magazine, Aug. 22, 2014, https://www.google.com/search?q= Andrew+Wagner,+Digital+vs.+Virtual+Currencies+(Aug.+22,+2014)+BITCOIN+MAGAZINE,

&rls=com.microsoft:en-US&ie=UTF-8&oe=UTF-8&startIndex=
&startPage=1&gws_rd=ssl

33. This segment relies heavily on the comments made by the latest update by the European Central Bank on Virtual Currencies. European Central Bank, *Virtual currency schemes – a further analysis*, Feb. 15, 2015, https://www.ecb.europa.eu/pub/pdf/other/virtualcurrencyschemesen.pdf

34. Vinay Gupta, *A Brief History of Blockchain*, Harvard Business Review, Feb. 28, 2017, https://hbr.org/2017/02/a-brief-history-of-blockchain

35. Becky Peterson, *Disney built a blockchain, and now its creators are trying to turn it into a commercial platform to compete with Ethereum*, Markets Business Insider, Oct. 1, 2017, http://markets.businessinsider.com/currencies/news/disney-blockchain-creators-build-commercial-platform-on-dragonchain-with-ico-2017-9-1002909421

36. *What is Bitcoin Mining?* https://www.bitcoinmining.com See, also, *Mining*, Blockchain, https://www.blockchaintechnews.com/topics/mining/

37. For a list of companies facilitating Bitcoin transactions, see Sofia, *22 Bitcoin Companies Allowing Merchants to Accept Payments in Cryptocurrency*, Let's Talk Payments, Mar. 11, 2016, https://letstalkpayments.com/22-bitcoin-companies-allowing-merchants-to-accept-payments-in-cryptocurrency/

38. There are many sites stating the uses and users of blockchain including the following: Blockchain Technologies, *Blockchain Applications: What are Blockchain Technology Applications and Use Cases?*, http://www.blockchaintechnologies.com and Andrew Meola, *The growing list of applications and use cases of blockchain technology in business & life*, Business Insider, Sept. 28, 2017, http://www.businessinsider.com/blockchain-technology-applications-use-cases-2017-9

39. *Understanding How a Cryptocurrency Wallet Works*, Crytocurrency Facts, http://cryptocurrencyfacts.com/what-is-a-cryptocurrency-wallet/

40. Stan Higgins, *NiceHash CEO Confirms Bitcoin Theft Worth $78 Million*, Dec. 7, 2017, Coindesk, https://www.coindesk.com/nicehash-ceo-confirms-bitcoin-theft-worth-78-million/

41. Samantha Bomkamp, *CBOE, CME to jump into bitcoin futures trading*, Chicago Tribune, Dec. 1, 2017, http://www.chicagotribune.com/business/ct-biz-cboe-cme-bitcoin-20171201-story.html

42. Lucinda Shen. *Bitcoin Just Surged on Futures Trading. Here's How That Actually Works*, Fortune, Dec. 11, 2017, http://fortune.com/2017/12/11/bitcoin-surge-futures-cboe-cme-price/

43. Oliver Dale, *Best Cryptocurrency Exchanges for Beginners,* Dec. 9, 2017, https://blockonomi.com/cryptocurrency-exchanges/ Additional discussions of cryptocurrencies exchanges include: Nitin Thappar, *Top 9 Cryptocurrency Platforms,* Quora, https://www.quora.com/What-is-the-best-cryptocurrency-trading-platform

44. U.S. FBI Honolulu, *FBI Warns Public About Platform Trading Investment Scams,* Honolulu Media Office, Jan. 5, 2015, https://www.fbi.gov/contact-us/field-offices/honolulu/news/press-releases/fbi-warns-public-about-platform-trading-investment-scams

45. *Overlooked and underserved,* The Economist, Sept. 9, 2017, at 57–58.

46. U.S. Commodity Futures Trading Commission, *A CFTC Primer on Virtual Currencies,* p. 5, LabCFTC, http://www.cftc.gov/idc/groups/public/documents/file/labcftc_primercurrencies100417.pdf

47. Volatility may be extreme as illustrated by the geometric rise in the price of Bitcoin which then fell by one-third in trading on December 22, 2017, with an estimated loss of some $200 billion or 45 percent of value. Frank Chung, *Bitcoin loses nearly half its value in $200 billion wipeout,* NZ Herald, Dec. 23, 2017, http://www.nzherald.co.nz/business/news/article.cfm?c_id=3&objectid=11965200

48. *Id.* and Peter Frank, Bruno Lopes, and Adam Taplinger, *The Pros and Cons of Digital Currencies,* TMI, Aug. 2014, https://www.treasury-management.com/article/1/310/2570/the-pros-and-cons-of-digital-currencies.html. One individual suffered a loss of millions of dollars of Bitcoin to a hacker who convinced T-Mobile that he was the customer and through the use of the individual's phone number that was transferred to another number thereby enabled the hacking and the loss of bitcoins, Mark Frauenfelder, *How One Guy Lost Millions of Dollars of Bitcoin to a Hacker,* Boing Boing, Dec. 20, 2016, https://boingboing.net/2016/12/20/how-one-guy-lost-millions-of-d.html

49. LabCFTC, *supra* note 46.

50. USDT (tether) is a cryptocurrency asset that is issued on the Bitcoin blockchain, each unit of which is secured by a U.S. dollar held by Tether Limited Reserves and redeemable through the Tether Platform. It is transferable and can be stored and spent like Bitcoin and other cryptocurrencies. Antonio Madeira, *What is USDT and how to use it,* Cryptocompare, Sept. 28, 2017, https://www.cryptocompare.com/coins/guides/what-is-usdt-and-how-to-use-it

51. Tether Critical Announcement https://archive.fo/ZFDBf which was cited by Stan Higgins, *Tether Claims $30 Million in U.S. Dollar Token Stolen,* CoinDesk, Nov. 21, 2017, https://www.coindesk.com/tether-claims-30-million-stable-token-stolen-attacker/

52. U.S. Consumer Financial Protection Bureau, *Risks to consumer posed by virtual currencies,* Consumer Advisory. Aug. 2014, http://files.consumer-finance.gov/f/201408_cfpb_consumer-advisory_virtual-currencies.pdf

53. Lily Katz and Julie Verhage, *Bitchin Exchange Sees Complaints Soar,* Bloomberg, Aug. 30, 2017, https://www.bloomberg.com/news/articles/2017-08-30/Bitcoin-exchange-sees-complaints-soar-as-users-demand-money

54. European Parliament, *Virtual currencies: what are the risks and benefits?* News (Jan. 26, 2016), http://www.europarl.europa.eu/news/en/head-lines/economy/20160126STO11514/virtual-currencies-what-are-the-risks-and-benefits

55. U.S. Office of the White House Press Secretary, *President Donald J. Trump Announces Nomination of Jerome Powell to be Chairman of the Board of Governors of the Federal Reserve System,* Nov. 2, 2017, https://www.whitehouse.gov/the-press-office/2017/11/02/president-donald-j-trump-announces-nomination-jerome-powell-be-chairman

56. Richard Leong, *A Top Fed official warns on the risks associated with Bitcoin and other digital currencies,* Reuters, Mar. 3, 2017, http://www.busines-sinsider.com/jerome-powell-warns-on-risks-of-Bitcoin-and-other-digital-currencies-2017-3 and Pymnts. *Federal Reserve Warns n Digital Currency* Mar. 6, 2017, https://www.pymnts.com/news/Bitcoin-tracker/2017/federal-reserve-warns-on-digital-currency/

57. U.S. Government Services Administration, *Blockchain,* https://www.gsa.gov/technology/government-it-initiatives/emerging-citizen-technology/blockchain

58. U.S. Securities and Exchange Commission, *Investor Bulletin: Initial Coin Offerings,* Jul. 25, 2017, https://www.sec.gov/oiea/investor-alerts-and-bulletins/ib_coinofferings

59. U.S. Securities and Exchange Commission, *Investor Alert: Public Companies Making ICO-Related Claims,* Aug. 28, 2017, https://www.sec.gov/oiea/investor-alerts-and-bulletins/ia_icorelatedclaims

60. European Union, *General Data Protection Regulation,* Regulation (EU), 2016/679.

61. European Union Agency For Network and Information Security, *ENISA Opinion Paper on Cryptocurrencies in the EU,* Sept. 2017, https://www.enisa.europa.eu/publications/enisa-position-papers-and-opinions/enisa-opinion-paper-on-cryptocurrencies-in-the-eu

62. Ceri Parker, *Robert Shiller, Bitcoin is just an 'interesting experiment',* Jan. 25, 2018, World Economic Forum, https://www.weforum.org/agenda/2018/01/robert-shiller-bitcoin-is-just-an-interesting-experiment/

63. Bloomberg, *Stiglitz and Shiller Slam Bitcoin,* Dec. 3, 2017, Wealthadvisor, https://www.thewealthadvisor.com/article/stiglitz-and-shiller-slam-bitcoin

Technology Underlying Cryptocurrencies and Types of Cryptocurrencies

Blockchain Technology

The underlying technology for digital currencies is *blockchain* which is an electronic distributed ledger technology (DLT) that forms the basis of Bitcoin and which now serves as the foundation for other cryptocurrencies. It has been defined in an article published by the Federal Reserve Board (FED) "as some combination of components including peer-to-peer networking, distributed data storage, and cryptography that, among other things, can potentially change the way in which storage, record-keeping, and transfer of a digital asset is done."[1] It is similar to a stock ledger maintained by various participants in a network of computers. Blockchain uses cryptography to process and verify transactions in a ledger (or register) thereby allegedly assuring users of the blockchain that their entries are secure and free from theft. "*Cryptography* is a branch of mathematics that is based on the transformation of data and can be used to provide several security services: confidentiality, data integrity, authentication, authorization, and non-repudiation. Cryptography relies upon two basic components: an *algorithm* (or cryptographic methodology) and a *key*. The algorithm is a mathematical function and the key is a parameter used in the transformation."[2]

© The Author(s) 2018
R. Girasa, *Regulation of Cryptocurrencies and Blockchain Technologies*, Palgrave Studies in Financial Services Technology, https://doi.org/10.1007/978-3-319-78509-7_2

Another comparable definition for blockchain, a DLT, is: "In the strictest sense, a distributed ledger is a type of database that is shared across nodes in a network. In a DLT arrangement, nodes are the devices running the DLT software that collectively maintain the database records. In this design, the nodes are connected to each other in order to share and validate information.".[3] It is "the data structure that records the transfer of scarce objects…With the blockchain, everything that was scarce now becomes programmable…cash, commodities, currencies, stocks, bonds which undergo the transformation."[4] Blockchain, as originally envisioned, is decentralized and adds changes to the database via a series of completed blocks of transactional data that are connected to each other in a chain in which transaction data is stored in a chronological order. Users of the technology automatically receive copies of the transactions. Each block contains a *hash* which is a one-way digital fingerprint that cannot be reversed, is timestamped, and inputs to a set of outputs. The prior block hash links the blocks together, preventing any block from being altered and actually enhances the links among the blocks.[5]

DLTs in the form of cryptocurrencies are mainly open systems operating without governmental permission, in contrast to banking systems that use the technology in a closed network. Thus, the parties avoid third persons and the costs associated with them; have certainty of the source, amount, and destination of the transaction (trust); are assured that the transaction may not be tampered with; and are made aware that all such transactions are final and cannot be reversed.[6] There are many variations of blockchain which are adapted to the particular uses of the numerous types of cryptocurrencies.

The history of blockchain (originally worded as "block chain") is somewhat uncertain with various claimants to aspects of the technology that forms its basis. Thus, there are articles that discuss brief histories of the Bitcoin Blockchain,[7] Blockchain from an investor's perspective,[8] Blockchain on trademarks,[9] and even a history of cryptography tracing back to Julius Caesar and to the Greeks before the Romans.[10] Although the current cryptocurrency mania emanates from Bitcoin, nevertheless, it appears that each technological advance is based upon the work of predecessors. According to Wikipedia, the initial concept of a cryptographically secured chain of blocks was created and described in an article by co-authors, Stuart Haber and W. Scott Stornetta in 1991.[11] The authors were concerned about securing digital documents which are easy to copy and alter. They proposed "a cryptographically verifiable label for any bit-string...by naming it according to its position in a growing, directed acyclic graph of one-way hash values." As described more fully in their article, they proved the security of the transmission.[12]

More than two decades later, in 2008, Bitcoin and its underlying blockchain were introduced to the public commencing with a White Paper written by "Satoshi Nakamoto," a pseudonym. Within a decade there was a frenzy of activity wherein sophisticated and much less knowledgeable investors have poured almost untold sums of money into well-known cryptocurrencies and there have been over a thousand other attempts to gain dominance in the market. In an article in the *Harvard Business Review*, there were five innovative blockchain occurrences, namely: (1) the initiation of Bitcoin; (2) blockchain; (3) "smart contracts" that arose with blockchain advancements particularly by Ethereum; (4) "proof of stake" and "proof of security" that threatens third-party data centers; and (5) "blockchain scaling" which accelerates the processing of transactions.[13]

The ramifications of blockchain were highlighted in an opinion article in the *Wall Street Journal* that expressed concisely the reasons for the import and extraordinary transformations that are and will come about, and which are comparable to the creation of the Internet. The interviewee, Balaji Srinivasan, co-founded 21.co with $115 million seed money from venture capitalists from Silicon Valley. Blockchain, he noted, is "programmable scarcity," i.e., everything that was scarce up to now, including cash, commodities, stocks, and bonds, is programmable. Blockchain will cause a major transformation in how we deal with money. The elimination in great part of third-party intermediaries and controllers, such as banks and governments, will bring about major adjustments due to the inherent statelessness of blockchain innovative technology that goes far beyond the initial impact of Bitcoin Blockchain to all segments of society.[14] Other commentators have noted that blockchain is not a "disruptive" technology that attacks existing business models but one that is "foundational," i.e., it will totally revolutionize how business is accomplished. The transitional period, however, will be delayed for decades to allow adjustments, learning curves, and adaptation, although companies and firms have already begun the process.[15] The degree to which publicity attendant to blockchain and to Bitcoin was highlighted by the irrational behavior of customers who caused the stock price of a tea company to rise by 200 percent from its change of name from the "Long Island Ice Tea Corp." to "Long Blockchain Corporation."[16]

A problem with Bitcoin and other similar cryptocurrencies is the degree of electrical power usage required to mine Bitcoin, which exceeds the total power needs and outputs of a number of countries such as Costa Rica, Jordan, and Iceland, particularly when coupled with Ethereum. Ethereum is now addressing the issue through its more energy-efficient "proof-of-stake" algorithm called Caspar. Many of the Initial Public Offering (IPO) startups have emphasized the much greater efficiency of their platforms *vis-à-vis* the dominant Bitcoin and Ethereum platforms.[17] It thus appears almost inevitably that there are hackers bypassing cyber-security to steal computing power for mining. It was first noted by an observer that the Showtime Anytime website possessed a tool that enabled hackers to secretly hijack visitors' computers to mine Monero, another cryptocurrency similar to Bitcoin.[18]

Types of Blockchain Technology

Bitcoin is one type of blockchain usage adapted for its unique platform. There are a number of types of blockchain technologies that fall within three main categories: private blockchains, hybrid blockchains, and public blockchains. *Private blockchain* or *permissioned ledger* is one favored by financial institutions and is used internally by an organization under its sole control for a variety of usages such as auditing, regulatory compliance, and other needs of the firm or institution. The advantages are security from external attack, low cost, sole control over who may access data, and it is more efficient for internal recordkeeping. *Public blockchain* or *permissionless ledger* is open source, permitting access to anyone and allowing blocks to be added to the blockchain. In addition, users can engage in transactions and validate them; remain anonymous particularly if decentralized such as Bitcoin; and there is security from hacking and other malfeasance. *Consortium blockchain* is exemplified by banks which communicate with each other within a closed environment. *Federated* and *hybrid* blockchains are broader in scope beyond the internal usage of a firm but are more limited in access than public blockchain, to designated persons only.[19]

Uses of Blockchain Technology

The potential uses of blockchain technology are extensive and include the following as exemplified, in part, in proposed Hawaiian legislation to regulate virtual currency:

1. *Identity and access management*—verification and identification using advanced cryptography and blockchain technology for digital IDs. Practical applications include verifiable identity for drivers' licenses, tax payments, voting, and other electronic government services.
2. *Health care*—revolutionary enablement of patients' rights to their health care records, and utilization of blockchain technology for "Internet of things" medical devices, increased accountability of health care providers via authentication, and record keeping.
3. *Legal*—tracking, verification, authentication, and record keeping of court orders, regulatory and anti-laundering compliance, contracts, loans, titles, mortgages, and records. This would allow "smart contracts" verified by and recorded on blockchain technology as immutable records, allowing transparency for users.
4. *Financial services*—blockchain technology is already widely used in the financial services industry for payments, capital markets, and trade finance and is poised to remove billions of dollars in overheads and intermediary fees and services.
5. *Manufacturing*—utilizing blockchain to provide accountability and transparency over the provenance of goods and services will reduce counterfeit products and improve competitiveness for local businesses and will be useful in supply chain management.

6. *Tourism*—digital currencies such as Bitcoin have broad benefits especially for travel destination states such as Hawaii. A large portion of Hawaii's tourism market comes from Asia where the use of Bitcoin as a virtual currency is expanding. Hawaii and other states have the unique opportunity to explore the use of blockchain technology to make it easier for visitors to consume local goods and services and to drive the tourism economy.[20]
7. *Government*—for voting, taxes, legislation. and regulatory oversight.
8. *Corporations*—maintenance of shareholder records, regulatory compliance.
9. Additional multi-uses include clearing and settlement of stock trades; audit trails; security of records for both governments and industry; trucking services (e.g., United Parcel Service (UPS) joined the Blockchain in Trucking Alliance for data collection, insurance, and compliance audits)[21]; capital markets (Credit Suisse is using it for capital markets and corporate banking); security; and other uses that will increasingly become known as the technology is enhanced and usage becomes more widespread as users learn and adapt to the new technologies.[22]

Banks and Blockchain Technology

After, perhaps with justification, expressing fear that cryptocurrencies and blockchain technology will replace many bank functions and profit centers, it appears that banks are adapting to the innovations that inevitably occur. Among the banks that have indicated their interest in Bitcoin and DLT are two French banks, BNP Paribas and Société Générale, the U.S. Citibank, the Swiss investment bank UBS, Barclays and Standard Charter Bank, both of the U.K., Goldman Sachs, and the Spanish Banco Santander. All of these banks operate internationally and have determined that the many advantages of blockchain technology would reduce their costs significantly as well as offering increased security against hacking, among other advantages.[23]

Types of Cryptocurrencies

Bitcoin

The most commonly known cryptocurrency that has received global attention is Bitcoin. Although Bitcoin has had a vast amount of publicity and is the largest of the cryptocurrencies, nevertheless, there are well over 1000 other currencies in existence that offer competing and varying alternative products, and offer services that differ from Bitcoin's. Among them are ZCash, Ethereum, Ripple, Litecoin, Dash, Manero, Hyperledger Fabric, Intel Sawtooth, and Corda.[24]

How Bitcoin Works

Bitcoin is the creation of one or more persons using the pseudonym Satoshi Nakamoto.[25] As there was wild speculation over the identity of "Deep Throat," the individual who exposed the Nixon Era Watergate scandal, later identified as Associate Director of the FBI, Mark Felt, comparable specualtion centers on the identity of Satoshi Nakamoto. Among others, it has been rumored that the person is Nick Szabo who first used the expression "smart contract" based on his polymath and legal background, and his lectures on Bitcoin, blockchain, and Ethereum and their supposed attribution to the writings of Friedrich Hayek and Ayn Rand famed for their antipathy to government interference in economic and social life.[26] Bitcoin and other cryptocurrencies are gradually being accepted as virtual legal tender for products and services. It had been reported that a prospective buyer could have purchased a new apartment in Dubai for 30 or 50 BTC (bitcoins) for a studio or one-bedroom apartment respectively (50 BTC was approximately $242,000 in early September, 2017).[27] Bitcoin is a decentralized virtual currency whose protocol allows for the storage of bitcoins in a "digital wallet" which are identified by the user's public key that may be transferred from one person to another anonymously without a central authority or other third party such as a bank to oversee or interfere with the transaction. Its value is based on whatever the customers determine and not by the input of external forces such as central banks, financial institutions, or governmental authorities. Bitcoin is not redeemable for another commodity, does not have a physical form, and has no government backing including the $250,000 insurance offered to depositors per bank account in U.S. insured banks and similarly in other countries.[28]

Transactions in Bitcoin are accomplished by use of the Internet and are based on the principles of cryptography. Each Bitcoin and each user is encrypted with a unique identity. The time and amount of each transaction together with its Bitcoin addresses are permanently recorded on the decentralized blockchain ledger which is visible to all computers using the network but reveals no personal information about the parties. Each Bitcoin is divisible to eight decimal places thereby permitting extensive use. The transaction is irrevocable and the use of cryptography ensures against wrongful intrusion. In order for a user to transfers bitcoins to the receiver, the latter provides his or her Bitcoin address and the sending user authorizes the transaction by the use of a private key, which is a random sequence of 64 letters and numbers and which unlocks the digital wallet.[29] As set up by the founder, a Bitcoin is issued every 10 minutes and this will continue until the total supply of 21 million bitcoins has been disseminated. Approximately, 12 million bitcoins having been issued to date (beginning of 2018). This is why, in part, there was frenzied financial activity around Bitcoin because there is a limited supply whose value is based on the supply and demand for bitcoins.

Mining

There are three ways to obtain bitcoins, namely: (1) by using one of the legally registered exchanges; (2) by mining new bitcoins; and (3) by the exchange of goods and services for bitcoins. *Mining*, defined as the process of adding transaction records (new blocks), that have been verified, to Bitcoin's public ledger of past transactions known as blockchain, is a concept unique to cryptography in which persons either alone or with other individuals located anywhere globally are encouraged to solve computational (mathematical) problems for which a reward (a "block reward") of newly minted bitcoins and transaction fees are given for the successful endeavor. The reward began at 50 BTC in 2009 which decreases by one-half (now 25 BTC) for every 210,000 blocks mined. The block rewards will end once a total of 21 million bitcoins has been released. The public ledger is important because it prevents forgery or counterfeiting and eliminates the need for a third party to oversee the transaction.

The *proof-of-work* relates to miners who find a random number known as *nonce* which when inserted into the current block makes the hash fall below the current target. This is then sent around the network whereby other miners check the proof-of-work by hashing the block and checking the result.[30] Mining is very difficult to accomplish due to the requirement that the SHA-256 hash of a block's header must be lower than or equal to the target. It requires that the hash commences with a certain number of zeros requiring many attempts to accomplish. The difficulty is apparently intentional to prevent inflation. As more miners attempt to join, the difficulty of the rate of block generation increases as well as the difficulty to compensate, in order to reduce the rate of block creation. The adjustments occur every 2016 blocks or approximately every two weeks.[31]

It has been calculated that to find a new block requires a degree of power than could run small countries. Mining can be successfully accomplished by either possessing equipment enabling the user to attempt the solution or join with others in sharing power needs.[32] Use of CPU (Central Processing Unit) mining is inefficient because it uses a general purpose processor whereas use of a GPU (Graphics Processing Unit) is greatly preferred because this is a special processing unit that gives more hashing power and is, thus, far more optimal for mining.[33] Currently coders, have turned to ASICs (Application Specific Integrated Circuits) for mining, which is much faster, designed for a specific purpose, and takes place in thermally-regulated data centers having access to low-cost electricity.[34] Another alternative is FPGA (Field Programmable Gate Array), an integrated circuit that can be programmed by the user) mining which was an improvement over CPU mining but is now obsolete due to the superior processing of ASICs. Because of the significant cost of electrical power needed, a possible alternative is to join people in countries with cheap power (e.g., Iceland). Chinese power would also have been a cheap alternative source but the government has banned its use for mining together with a ban on cryptocurrencies. Some miners have looked to cheaper U.S. electrical power sources such as Chelan County, Washington. Whether improvements and innovations in solar power, cold fusion, or other sources will replace current power sources remains for the future.

Although blockchain use and the underlying cryptography preserve the anonymity of the parties to the transaction, as stated below, there are means by which governments can ascertain the identities of the users such as: tracking withdrawals and deposits of large sums of fiat money resulting from the transactions; subpoenas of computer and smartphone records; whistleblowing; and other backdoor techniques. A number of prosecutions and litigation are discussed in subsequent chapters.

A classic issue that inevitably arises in finance is whether a spectacular rise in the price of shares, the price of homes, and other assets will lead to an equally spectacular crash. The price of Bitcoin has risen so dramatically that a comparison to "tulipmania"[35] is inevitably made. The most recent example of a price bubble occurred a decade ago when the U.S. housing market witnessed an extraordinary rise in house prices in certain parts of the country only to then fall dramatically. At a meeting of the SEC Investor Advisory Committee on October 12, 2017, this issue, among others, was raised in connection with Bitcoin and typically committee members could only speculate whether the run-up in its price will follow along similar lines to such historical events.[36] Ultimately, after rising to an almost unconscionable price level approaching $20,000, there was a drop of some 45 percent in value followed by a less spectacular recovery. There are innumerable naysayers that predict a major downturn for 2018. One commentator, when adroitly summarizing Bitcoin mania, divided investors (customers) into "devotees" who purchase Bitcoin as a rebellion against government controlled currency by substituting the decentralized anonymous currency and "sheep" who follow the devotees' lead on seeing how the price has risen so dramatically.[37] Most economists and financiers agree that when the average person begins investing in a particular asset class whose value has risen dramatically, whether it be stocks, real estate, or other assets, it is then inevitable that a significant drop will take place. A diagram of how Bitcoin is transacted may be found in Appendix 1.

Ethereum

Whereas Bitcoin is digital money or currency that can be exchanged without third-party involvement, such as a bank, and is not subject to banking regulations, Ethereum is also a form of cryptocurrency that uses blockchain as its underlying technology but which possesses much broader uses, allowing other decentralized applications to be erected upon it such as smart contracts. It was created by a 19-year-old programmer from Toronto, Vitalik Buterin, who was highly critical of the limited use of Bitcoin and sought a means to enlarge the capability of blockchain to encompass numerous additional features. As a co-founder of Ethereum with three other members, he worked in conjunction with a major proponent, Gavin Wood, who published an article detailing the mathematical and scientific aspects of Ethereum.[38] Wood stated that Ethereum is "a transaction-based state machine" that may encompass a broad spectrum of account balances, reputations, trust arrangements, and almost anything that can emanate from a computer. "Ethereum is a project which attempts to build the generalised technology; technology on which all transaction based state machine concepts may be built. Moreover it aims to provide to the end-developer a tightly integrated end-to-end system for building software on a hitherto unexplored compute paradigm in the mainstream: a trustful object messaging compute framework."[39]

Ethereum possesses a support system known as the Enterprise Ethereum Alliance which, according to its website, connects Fortune 500 enterprises, startups, academics, and technology vendors to manage highly complex applications expeditiously.[40] Both Bitcoin and Ethereum are revolutionary digital applications but, as one author stated, "Whereas Bitcoin is disrupting currency, Ethereum is disrupting equity."[41] A future application, as envisioned by another author, is the elimination of third parties, including attorneys and escrow agents, in real estate transactions whereby home ownership and purchase moneys can be transferred using smart contracts by means of a piece of code that automatically accomplishes the transfer. Removing third parties from many forms of financial transactions such as Uber, Airbnb, eBay, etc. results in lower costs for participants, as well as speed, control, limitation of collusion, and other benefits.[42]

Comparison of Bitcoin and Ethereum

Whereas Bitcoin was the first major effort to encompass blockchain attributes, nevertheless, it is limited in scope and size. Ethereum thus fills a need that Bitcoin cannot. A comparison of some of their attributes is as follows:

- Bitcoin and Ethereum are decentralized (no third party is in control), are open-sources, and offer a secure anonymous access that cannot be compromised.
- Bitcoin is a payment system while Ethereum is a decentralized platform that has far more extensive applications and one that runs smart contracts and allows numerous other applications.
- Bitcoin's block time is about 10 minutes whereas Ethereum's average block time is around 14 seconds (14.38 seconds on December 26, 2017).
- The "rewards" differ—Bitcoin offers a "block reward" of BTC (unit of currency or amount) to miners who create a block. This was originally 50 BTC per 10 minutes but which halves over time (and is presently 25 BTC). Ethereum's reward consists of 5 Ether (the "fuel" for operating the Ethereum platform) which remains the same and does not diminish over time plus 1/32th per Uncle block. (Uncles are stale blocks with parents that are a maximum of six blocks back from the present block.)[43]
- The underlying protocol differs in that Bitcoin is written in C++ computer code while Ethereum uses Turing complete internal code.
- Bitcoin mining is by ASIC, a specific integrated circuit that was customized for Bitcoin's particular use; whereas Ethereum is by GPUs (graphics processing units), found in smart phones and personal computers), originally used for computer graphic computations and are specialized electronic circuits for the creation of images.
- Bitcoin's initial distribution was by mining, while Ethereum did so by ICOs.
- Bitcoin's hash rate is 1.8 Exahash (extraordinary processing of transactions—proof of work) while Ethereum is 3 TeraHash (a measure of mining performance).[44]

- Bitcoin's cost is based on competing with one another while Ethereum's cost is based on the amount of "gas" used for each computational step and is set between the miners and the users.[45]
- Bitcoin was the creation of Satoshi Nakamoto, an unknown person or persons, while Ethereum was created by Vitalik Buterin and the expansion of Ethereum was financed by crowdfunding (described in the chapter on "Crowdfunding and the Taxation of Virtual Currencies").[46]

Other Variations of Cryptocurrencies

Litecoin

Litecoin was created by Charlie Lee on October 7, 2011. His goal was to create "a lighter type" of Bitcoin, alleging it is silver compared to Bitcoin's gold. It is open-sourced on GitHub and its aim is to provide a cheaper and more everyday-purposed currency. According to its website,[47] Litecoin's market capitalization (when downloaded on December 29, 2017) was over a half billion dollars or about 1/11th that of Bitcoin's; its coin limit is 84 billion vs. 21 billion for Bitcoin; its algorithm is Scrypt (a memory hard key-derivation function) vs. SHA-256 for Bitcoin; its block reward is halved every 840,000 blocks vs. every 210,000 for Bitcoin; its block time is one-fourth that of Bitcoin's (2½ minutes vs 10 minutes); and its block explorer is block-explorer.com vs. blockchain.infor. Like Bitcoin, its value has risen extraordinarily and investors may question whether it is one of the numerous tech shares and currencies that are evidence of a major bubble. Its main advantage is less energy use, allowing a greater number of miners to partake.[48]

IOTA

IOTA's website[49] alleges that it is scalable, decentralized, modular, and without fees. It claims that it enables companies to explore new Business-to-Business (B2B) models through its service to be traded in an open market, in real time, and without cost. By means of its "Autonomous Machine Economy" it is able to settle transactions without fees or use of blocks that enables devices to trade exact amounts of resources on demand and store data from sensors and dataloggers securely and verifiable on the ledger. In a White Paper by Serguei Popov, the mathematical foundations of IOTA are discussed. In it he states the main feature of this cryptocurrency is the "tangle," which is a directed acyclic graph for storing transactions. It purports to be the next evolutionary step in blockchain that offers features to establish a machine-to-machine micro-payment system.[50] It is the "Internet of things." Its credibility lies in the fact that it has partnered with Microsoft and one of the "Big 4" accounting firms (PricewaterhouseCoopers) and has been heavily invested in by other major companies. With a market cap of $14 billion, it is the sixth largest cryptocurrency globally.[51]

Golem

Golem also alleges that it is scalable, decentralized, secure, open to development, without a single point of failure, and capable of connecting millions of nodes using a P2P (Peer-to-Peer) architecture. According to its website,[52] developers are able to deploy their own integration on Golem and implement an appropriate monetization mechanism through personal laptops and data centers. Users can earn money by "renting" out their computing power or by developing and selling software. Golem utilizes an Ethereum-based transaction system that clears payments between providers, requesters, and software developers. Its application and transaction framework enable anyone to deploy and distribute applications on the site's network. Called the Airbnb of cryptocurrencies, it is the tenth most valuable cryptocurrency with a market capitalization of approximately $113 million, which, like other like cryptocurrencies, has risen in value dramatically.[53]

Request Network

In the Request White Paper,[54] it alleges that Request is a decentralized network that permits anyone to ask for a payment (a Request Invoice) that can be accomplished in a secured way. The information is stored in a decentralized authentic ledger which is universal, i.e., is designed to support all global transactions regardless of the type of currency, legislation, or language. It is allegedly cheaper and more secure than existing payment mechanisms allowing a wide range of automation possibilities. It seeks to become the backbone of world trade and is at the origin of exchanges integrating a computerized trade code, and acts as the management of a multitude of payment terms. It is yet another layer on top of Ethereum2 which permits requests for payments that satisfy existing legal frameworks. Its advantages, according to its White Paper, is security that is without risk of interception, unlike banks; its simplicity with a one-click operation to pay without the possibility of manual input error; and lower cost in comparison with third parties such as Paypal, Bitpay, or Stripe which charge between 1 and 7 percent for their services.[55] Its market cap at the time of its ICO was $59 million. Some of the intended uses and future consequences include the automation of accounting processes such as payments and Value Added Tax (VAT) refunds, auditing through use of blockchain to simplify compliance, and simplification of commercial tools for easy access to tools such as those used for escrow payments or factoring.[56]

Dash

As with other cryptocurrencies, Dash is an open-sourced and P2P cryptocurrency. Its mission, according to its website, is to make digital cash easy to use and accessible to all users including those with limited technological backgrounds. It alleges that anyone will be able to set up an account on blockchain, add contacts, and pay for purchases from websites or mobile apps with a one-click process. The value of a Dash coin had risen from $10 to $1531 by December 21, 2017.[57] Initially called XCoin and later, Darkcoin, its dominant feature is the enabling of users to engage in payments for goods and services with merchants who have adopted its use in a much more expedited manner than other cryptocurrencies.

Ripple

At the time of writing (February 17, 2018), Ripple was the second largest cryptocurrency by market cap at almost $47 billion (was $86 billion in late December, 2017) having surpassed Ethereum.[58] Started in September 2013, by its creator, Jed McCaleb, it is a payment network that is currently being used by many banks such as the Bank of America, Santander, American Express, and UBS. Its code is not open-sourced but rather is privately owned by Ripple.[59] Unlike Bitcoin which is decentralized—i.e., users obtain units by mining—Ripple is centralized meaning that only it may issue units as it so chooses, and this is done by the Ripple Foundation which has created 100 billion units (XRP). According to its website, it is scalable, secure, and interoperates different networks. Its software solution, xCurrent, enables banks to instantly settle cross-border payments with end-to-end tracking. Banks message each other in real-time confirming payment details before initiating the transaction and then confirm delivery after settlement. It minimizes costs and capital requirements for liquidity. It uses a standard interface, xVia's simple API (Application Programming Interface) that requires no software installation and enables users to seamlessly send payments globally with transparency of payment status.[60] As of the end of December, 2017, a co-creator, Chris Larsen, the largest holder of Ripple tokens, rivaled Jeff Zuckerberg for financial supremacy based on Ripple's growth of 30,000 percent in a year.[61]

Monero

Monero is a leading cryptocurrency that claims it is "secure, private, and untraceable." Open-sourced, the Monero website alleges it is decentralized, accessible to all and so permitting users to be their own bank, allowing them to maintain accounts and transactions anonymously, be secure owing to the use of ring signatures and other means to prevent third parties from prying, and fungible in that it cannot be blacklisted by vendors or exchanges. Allegedly, it has been used by darknet markets as well as people with legitimate interests.[62]

Digital Tokens (Cryptotokens)

Digital tokens are the basis for the latest get-rich-quickly mania. They are used by startup companies to raise capital for technology being developed by coders. As with bitcoins, their value is what the investors give to them. To date, many billions of dollars have been invested in tokens' ICOs for startup companies wherein the purchasers of the tokens contribute capital to these digital enterprises in the hope that the tokens will substantially rise in value and the digital products emanating from their investments will result in monetary gain.[63] Although venture capitalists have invested in these ICOs, unlike in the past when new startup companies often relied on them to fund their proposed ventures, these tokens may be purchased by ordinary investors in much smaller amounts that collectively not only rival sums invested by venture capitalists but now greatly exceed those sums. Many ICOs limit the tokens that can be purchased in the hope of encouraging investors who will contribute more than monetary sums but assist in the development of their products.[64] They generally limit their offerings to non-U.S. purchasers due to fears that the SEC and U.S. tax authorities may intervene. The ICOs often have check boxes whereby the purchasers of tokens state they are not U.S. residents or green card holders.[65]

Tokens represent an asset, such as property or utility, or act as securities. They are fungible and may offer income or rewards. The best known is Ethereum which offers tokens whereas Bitcoin offers coins. They are generally tradable and usually reside on top of the blockchain thereby making it unnecessary to modify the existing protocol or blockchain. They are created in an ICO and may be considered as a security requiring registration and conformity to other laws and regulations as illustrated in the DAO litigation discussed hereinafter.[66]

Types of Tokens

Although ICOs have raised only a small percentage of capital (2 percent) compared to overall sums raised by IPOs globally, nevertheless, they have expanded exponentially going from a small sum in 2015, to approximately $96.3 million in 2016, to $4 billion in 2017, and to an expected 180 new offerings in 2018.[67] The market cap for the 1453 cryptocurrencies as of January 19, 2018 was $583 billion with a Bitcoin dominance of 33.8 percent.[68]

Traditionally, IPOs were relegated to sophisticated hedge fund investors, venture capitalists, and others having substantial capital to invest in exchange for a percentage share in the company's equity (shares of stock). ICOs differ from IPOs by offering products or services. They are becoming mainstream where even those persons with meagre incomes and capital are engaged in the purchase of interests in newly emerging startups. For example, this author when discussing Bitcoin and other cryptocurrencies with an undergraduate class, was astonished to hear a number of students stating that they have invested in companies offering cryptocurrencies, which has never occurred in several decades of lecturing. Investments were made by the offering of tokens through the blockchain-based offerings that enabled the creation of new currency offerings and the raising of capital almost literally overnight, avoiding the regulatory time-consuming roadblocks of traditional offerings.

There are several types of tokens that can be purchased: from utility tokens. They are from, to equity and debt security tokens, and other cryptocurrencies, each offering a type of benefit to the purchaser in a multitude of products and/or services. They often arise from crowdfunding (discussed in the chapter on "Crowdfunding and the Taxation of Virtual Currencies"). They are transferable to others in a secondary market and are unlike traditional venture capital investments and IPOs which are subject to time constraints under the 1933 and 1934 Securities Acts. The ICOs pre-sell coin tokens to potential investors in accordance with a concept generally laid out by the firm in a White Paper that contains both conceptual and mathematical algorithm jargon. The discussion generally states the mission, timeline, target budget, and the manner of coin sales to take place. Examples are Ethereum's cryptocurrency tokens, Golem's tokens received by selling computing capacity, Anryze's use of tokens to decode audio files, and stock tokens sold on exchanges.[69]

An excellent example of a White Paper discussing token sales is that of the Ethereum and TrueBit founders and chief architects, who discuss

Ethereum's token offerings.[70] They state that typically buyers desiring to purchase Ethereum's ERC20 tokens over the Ethereum network do so in exchange for Ethereum's own currency. Unlike equity sales in IPOs, these tokens have no known initial market valuation and buyers must rely on projections and possibilities. Ethereum has made *capped offerings*, i.e. capped at a determined maximum or minimum number of tokens for sale, and *uncapped offerings* whereby the sales are potentially unlimited. Other types of token sales can involve hidden caps and reverse Dutch auctions. (A *Dutch auction* is when an initial high offering sum is gradually lowered until a sufficient number of buyers agree to purchase.)

Forks

Complicating the various types of digital currencies are alternatives to Bitcoin and its underlying blockchain technology known as *altcoins*, *coins* or *forks* which in turn may be subdivided into *hard forks* and *soft forks* such as Litecoin, Namecoin, and Dogecoin each of which has its own variant of the underlying blockchain technology. A *fork* in connection with cryptocurrency occurs when alternative versions of the particular currency are created. The problem is that there are different versions of the currency (e.g., Bitcoin split into Bitcoin and Bitcoin Cash) and the issue of compatibility arises. By being open-source, modifications can be made ostensibly by any user. The fork may arise either by the particular blockchain used, as in Bitcoin, which may then be split into alternative but compatible versions, or where a new version of the technology arises that alleges it is either better or seeks to apply it to other uses (Litecoin, IOTA, Ripple, etc.). A *hard fork* occurs when the cryptocurrency is split into two different cryptocurrencies, generally due to the inability of non-upgraded nodes (persons in possession of a copy of a blockchain) to validate blocks created by newer upgraded nodes, while a *soft fork* refers to a divergence in an updated version of the blockchain that modifies the earlier version but remains compatible.[71] A number of coins use the SHA-256 algorithm that also underlies Bitcoin while many other use script algorithm, and hybrid and CPU alternative cryptocurrencies.

Altcoins

Altcoins are alternative cryptocurrencies not compatible with Bitcoin but emulate it generally by using the same hashing algorithm as Bitcoin, i.e., SHA-256. They are P2P, using a mining process to generate new blocks based on blockchain technology. They may be considered "hard forks" to Bitcoin and it is often claimed that they are an improvement over it by performing different functions or constitute an improvement of some component of Bitcoin. There are several hundred altcoins that have emerged as alternatives ("forking the code") and a number of ICOs that will be offered in the near future.[72] Exemplified by Ethereum, Dogecoin, Feathercoin, and Peercoin, they attempt to offer cheaper alternatives to Bitcoin using less computer power to generate blocks.[73] A major altcoin is Litecoin with its different hashing algorithm and higher currency units. It alleges, as stated previously, that it is "silver to Bitcoin's gold."[74] Other alternative altcoins include Namecoin (a domain registration system), Dogecoin, Manero, and Peercoin, A well-known online store which sells a large variety of consumer goods, Overstock, stated on August 8, 2017, that it would accept payment by altcoins such as Ethereum, Litecoin, Dash, and every other major currency as payment from its customers. Its CEO, Patrick Byrne, who is also an economist, said to a *Fortune* magazine interviewer that it would accept 40 or 45 digital currencies at any given time.[75]

Meta Coins

Meta coins are protocols built on an existing cryptocurrency platform. A prime example is that of Counterparty, which is a P2P financial platform using its own currency XCP, and shares the same benefit in not needing a trusted third party: its goal is to "democratize finance in the same way the Internet itself democratized the creation and sharing of information." It is built on the Bitcoin platform that permits users to engage the financial sector in an inexpensive way, sharing the same features of being user-friendly, open, safe, and secure. It can make bets, construct smart contracts, create and sell one's own tickets for particular functions, broadcast information, and perform a multitude of other financially related tasks.[76]

Sidecoin

Sidecoin is a fork of Bitcoin which, according to a Side Bitcoin White Paper, "is a mechanism that allows a snapshot to be taken of Bitcoin's blockchain."[77] The developers stated that they compiled a list of unspent transaction outputs which they then utilized with corresponding balances to bootstrap a new blockchain. The developers took a snapshot of available public addresses in the Bitcoin network by downloading the Bitcoin blockchain with their public keys and converted the hash 160s into commonly used Bitcoin addresses, then "parsed" the balances in the Bitcoin blockchain. Its alleged use of the sidechain is to enable those who wish to make an altcoin and dramatically increase community adoption.[78]

Sidechain

A sidechain is the use of a separate blockchain but one wherein the user may revert back to the original blockchain (main chain). When used in Bitcoin, the user sends bitcoins to a special address on the Bitcoin blockchain that is set off from the original blockchain. Ethereum has a private Ethereum-based network that permits its ether to be sent to a private blockchain away from the public Ethereum main chain.[79]

Having briefly explored the nature of digital currencies, we will now examine, in the chapter on "Legal Issues of Digital Technology", the legal issues and how the legal systems, both domestically and internationally, deal with the new technology. Typically, the law moves slowly when confronted with new developments as illustrated by the issues raised by the Internet's development. Judges and legislatures often attempt to apply existing legal doctrines to solve problems that require the same degree of innovative legal strategies as the new developments, much like trying to apply traditional legal principles to new innovations. As seen later, legislatures everywhere are attempting to move beyond their normal snail-like pace to meet the challenges, especially after the extraordinary price rise of Bitcoin which almost all commentators agreed would face an inevitable collapse, as experienced in recent years by other bubbles in the financial sector. Whenever there are innovations that seriously affect financial markets, governmental authorities will inevitably intervene in an endeavor to prevent fraud and other malfeasance. We will review how government is becoming concerned, as illustrated by its attempts to curb abuses or strongly advise customers of the dangers inherent in the ultra-new technologies.

Notes

1. David Mills, Kathy Wang, Brendan Malone, Anjana Ravi, Jeff Marquardt, Clinton Chen, Anton Badev, Timothy Brezinski, Linda Fahy, Kimberley Liao, Vanessa Kargenian, Max Ellithorpe, Wendy Ng, and Maria Baird (2016). *Distributed ledger technology in payments, clearing, and settlement*, Finance and Economics Discussion Series 2016-095. Washington: Board of Governors of the Federal Reserve System, at p. 8. https://doi.org/10.17016/FEDS.2016.095
2. E. Barker and W.C. Baker, *Guideline for Using Cryptographic Standards in the Federal Government: 175A – Directives, Mandates and Policies; 175B – Cryptographic Mechanisms,* NIST Special Publications 800-175A and 800-175B, Aug. 2016, https://doi.org/10.6028/NIST.SP.800-175B
3. *Federal Reserve Publishes Paper on Bitcoin's Blockchain Technology,* Bitconist, *I.S.,* Dec. 6, 2016, https://www.ccn.com/federal-reserve-blockchain-paper-use-banks-conduct-payments-become-obsolete/
4. Tunku Varadarajan, *The Blockchain Is The Internet of Money,* Wall Street Journal Opinion, Sept. 23–24, 2017, quotes from an interview with Balaji S. Srinivasan, https://www.wsj.com/articles/the-blockchain-is-the-internet-of-money-1506119424
5. Manav Gupta, IBM Blockchain for Dummies, at 13–14. https://bertrandszoghy.files.wordpress.com/2017/05/ibm-blockchain-for-dummies.pdf
6. Tunku Varadarajan, *supra,* note 4.
7. Tiana Lawrence, *A Brief History of the Bitcoin Blockchain*, Dummies, http://www.dummies.com/personal-finance/brief-history-bitcoin-blockchain/
8. Cameron McLain, *A Brief History of Blockchain: An Investor's Perspective,* The Mission, originally posted in Thoughts and Ideas, https://medium.com/the-mission/a-brief-history-of-blockchain-an-investors-perspective-e9b6605aad68

9. Nadaline Webster, *A Brief History of Blockchain in Trademarks,* Trademark Now, https://www.trademarknow.com/blog/brief-history-of-blockchain-in-trademarks

10. Come Jean Jarry and Romain Rouphael, *From Julius Caesar to the Blockchain: A Brief History of Cryptography,* https://cib.bnpparibas.com/documents/6-From_Julius_Caesar_to_the_blockchain_a_brief_history_of_cryptography.pdf. The authors are the co-founders of the cryptocurrency Belem.

11. Stuart Haber and W. Scott Stornetta, *How to time-stamp a digital document,* Journal of Cryptology 3(2), 99–111, Jan, 1991, cited in Wikipedia, *Blockchain,* https://en.wikipedia.org/wiki/Blockchain

12. Scott Haber and W. Scott Stornetta, *Secure Names for Bit-Strings,* http://nakamotoinstitute.org/static/docs/secure-names-bit-strings.pdf

13. Vinay Gupta, *A Brief History of Blockchain,* Harvard Business Review, Feb. 28, 2017, https://hbr.org/2017/02/a-brief-history-of-blockchain

14. Tunku Varadarajan, *The Blockchain Is the Internet of Money,* The Wall Street Journal, at A11, Sept. 23–24, 2017.

15. Marco Iansiti and Karim R. Lakhani, *The Truth About Blockchain,* Harvard Business Review (Jan–Feb, 2017), https://hbr.org/2017/01/the-truth-about-blockchain

16. William White, *Long Iced Tea Stock Skyrockets on 'Blockchain' Rebranding,* Investorplace, Dec. 21, 2017,, https://investorplace.com/2017/12/long-island-iced-tea-corp-rebranding-for-blockchain/#.WkO4sLpFzIU

17. Digiconomist, *Ethereum Energy Consumption Index(beta),* https://digiconomist.net/ethereum-energy-consumption

18. Mike Orcutt, *Highjacking Computers to Mine Cryptocurrency Is All the Rage,* MIT Technology Review, Oct. 5, 2017, https://www.technologyreview.com/s/609031/hijacking-computers-to-mine-cryptocurrency-is-all-the-rage/

19. *Blockchains & Distributed Ledger Technologies,* BlockchainHub, https://blockchainhub.net/blockchains-and-distributed-ledger-technologies-in-general/

20. Hawaii House Bill 1481, 2017, https://legiscan.com/HI/text/HB1481/id/1481334

21. Jonathan Camhi, *UPS joins blockchain initiative,* Business Insider, Nov. 13, 2017, http://www.businessinsider.com/ups-joins-blockchain-initiative-2017-11

22. *What Are the Applications and Use Cases of Blockchains?*, Coindesk, https://www.coindesk.com/information/applications-use-cases-blockchains/ and Andrew Meola, *The growing list of applications and use cases of blockchain technology in business & life*, Business Insider, Sept. 28, 2017, http://www.businessinsider.com/blockchain-technology-applications-use-cases-2017-9

23. Yessi Bello Perez, *8 Banking Giants Embracing Bitcoin and Blockchain Tech*, Coindesk, July 27, 2015, https://www.coindesk.com/8-banking-giants-bitcoin-blockchain/

24. For a discussion, Gaurang Torvekar, *7 blockchain technologies to watch out for in 2017*, Medium, Jan. 23, 2017, https://medium.com/@gaurangtorvekar/7-blockchain-technologies-to-watch-out-for-in-2017-4b3fc7a85707. A comparison of several of these cryptocurrencies may be found in *Bigger Than Bitcoin: Cryptocurrency Statistics*, https://bitinfocharts.com/

25. P2P Foundation, *Satoshi Nakamoto's Page*, http://p2pfoundation.ning.com/profile/SatoshiNakamoto. The site states he is from Japan and is aged 42. There is no confirmation and commentators reiterate that the comment and the name are fictitious.

26. Rob Price, *The man everyone thinks is the creator of bitcoin gave a speech discussing the history of the technology*, Business Insider, *Nov.* 13, 2015, http://www.businessinsider.com/nick-szabo-ethereum-bitcoin-blockchain-history-satoshi-nakamoto-2015-11

27. Zahraa Alkhalisi, *You can buy a new Dubai apartment for 50 Bitcoin*, CNN Tech, Sept. 6, 2017, http://money.cnn.com/2017/09/06/technology/dubai-bitcoin-apartments/index.html

28. For a discussion, see U.S. Federal Deposit and Insurance Corporation, *Who is the FDIC?*, https://www.fdic.gov/about/learn/symbol/

29. U.S. Government Accountability Office, Virtual Currencies: Emerging, Law Enforcement, and Customer Protection Challenges, Report to the Committee on Homeland Security and Governmental Affairs, U.S. Senate, May, 2014, GAO-14-496, https://www.gao.gov/assets/670/663678.pdf

30. *Bitcoin*, Stack Exchange, https://bitcoin.stackexchange.com/questions/9078/what-is-proof-of-work

31. *Mining*, Bitcoin Wiki, https://en.bitcoin.it/wiki/Mining and *Bitcoin Mining*, Investopedia, https://www.investopedia.com/terms/b/bitcoin-mining.asp

32. For a definition and equipment that can be purchased for mining, see *What is Bitcoin Mining?*, https://www.bitcoinminibng.com/
33. Erik Fair, *What's the difference between a CPU and a GPU? When I Switch on my computer, it shows GPU information. What does it mean?*, Quora, Jan. 16, 2017, https://www.quora.com/Whats-the-difference-between-a-CPU-and-a-GPU-When-I-switch-on-my-computer-it-shows-GPU-information-What-does-it-mean
34. Jordan Tuwiner, *What is Bitcoin Mining? (/mining/)*, Buy Bitcoin Worldwide, June 28, 2017, https://www.buybitcoinworldwide.com/mining/profitability/
35. Tulipmania is a reference to the events in the Netherlands that took place when tulip bulbs became extraordinary in demand in Europe causing the prices of the bulbs to escalate dramatically and which then led to perhaps the first major financial crash in February, 1637. Andrew Beattie, *Market Crashes: The Tulip and Bulb Craze (1630s)*, Investopedia, https://www.investopedia.com/features/crashes/crashes2.asp
36. Kari S. Larsen and Michael Selig, *SEC Investor Advisory Committee Considers Blockchain Technology and Securities Markets*, Reed Smith Client Alerts, Oct. 13, 2017, https://www.reedsmith.com/en/perspectives/2017/10/sec-investor-advisory-committee-considers-blockchain-technology
37. Palwasha Saaim B.Sc., *Bitcoin Crash Fears Rise:Will Bitcoin Crash in 2018?*, Profit Confidential Dec. 15, 2017, https://www.profitconfidential.com/cryptocurrency/bitcoin/will-bitcoin-btc-crash-2018/
38. *Who Created Ethereum?*, Bitcoin Magazine, https://bitcoinmagazine.com/guides/who-created-ethereum/
39. Gavin Wood, *Ethereum: A Secure Decentralised, Generalized Transaction Ledger*, Ethereum, Aug. 7, 2017, https://ethereum.github.io/yellowpaper/paper.pdf
40. Enterprise Ethereum Alliance, https://entethalliance.org/
41. Samantha Radocchia, *How is Ethereum Different from Bitcoin?*, Quora, Forbes, Sept. 9, 2017, https://www.forbes.com/sites/quora/2017/09/14/how-is-ethereum-different-from-Bitcoin/#1a765248502b
42. Vincent Briatore, *What is Ethereum and how is it different from Bitcoin?*, Quora, https://www.quora.com/What-is-Ethereum-and-how-is-it-different-from-Bitcoin
43. *What are Mining Rewards in Ethereum?* Cryptocompare, https://www.cryptocompare.com/mining/guides/what-are-mining-rewards-in-ethereum/

44. Vangie Beal, *hashing*, Webopedia, https://www.webopedia.com/ TERM/H/hashing.html; and JP Buntinx, *Bitcoin Cash Hashrate Surpasses 2.4 Exohash per second*, Bitcoin Interest, Dec. 20, 2017, http://www.livebit-coinnews.com/bitcoin-cash-hashrate-surpasses-2-4-exohash-per-second/

45. *How do Ethereum's Transaction fees compare to Bitcoin?*, Ethereum, https:// ethereum.stackexchange.com/questions/11/how-do-ethereums-transaction-fees-compare-to-bitcoin

46. Antonio Madeira, *Why is Ethereum different to Bitcoin?* Cryptocompare, Sept. 27, 2017, https://www.cryptocompare.com/coins/guides/why-is-ethereum-different-to-bitcoin/

47. *What is Litecoin? A Basic Beginner's Guide*, Blockgeeks, Inc. (Ca), https:// blockgeeks.com/guides/litecoin/

48. *What is Scrypt?*, Cryptocompare, https://www.cryptocompare.com/ coins/guides/what-is-scrypt/

49. *The Backbone of IOT Is Here*, IOTA, https://iota.org/

50. Serguei Popov, *The Tangle*, IOTA, Oct. 1, 2017, https://iota.org/IOTA_Whitepaper.pdf

51. Wayne Duggan, *Meet IOTA: The Cryptocurrency For The Internet-Of-Things*, Benzinga, Dec. 26, 2017, https://www.benzinga.com/general/ education/17/12/10946936/meet-iota-the-cryptocurrency-for-the-internet-of-things

52. *Worldwide Supercomputer*, GOLEM, https://golem.network/

53. Frisco d'Anconia, *Golem Is 10th Most Valuable Crypto*, The Cointelegraph, Apr. 28, 2017, https://cointelegraph.com/news/golem-is-10th-most-valuable-crypto

54. *Whitepaper: The future of commerce: A decentralized network for payment requests*, Request Network, Oct. 25, 2017, https://request.network/ assets/pdf/request_whitepaper.pdf

55. *Id.*, at pp. 10–11.

56. *Analysis of Request Network – Decentralized Network for Payment Requests*, Crushcrypto, https://crushcrypto.com/analysis-of-request-network/

57. Dash, https://www.dash.org/2017/12/22/ceoofdash.html

58. Kailey Leinz, *Ripple's 53% surge makes it the second-biggest cryptocurrency*, Moneyweb, https://www.moneyweb.co.za/news/markets/ripples-53-surge-makes-it-the-second-biggest-cryptocurrency/

59. *Ripple News*, The Coin Telegraph, https://cointelegraph.com/tags/ripple

60. Ripple, https://ripple.com/

61. Nathaniel Popper, *Rise of Bitcoin Competitor Creates Wealth to Rival Zuckerberg*, New York Times, Jan. 4, 2018, https://www.nytimes.com/2018/01/04/technology/bitcoin-ripple.html?ref=todayspaper

62. Monero, https://getmonero.org/

63. Joan Ian Wong, *The new cryptocurrency gold rush: digital tokes that raise millions in minutes*, Quartz, June 5, 2017, https://qz.com/994466/the-new-cryptocurrency-gold-rush-digital-tokens-that-raise-millions-in-minutes/

64. Gertrude Chavez-Dreyfuss, *U.S. venture capital's digital coin quandary: cash-rich startups*, Reuters, July 24, 2017, http://www.reuters.com/article/us-usa-venturecapital-digitalcurrency/u-s-venture-capitals-digital-coin-quandary-cash-rich-startups-idUSKBN1A90CR

65. Evelyn Cheng, *This hot digital currency trend is minting millions but U.S. investors aren't allowed to play*, CNBC, July 18, 2017, https://www.cnbc.com/2017/07/18/hot-digital-currency-trend-minting-millions-off-limits-to-us-investors.html

66. For a summary, see Aziz, *Coins, Tokens & Altcoins: What's the Difference?*, https://masterthecrypto.com/differences-between-cryptocurrency-coins-and-tokens/

67. Sergi Dromo, *ICOs Raised Bln in 2017, What 2018 Has in Store*, The Cointelegraph, Dec. 31, 2017, https://cointelegraph.com/news/icos-raised-4-bln-in-2017-what-2018-has-in-store

68. *Cryptocurrency Market Capitalizations*, Coin Market, Jan. 19, 2018, https://coinmarketcap.com/

69. *Initial Coin Offerings (ICOs)*, BlockchainHub, https://blockchainhub.net/ico-initial-coin-offerings/

70. Jason Teutsch, Vialik Buterin, and Christopher Brown, *Initial coin offerings*, Dec. 11, 2017, https://people.cs.uchicago.edu/~teutsch/papers/ico.pdf

71. *What Are Forks?* World Crypto Index, https://www.worldcrypto-index.com/what-are-forks/, and *The Differences Between Hard and Soft Forks*, WeUseCoins, https://www.weusecoins.com/hard-fork-soft-fork-differences/

72. For a listing of Altcoin offering, see Altcoins, http://altcoins.com/

73. Ofir Beigel, *What are Altcoins?*, Bitcoins, Aug. 31, 2016, https://99bitcoins.com/altcoins/

74. *What is an Altcoin?*, CCN, Sept. 12, 2014, https://www.ccn.com/altcoin/

75. Jeff John Roberts, *Beyond Bitcoin: Overstock Lets Customers Pay With More Than 40 Alt Coins,* Fortune, Aug. 8, 2017, http://fortune.com/2017/08/08/overstock-digital-currency/

76. *Counterparty – Pioneering Peer-to-Peer Finance,* Bitcoin Forum, Jan. 2, 2014, https://bitcointalk.org/index.php?topic=395761.0. An excellent summary of the diverse platforms is discussed by Peter Van Valkenburgh, *What are Forks, Alt-coins, Meta-coins, and Sidechains?,* Coin Center, Dec. 8, 2015, https://coincenter.org/entry/what-are-forks-alt-coins-meta-coins-and-sidechains

77. Joseph Krug and Jack Peterson, *Sidecoin: a Snapshot Mechanism for Bootstrapping a Blockchain/*Sidecoin: The sidecar to Bitcoin's motorcycle, http://www.sidecoin.net/

78. *Id.*

79. Ethereum, *What is a sidechain?,* https://ethereum.stackexchange.com/questions/379/what-is-a-sidechain

Legal Issues of Digital Technology

Legal issues arising from blockchain technology and other advancements in the digital arena are reminiscent and comparable to the rise of the Internet some two decades ago. Among the difficulties presented in the civil and criminal arenas are the adjustments required by legislators, regulators, and judges to address new challenges posed by innovative technologies. The following areas are some that have to be determined.

Jurisdiction

Jurisdiction is based on the concept of boundaries; it is the power of a particular court to exercise its authority in a given case. In the United States, there are multiple levels of jurisdictional issues that may arise dependent on the nature of the parties, i.e., where they reside and where the controversy arose or is based on, and disputes called subject-matter that concern the laws and regulations therein. In the United States there are 51 government entities that exercise jurisdiction within their domain, namely, the federal government, based in Washington, D.C., and the 50 states. Each of the governmental entities possesses a judicial system

© The Author(s) 2018
R. Girasa, *Regulation of Cryptocurrencies and Blockchain Technologies*, Palgrave Studies in Financial Services Technology, https://doi.org/10.1007/978-3-319-78509-7_3

unique unto itself and each exercises jurisdiction or power over its inhabitants according to the laws and regulations promulgated therein. Federal subject-matter jurisdiction is based upon Article 3, §2 of the U.S. Constitution, which states: "The judicial Power shall extend to all Cases, in Law and Equity, arising under this Constitution, the Laws of the United States, and Treaties made…to Controversies between two or more States; between a State and Citizens of another State; between Citizens of different States;…and between a State, or the Citizens thereof, and foreign States, Citizens or Subjects."

Federal jurisdiction is very broad, extending to all laws passed by Congress, issues related to federal questions, to cases involving ambassadors and other foreign diplomatic personnel, to disputes between states, and matters arising out of the U.S. Constitution. Its jurisdiction may be *exclusive*, meaning that only federal courts may hear the cases or controversies, or *concurrent*, whereby jurisdiction is shared with state courts according to the laws and regulations enacted therein. Generally, when a federal statute is enacted, it will provide for whether it is to be enforced exclusively or permissively with the states. Exclusive jurisdiction would include subject areas such as bankruptcy, federal crimes, and international treaties. Federal courts may share jurisdiction in cases where a citizen of one state sues a citizen of another state. Jurisdiction may exist in state courts wherein the cause of action has its main locus or may be exercised in the federal court provided the controversy is for more than $75,000. States also have both exclusive and concurrent jurisdiction with the federal government and also with other states depending on the nature of the litigation. If the controversy is between citizens of different states and the sum in question is for $75,000 or less, than the litigation is reserved to the states.

Jurisdiction may also be based by service of a summons upon the party being sued either within the state (*in personam jurisdiction*) or by service outside the state (*long-arm jurisdiction)* provided certain due process constitutional requirements are met. Other bases for jurisdiction may be obtained *in rem,* that is, by be the assertion of authority over property located therein and also *attachment jurisdiction* that permits the seizure of in-state property belong to out-of-state persons.

Comparable to cyberlaw concerns, courts will need to address the locus of activities and whether a particular court may entertain a lawsuit arising out of alleged contractual or tortious breach inasmuch as blockchain usage may take place at any site globally[1] The issue and determination are more complex than cyberlaw cases where, in most cases, the parties and their locations are known. In the virtual arena the parties act anonymously. Nevertheless, the location of federal and state courts have evolved a variety of concepts having at their bases due process obligations under the 5th and 14th Amendments of the U.S. Constitution as exemplified by the "minimum contacts" requirements as set forth in *International Shoe Co. v. Washington*[2] and *Asahi Metal Industry Co. v. Superior Court.*[3] Federal courts have adopted a "sliding scale" based on active or passive use of the Internet to determine whether they will entertain jurisdiction as illustrated in *Zippo Mfr. Co. v. Zippo Dot Com, Inc.*[4] It would appear that these precedents will be applicable to litigation arising from digital currency-based disputes.

Due to the anonymity of blockchain users, enforcement authorities are at a loss as to how to oversee and enforce legal obligations to protect investors and other parties to particular transactions. Jurisdiction can be asserted successfully over firms acting as brokers or exchanges provided their activities are within the national boundaries of the courts, or even worldwide if multi-national co-operative agreements are secured. The global nature of these transactions and the vast array of statutory, regulatory, and customs of particular national and local authorities render enforcement often improbable. For example, owing to twentieth century historical conflicts, the European Union (EU) is exceptionally concerned with privacy matters, as evidenced by the new EU Data Protection Regulation.[5] The fear is that wrongdoers may be exempt from lawful regulatory regimes.[6]

Scholars have offered a variety of possible solutions to the conundrum. Among them include the suggestion that there be "an open source platform ecosystem of smart contracting dispute resolution" whereby parties to the contract can opt into particular dispute resolution mechanisms. They would be platform-based ecosystems for dispute resolution of "cryptotransactions" that would facilitate anonymity but also permit users to choose which judges or arbitrators are to decide conflicts among the parties.[7] The Aragon Jurisdiction Network offers a possible alternative decentralized dispute mechanism by defining a set of contracts open to arbitral resolution wherein an individual having a dispute posts a bond with the Network, which will be returned only if the party is successful but forfeited if unsuccessful. Thereafter, a panel of five judges will review the rules and materials forming the basis of the claim dispute and make a decision, which may either be accepted by the applicant or disputed, at which time a larger bond is to be posted. Ultimately, the case can be elevated to the Network's nine-member Supreme Court which makes the final decision that may not be appealed. Unlike the traditional norm of judicial decision-making, prior judges of the Network are rewarded or penalized for their proper or wrongful determination.[8]

SEC v. Shavers

There is a paucity of cases that concern the issue of jurisdiction particularly relating to bitcoins. An important early case where the court discussed whether it possessed jurisdiction in a Bitcoin-related litigation was *SEC v. Shavers.*[9] In its decision, the court determined that jurisdictional requirements had been met which resulted in a decision granting summary judgment to the Securities and Exchange Commission (SEC) that decreed the disgorgement of $40 million from the defendants, Trenton T. Shavers and his unincorporated affiliated entity, and a fine of $150,000. Shavers and his unincorporated online entity, in essence operated a Ponzi-type scheme where investors were told that he was in the business of selling Bitcoin to local people and offered investors up to 1 percent interest daily until the funds were either withdrawn or the host's dealings were no longer profitable. Shavers obtained 700,467 bitcoins from investors valued at $4.592,806. The investors lost 263,104 bitcoins, equivalent to $1,834,303 (at the then value) when invested.

With respect to jurisdiction, the court determined that the Bitcoin constituted investments over the Internet operating under the Internet name of "pirateat40"; that solicitation was made in online chat rooms and on the Bitcoin Forum, an online forum with a promise of a 7 percent return weekly; that Shavers used new bitcoins received from investors to pay purported returns on outstanding investments; and that he diverted investors' bitcoins to his personal use. Shavers was, at all times, a Texas resident soliciting investors to invest in the Bitcoin-related investment scheme and Bitcoin is an electronic form of currency not backed by any real assets and without specie. Contrary to Shavers' contention that bitcoins were not money and thus not securities, the court determined that the investments were securities holdings and that they were investment contracts having met the three-fold requirements of a security under the *SEC v. Howey* case, namely (1) an investment of money, (2) in a common enterprise, (3) with the expectation that profits will be derived from the efforts of the promoter or a third party.[10] The court concluded that the scheme was a Ponzi scheme constituting a fraud on investors all in violation of §5 and §17(a) of the Securities Act of 1933 and §10(b) of the Securities Exchange Act of 1934 and Rule 10b-5 thereunder. Thus, the court determined that it had subject-matter jurisdiction under §20 and §22 of the 1933 Act and §§21 and 27 of the 1934 Act.[11]

Gordon v. Dailey

In a New Jersey federal case, *Gordon v. Dailey*[12] the court also determined it possessed jurisdiction in a civil case wherein the plaintiffs complained that the defendants' sale of securities violated the provisions of the Securities Act of 1933 and the Securities Exchange Act of 1934 based upon diversity of citizenship and the sum complained exceeded the required jurisdictional sum of $75,000, to wit, over $1 million in Bitcoin value. The complaint, in essence, stated that the defendants offered 100,000 bonds to the public that were tiered in value to be purchased in Bitcoin. All dividends received for mining Bitcoin would be paid in Bitcoin, although no guarantee of value was made respecting the said offering. The complaint further alleged that the IPO offering of Bitcoin securities was never registered as required by the said securities statutes.[13]

Virtual Currencies as Money

Virtual currencies, and in their major incarnation as Bitcoin, are not fiat money, and possess no backing from the Federal Reserve, but the issue remains whether they are considered to be moneys exchanged from one party to another by digital means. The IRS considers them as property and taxable when exchanged at a profit (see the chapter on "Crowdfunding and the Taxation of Virtual Currencies"). Although governmental entities may deny virtual currencies as "money" for tax purposes, nevertheless, they may hold that status in the minds of their holders. They are considered as monetary assets that are used for the payment of goods and services, which begs the question at the outset of the fundamental meaning of the word "money."

The confusion is reflected in scholarly articles wherein authors cite the basis for holding virtual currency, particularly Bitcoin, as either "money" or "property." The argument for its status as "money" is illustrated by the purpose of Bitcoin to act as an alternative currency that avoids the need for third parties such as governments, central banks, and "shadow" (non-bank) banks. It is used currently in some quarters as a medium of exchange, albeit not universally, but is increasingly common as merchants become accustomed to the new technologies and willing to accept non-fiat money. The advantages are the avoidance of credit card fees of generally 2–4 percent to the merchant, and monthly interest to the consumer, which enables the former to discount merchandise. The obvious problems that arise are the volatility of the virtual currency and how to deal with returns. Some merchants resolve the issue of returns by offering credit on store-based credit cards. In addition to acting as a possible medium of exchange, the virtual currency may act as a store of value, i.e., an asset to be retained pending an expected rise in value.[14]

Virtual currency as "property" is illustrated by federal and state laws that treat Bitcoin and other virtual currencies as intangible property. It is so designated by the IRS, by FinCEN, by the CFTC as a commodity under the CEA; under bankruptcy laws; as part of equitable distribution or division under divorce laws; by the New York "BitLicense Requirement"; under trust and estates laws that concern inheritance; under the Uniform Commercial Code Article 9 as a security interest in personal property;

and under other diverse statutes and regulations.[15] Confusion thus remains and future regulatory agencies will have to decipher it.

Smart Contracts

Smart contracts are virtual contracts using and are atop the Ethereum platform, which are entered into without human intervention. They are based on a sequence of coded events that automatically verify and execute the agreed terms of the contract.[16] The terms therein are recorded in a computer rather than hard-copy legal language. The concept of a "smart contract" was conceived by Nick Szabo, cited previously, who is a polymath, computer scientist, and legal scholar who was interested in the interrelationship between contracts and digital technology.[17] The system involves a decentralized platform run on a custom-built blockchain that has smart contracts and which Ethereum alleges is run "exactly as programmed without any possibility of downtime, censorship, fraud or third-party interference."[18] There are no intermediaries such as clearing houses inasmuch as they are linked to DLT.

Among the benefits of a smart contract is its coding that is less ambiguous than verbal language, verifiable, self-executing, and integrates with IT systems. However, it also has negative aspects such as the lack of knowledge concerning its methodologies, privacy and transparency concerns, and the need for continuous updates.[19] Thus, the federal government is exploring the use of smart contracts internally which offer considerable savings, time, and ostensible freedom from hacking.[20] The government has awarded $1.3 million in blockchain contracts in 2017 and will likely substantially increase its investment in the technology, particularly to streamline record-keeping and promote transparency and accountability. States, such as Arizona, Illinois, Maine, and Vermont, are beginning to adapt blockchain for permanency in record-keeping and security.[21]

Unlike the traditional contract whereby a party may commence litigation to enforce it, including seeking damages for non-fulfillment or requesting a court to exercise its equitable powers in granting specific performance, a smart contract by definition has already been executed and a party suing essentially requests a court to undo what has already been accomplished. It is the performance of the contract that signifies its acceptance. Once the agreement has been encoded, a party may not undo it unless the agreement so permits. There are judicially permitted exceptions for illegality, lack of capacity, and other such defenses, but smart contracts adapted to particular needs, such as the purchase of real estate, pre-nuptial agreements, construction, and other financial areas, are likely to be the future trend making traditional contractual arrangements less common.[22]

Smart contracts will require law firms to adapt to the new technologies. Among the personnel required to make the transformation in larger firms are attorneys knowledgeable about contracts, software developers who assist in providing the technical expertise of transformation using blockchain, and software coders and programmers who will code the various terms of the contract. Law schools, in conjunction with information systems professionals, will have to train future attorneys in making the transition. There will be new terms such as "dynamic transaction" and "smart contract mediator." The smart title company of the future will see the elimination of current title searches and recording processes, and other changes which will reduce costs and time, and lessen the possibility of fraudulent activity. The need for title searchers and title companies themselves may be eliminated together with third parties who participate in the process of conveying title from one party to another.[23]

There are consumer protection risks due to the complex nature of the technology for ordinary consumers who may not understand the terms to which they are agreeing. Other fears include financial instability brought about by the non-reversible nature of the contracts which could enforce adverse terms automatically through the financial system. Additional practical issues include the admissibility of the contracts under existing rules of evidence; the application of burden of proof to the accuracy and authenticity of the agreements; who is accountable for an alleged breach; the application of rules of evidence such as the parol evidence rule and the dead man's statute; legal defenses such as minority, fraud, mutual mistake, identity of the parties; and bringing both attorneys and judges up to speed in understanding their technology-based nature.[24]

Intellectual Property

Are the many forms of virtual currency and the underlying technology protected by intellectual property (IP) in the form of patents, copyrights, trademarks, and/or trade secrets? It would appear that they may come within the parameters of protection, at least within the United States. The basic definitions are as follows. A *patent* is a grant of property rights by the U.S. Patent and Trademark Office to whoever invents or discovers any new and useful process, machine, manufacture, or composition of matter, or any new and useful improvement thereof. Its protection is dependent on whether it is a utility patent, which is good for 20 years from date of filing, or a design patent which has a 14-year protection. A *copyright* is a form of protection provided to authors of original works of authorship such as literary, dramatic, musical, artistic, and other such forms, and is protected for the life of the author plus 70 years. A *trademark* is any word, name, symbol, or device, or any combination thereof, that is used, or intended to be used, in commerce to identify and distinguish the goods or services of the holder thereof and is protected for an initial 10-year period and renewable indefinitely for additional 10-year timeframes. A *trade secret* is any information that provides economic value that is not in the public domain and that has been a reasonably kept secret. It protects formulas, patterns, compilations, programs, devices, methods, techniques, or processes as long as they remain secret.[25]

Ordinarily, when discussing IP, we discuss whether a particular invention, idea, or symbol qualifies for statutory protection, but blockchain technology is an innovative benefit in that it may act as registry for IP rights permitting users to file and catalog their creations. It can act as evidential proof of ownership of copyright-protected original works in contested proceedings not only in the United States but also worldwide. The use of blockchain prevents vulnerability of the works by other persons alleging ownership because it is stored on a main centralized register that is part of a connected, publicly distributed, system of registers.[26] Currently, there are platforms already making use of the technology such as Binded,[27] formerly known as Blockai, which is a copyright service using Bitcoin blockchain to create legally binding records. Although its use is free, the site offers to register the copyright with the U.S. Copyright Office for the cost of the filing fee using a one-click process.[28] There are numerous other websites offering comparable services that, for example, include securing trade secrets, establishing prior art in patent cases, and enhancing contracts by alleged "decentralized, uncensorable, permission-less, resilient" platforms.[29]

Blockchain technology may be used for smart contracts in relation to IP whereby persons wishing to use copyrighted works could secure permission from owners by making micro-payments directly, thereby avoiding significant transactional fees that often accompany such usage. Licenses in IP could be made self-executing, especially in the music industry, so that the owners would possess greater control over their works in addition to having unassailable proof of their creative works.[30] The fashion industry is particularly vulnerable to misuse with theft of designs and other IP protected works, often by larger, well-financed enterprises which have the resources to defend against litigation by less-well-financed enterprises. Blockchain has made proof of misuse much easier to establish with less costly outlays for proof in litigation. It is invaluable for its record-keeping capabilities, registration, ability to detect forgeries, fake goods, gray goods (goods sold in violation of contractual obligations, generally, beyond the intended national borders for resale), evidence of first use, payments, and other uses.[31]

Governments faced with newly innovative financial products or services are understandably unable to react until a learning process has taken place and abuses begin to emerge. In the chapter on "Federal Regulation of Virtual Currencies", we will examine the federal regulation of virtual currencies and the agencies that are presently engaged in overseeing those aspects that come within their domain.

Notes

1. For a discussion of the complexity jurisdiction in cyberlaw cases and how courts exercise it, see Roy J. Girasa, Cyberlaw: National And International Perspectives, Ch. 2, Prentice-Hall, 2010.
2. *International Shoe Co. v. Washington*, 326 U.S. 310 (1945).

3. *Asahi Metal Industry Co. v. Superior* Court, 480 U.S. 102 (1987). For a discussion of jurisdictional basics see, Betsy Rosenblatt, Principles of Jurisdiction, https://cyber.harvard.edu/property99/domain/Betsy.html
4. *Zippo Mfr. Co. v. Zippo Dot Com, Inc.*, 952 F. Supp. 1119 (W.D. Pa. 1997).
5. Regulation EU 2016/679.
6. Gregory Brandman and Samuel Thampapillai, *Blockchain – Considering the Regulatory Environment*, University of Oxford Law Faculty, July 7, 2017, https://www.law.ox.ac.uk/business-law-blog/blog/2016/07/blockchain-%E2%80%93-considering-regulatory-horizon
7. Wulf Kaal and Craig Calcaterra, *Cryptotransaction Dispute Resolution*, University of Oxford Law Faculty, July 13, 2017, https://www.law.ox.ac.uk/business-law-blog/blog/2017/07/cryptotransaction-dispute-resolution
8. *Digital Decision,* Aragon Network, https://blog.aragon.one/aragon-network-jurisdiction-part-1-decentralized-court-c8ab2a675e82
9. *SEC v. Shavers,* No. 4:13-CV-416 (E.D. Tex. Aug. 6, 2013).
10. *SEC v. W.J. Howey & Co.,* 328 U.S. 293, 298–99 (1946); *Long v. Shultz Cattle Co,* 881 F.2d 129, 132 (1989).
11. *SEC v. Shavers, supra* at note 9, https://www.sec.gov/litigation/complaints/2013/comp-pr2013-132.pdf. See also U.S. Securities and Exchange Commission, *Litigation Release.* No. 23090 (Sept. 22, 2014), https://www.sec.gov/litigation/litreleases/2014/lr23090.htm
12. *Gordon v. Dailey,* No. 14-cv-7495 (JHR) (JS) (D.C.N.J., July 25, 2016).
13. *Federal Court Allows Bitcoin Investor Suit to Proceed,* Internet Law Commentary, March 30, 2017, https://internetlawcommentary.com/2017/03/30/federal-court-allows-bitcoin-investor-suit-proceed/
14. Stephanie Lo and J. Christina Wang, *Bitcoin as Money?,* Federal Reserve Bank of Boston: Current Policy Perspectives, Sept. 4, 2014, https://www.bostonfed.org/publications/current-policy-perspectives/2014/bitcoin-as-money.aspx
15. J. Dax Hansen and Joshua L. Boehm, *Treatment of Bitcoin Under U.S. Property Law,* Perkins Coie, March 2017, https://www.virtualcurrencyreport.com/wp-content/uploads/sites/13/2017/03/2016_ALL_Property-Law-Bitcoin_onesheet.pdf
16. Cynthia Gayton, *Smart Contracts, Cryptocurrency and Taxes,* July 26, 2016, https://medium.com/@squizzi3/smart-contracts-cryptocurrency-and-taxes-6050f1f5308e

17. Search Complaince, *Smart contract,* Tech Target, http://searchcompliance.techtarget.com/definition/smart-contract
18. Ethereum, https://ethereum.org/
19. Iltacon, *What are Blockchain and Smart Contracts and When Will They Be Important,* Panel Discussion, Sept. 30, 2016, https://www.iltanet.org/HigherLogic/System/DownloadDocumentFile.ashx?DocumentFileKey =bde36e05
20. U.S. Government Services Administration, *Blockchain,* https://www.gsa.gov/technology/government-it-initiatives/emerging-citizen-technology/blockchain
21. Michaela Ross, *Tech Giants Eye Government Blockchain Use as Business Boost,* Bloomberg, Aug. 25, 2017, https://www.bna.com/tech-giants-eye-n73014463697/
22. For a history of smart contracts and their implications, see Max Raskin, *The Law and Legality of Smart Contracts,* 1 GEO. L. TECH. REV. 304 (2017), https://www.georgetownlawtechreview.org/the-law-and-legality-of-smart-contracts/GLTR-04-2017/
23. Caitlin Moon, *Blockchain for Lawyers 101: Part 2,* Law Technology Today, Jan. 31, 2017, http://www.lawtechnologytoday.org/2017/01/blockchain-lawyers-101-part-2/
24. Kate H. Withers, *Smart Contracts: Opportunities and Legal Risks in Fin Tech,* Nov. 8, 2016, National Law Review, Jan 15, 2018, https://www.natlawreview.com/article/smart-contracts-opportunities-and-legal-risks-fintech
25. Sue A. Purvis, *The Fundamentals of Intellectual Property for the Entrepreneur,* U.S. Patent and Trademark Office, https://www.uspto.gov/sites/default/files/about/offices/ous/121115.pdf
26. Amanda G. Ciccotelli, *How blockchain is critical to the securitization of IP,* IPWatchdog, Oct. 9, 2017, http://www.ipwatchdog.com/2017/10/09/blockchain-critical-securitization-ip/id=88179/
27. Binded, www.binded.com
28. Michael Zhang, *Binded Unveils One Click US Copyright Registration for Photos at No Extra Fee,* Petapixel, Aug. 8, 2017. https://petapixel.com/2017/08/08/binded-unveils-one-click-us-copyright-registration-photos-no-extra-fee/
29. Bernstein, https://www.bernstein.io/

30. Suzy Shinner *Blockchain Technology and IP,* Lexology, Feb. 3, 2017, https://www.lexology.com/library/detail.aspx?g=755d3893-a5fb-43d7-86f7-c4b842641bbf

31. Ruth Burstall and Birgit Clark, *Blockchain, IP and the Fashion Industry,* Managing Intellectual Property, March 23, 2017, http://www.managingip.com/Article/3667444/Blockchain-IP-and-the-fashion-industry.html

Federal Regulation of Virtual Currencies

Introduction

National and local governments, both in the United States and abroad, are attempting to understand and regulate these virtual currencies which raise issues affecting investors and consumers using them. Among the issues are potential fraud, use by drug dealers and other criminal elements for money laundering, etc. due to the current near impossibility of tracing, tax aspects, the displacement of national currencies, and other concerns. It has been reported that ostracized governments, due to the sanctions imposed upon them, including bank restrictions, have amassed large sums of Bitcoin and other currencies which serve as hard currencies for their endeavors.[1] Due to its open-source software as a decentralized model, North Korea, in order to overcome United Nations, U.S., and other governmental restrictions, has engaged in Bitcoin mining to add to Bitcoin's blockchain in an endeavor to raise funds that have been blocked for its missile and nuclear programs. North Korea began its mining on May 17, 2017, continuing in its efforts exponentially to avoid restrictions and have access to global capital.[2]

Bitcoins were earlier adopted by criminal elements because of the anonymity and inherent difficulty of determining whether law enforcement

© The Author(s) 2018
R. Girasa, *Regulation of Cryptocurrencies and Blockchain Technologies*, Palgrave Studies in Financial Services Technology, https://doi.org/10.1007/978-3-319-78509-7_4

had the power to regulate activities that most often were borderless. Some commentators have asserted that the only or most noteworthy value of Bitcoin is its "underlying value as a medium of exchange by lawbreakers."[3] The surge in the value of Bitcoin may be attributable, in substantial part, because of its use by drug kingpins, terrorists, white-collar criminals, and Russian cybercriminals.[4] Bitcoin and other cryptocurrencies have also gained the attention of Islamic terrorists as a means of receiving financial contributions from sympathizers while preserving their anonymity.[5]

In a detailed study of terrorist use of virtual currencies, it was found that ISIS (Islamic State in Iraq and Syria) members have made use of virtual currencies to fund their operations but, unlike other criminal enterprises, are limited particularly to countries where the infrastructure supports the exchange of virtual currencies. The advantage of such use, of course, is the global nature of currency exchange in an anonymous manner. The authors suggest a series of policy recommendations: (1) a better understanding of the evolving threat of virtual currencies financing terrorism; (2) prioritizing terrorist financing as a matter of public policy and law enforcement significance; and (3) prioritizing terrorist financing as a compliance matter within private institutions.[6] Nevertheless, it appears that cash still remains the major source of terrorist financing owing to the lack of technological infrastructure especially where such terrorism is dominant in underdeveloped regions such as northern Nigeria and Yemen.

On the other hand, it appears that governmental agencies are beginning to crack the wall of anonymity by partnering with companies able to analyze data, often from anonymous sources using Bitcoin, that draws inferences from persons using the blockchain technology and its products. One company, Chainalysis, is working with U.S. and foreign governments to track the flow of funds, aided by the discovery of Bitcoin addresses found in a suspect's possession which then may be used to secure court orders for further discovery.[7] Researchers at the University of Luxembourg, using relatively inexpensive equipment, allege that they are able to ascertain the identity of between 11 percent and 60 percent of all Bitcoin transactions. The method used is by "abusing" the firewalls protecting anonymity and de-anonymizing the network protecting the identity of those using the network to conceal their transactions.[8]

A number of U.S. and international governmental agencies have begun to focus major financial resources to assure compliance with existing laws and regulations and to ascertain and punish criminal behavior. The U.S. federal and state agencies concerned with cryptocurrencies are discussed below. A critical question that has arisen for regulatory purposes is whether virtual currency is currency or property and whether the offerings are securities. The U.S. government, as previously stated, has determined that virtual currencies such as Bitcoin are deemed to be property rather than currencies.[9] The tax treatment of virtual currency efforts discussed in the chapter on "Crowdfunding and Taxation of Virtual Currencies."

U.S. Government Agencies Concerned with Virtual Currencies

Securities and Exchange Commission (SEC)

The SEC is the primary regulator of the securities market including securities exchanges, securities brokers and dealers, investment advisers, and mutual funds, for the protection of investors and the general public against fraud.[10] The basic question is whether it deems cryptocurrencies as "securities," thus granting it jurisdiction to regulate. The seminal case of *SEC v. Howey*, cited previously, is the basis for the assertion of authority by the SEC.

The SEC, which has been unusually reticent concerning regulation of Initial Coin Offerings (ICOs), has begun to weigh in with comments and investigations as to their character and the need for oversight. It noted that some promoters of ICOs have told potential investors that they may expect a sizeable return on their investments or participate in a share of returns from capital raised from the sales of coins to fund development of a digital platform, software, or projects. In so doing, they may fall under the *Howey* definition of a *security* and thus be subject to possible regulation by the SEC by (1) its investment in a common enterprise, (2) through the efforts of others, (3) with the expectation of earning a profit.[11]

Enforcement of securities laws has to date been undertaken by the newly formed Cyber Unit of the SEC's Enforcement Division. The Unit was created to focus on cyber-related misconduct including market manipulation, hacking, use of the dark web for unlawful conduct, violations involving DLT and ICOs, and other cyber-related threats to investors and to the general public.[12] Much of the confusion may also be attributable to the exemption from securities registration given to crowdfunding efforts discussed in the chapter on "Crowdfunding and Taxation of Virtual Currencies." Unlike typical IPOs that raise capital by the sale of shares of stock, ICOs may offer tokens that have a variety of other incentives such as social causes, games, or the receipt of present or future products or services. There are a number of excellent analyses of whether tokens distributed on virtual currency websites are securities offerings subject to SEC registration requirements or are exempt from the said regulations.[13]

Distinguishing between legitimate and illusory offers may bring about SEC enforcement based on the Securities Exchange Act of 1934 for fraud. Examples of prosecutions are the PlexCoin ICO and the Munchee ICO discussed below.[14]

SEC First Enforcement Action: REcoin

On September 29, 2017, the SEC filed a complaint seeking a temporary stay and final injunction, disgorgement of profits, and other relief against REcoin Group Foundation, DRC World, Inc., and Maksim Zaslavskiy. The complaint alleged that Zaslavskiy, who was president of the two companies, had raised $300,000 in ICOs from investors through misrepresentations and deceptive acts relating to alleged investments in tokens or coins offered by the companies. The SEC claimed that the tokens or coins were unlawful offerings of securities for which no registration statement was filed as required by law. The purpose of each ICO, according to the complaint, was to convert "fiat currency" or "digital currency" obtained into "tokenized" currency backed by investment in assets, to wit, real estate for REcoin, and diamonds for its Diamond Reserve Club.

The defendants' posting characterized the offering as "The First Ever Cryptocurrency Backed by Real Estate." It was expected that the investments would generate returns from their appreciation in value and the appreciation in value of the tokens by reason of increased demand.

It was alleged that the false and misleading statements included claims made by Zaslavskiy that investors were in fact purchasing tokens or coins; that defendants raised over $2 million, later raised to $4 million, from REcoin; that REcoin had a team of lawyers, professionals, brokers, and accountants that would invest the proceeds into real estate, and that Diamond had experts to select the best diamonds; that REcoin had to shut down because the government compelled it to do so; and that investors could expect to reap rewards of 10–15 percent on their investments. The statements were allegedly untrue. The complaint further stated that defendants also attempted to evade registration requirements by refashioning the sale as memberships in a club which had the same attributes of securities that required registration under both the Securities Act of 1933 and the Securities Exchange Act of 1934 and regulations issued thereunder.[15]

It is becoming increasingly evident that ICOs, which, unlike IPOs, were perceived by investors to be unregulated, are now facing governmental scrutiny. It is estimated that the ICO market will have received some $1 billion to –$1.5 billion from investors by the close of 2017.[16] The confusion attendant to virtual currencies initially led to a lack of regulatory intervention but whether perceived as currency or as securities or other forms of monetary mechanisms, the potential and actual loss of investments to unscrupulous entrepreneurs has now caught the attention of federal and state regulatory authorities. The chairperson of the SEC identified ICOs as a priority for enforcement. The characterization by companies engaged in ICOs pertaining to sales of tokens or coins will be left to Congressional authorization and judicial interpretations.[17] Issuers of offerings of utility tokens will have to carefully scrutinize compliance regulations, both of the SEC and of the CFTC that oversees futures offerings. State law observance, especially as to banking and payments requirements, also adds to the confusing current state of ICOs.[18]

The DAO Conundrum

The SEC investigated a new cryptocurrency offering to determine whether the Decentralized Autonomous Organization (DAO) violated U.S. securities laws through its sales of DAO Tokens to investors to be used to fund projects. The DAO is an organization created by German nationals that arose from the crowdfunding exception to the Securities Act of 1933[19] which implemented the requirements of Title III of the Jumpstart Our Business Startups Act.[20] The Act, discussed in the chapter on "Crowdfunding and Taxation of Virtual Currencies," facilitated new ventures by removing many of the onerous filing requirements of the securities laws and provided a framework for the regulation of registered funding portals and broker-dealers that issuers are required to use as intermediaries in the offer of sale of securities.[21] The DAO, during the "Offering Period" of April 30, 2016 through May 28, 2016, offered and sold "pseudonymously" 1.15 billion DAO tokens in exchange for a total of approximately 12 million Ether, a virtual currency based on the Ethereum blockchain. Holders of the DAO tokens had unrestricted rights to resell them.

The DAO initially sought to create a crowdfunding smart contract using the blockchain to execute and record the contracts. The purchase of DAO tokens with Ether entitled participants to vote on projects funded by the purchases and to "rewards" which were akin to dividends. Funds raised from investors were held at an Ethereum blockchain address associated with DAO. Promotion of the DAO was through its website "The DAO Website" which described its intended purpose, how it operated, and provided a link through which purchase of tokens could be made. The company also posted almost daily updates through the media and conducted online forums. Ether raised and future profits were to be maintained in the DAO's Ethereum blockchain address. Individuals seeking funding from the DAO were to submit a proposal for projects, which involved a smart contract published on the Ethereum blockchain, and had to provide details of the proposal which would be reviewed and published on the DAO Website and required approval by a majority of holders of the DAO tokens. The proposals were to be initially reviewed by one or more of the DAO's "Curators" who had the ultimate power to decide whether to submit a proposal for a vote.[22]

The SEC conducted an investigation to determine whether the DAO violated U.S. securities laws by failing to register the purchase and sale of tokens as securities. In its Report of Investigation dated July 25, 2017, the SEC concluded that DAO Tokens are securities under the Securities Act of 1933 and the Securities Exchange Act of 1934. It stated that the foundational principles of the securities laws apply to organizations or capital-raising entities making use of distributed ledger technology. Citing the *Howey* seminal case and other precedents, it noted that the DAO Tokens sale is an investment in a common enterprise premised on a reasonable expectation of profits to be derived from the entrepreneurial or managerial efforts of others.

The definition of a security, the SEC noted, is based on a flexible rather than static principle. In the DAO offerings, investors invested money which need not take the form of cash. Investors used Ether to make their investments in exchange for DAO Tokens. There is a reasonable expectation of profits inasmuch as investors who purchased DAO Tokens were investing in a common enterprise and reasonably expected to earn a profit from the enterprise in the form of dividends, other periodic payments, or the increased value of their investments. The profits were derived from the managerial efforts of others, specifically from the decisions and activity of Slock.it, its co-founders, and the DAO's Curators. Investors were urged to make their investments by the marketing of the DAO and active engagement of the company's co-founders with token holders. Control was centered on Slock.it, a German corporation, and the co-founders and the Curators who made the fundamental decisions whether or not to submit proposals for a vote by the token holders. The token holders' voting rights were limited and dependent on the efforts of the Curators, etc.[23]

The SEC concluded that issuers must register offers and sales of securities unless a valid exemption exists. The SEC defines *issuer* to include "every person who issues or proposes to issue any security" and persons to include "any incorporated organization."[24] It also includes issuers who "devise new ways to issue their securities and the definition of a security itself expands."[25] Thus, the DAO, an unincorporated organization, was an issuer of securities and was responsible for the success or failure of the enterprise, for which concern investors needed information materials to make their investment decisions. Section 5 of the Securities Exchange Act of 1934 makes it unlawful for any broker, dealer, or exchange, directly or indirectly, to effect any transaction in a security, or to report any such transaction, in interstate commerce, unless the exchange is registered as a national securities exchange under §6 of the Exchange Act, or is exempted from such registration. The DAO Platforms that traded DAO Tokens, according to the SEC, appear to fully meet the criteria of Rule 3b-16(a) which recites a functional test for determining whether a trading system meets the definition of an *exchange*. The test includes any organization, association, or group of persons bringing together the orders of multiple purchasers and sellers of securities and uses established, non-discretionary methods under which such orders interact with each other, and the sellers and buyers agree to the terms of the trade. The SEC concluded that the platforms that traded DAO Tokens satisfied the Rule and were not within the exemptions.[26]

Nevertheless, the SEC decided not to institute enforcement action at this time and advised the issuers of distributed ledger or blockchain technology, as well as investors in the DAO, to comply with the appropriate registration requirements.[27] The SEC apparently was keen to foster the new technology, and, as stated by SEC chairperson, Jay Clayton, "We seek to foster innovative and beneficial ways to raise capital, while ensuring – first and foremost – that investors and our markets are protected."[28] In addition, a problem arose in June 2016 when a DAO that was built on Ethereum started with $150 million in crowdfunding but a third of the virtual currency (Ether), some $50 million to 55 million, was hacked but later restored on the Ethereum blockchain.[29] The identity of the thief has not been discovered although it is believed that there was no actual loss.[30]

SEC v. Munchee Inc.

In an administrative proceeding that has caused noteworthy comments concerning the expansion of SEC authority, the agency issued a cease-and-desist order and commencement of proceedings against Munchee pursuant to §8A of the Securities Act of 1933 that requires registration of certain securities offerings and which order was consented to by the respondent. Munchee commenced a business in California that created an iPhone application allowing users to review restaurant meals. In October and November, 2017, the company offered and sold digital tokens to be issued on a blockchain in order to raise $15 million for the purpose of buying advertisements, writing reviews, selling food, and other related applications. The company alleged that it was anticipated the tokens would increase in value and later be traded on secondary markets. The SEC, in an Order dated December 11, 2017, based on the *Howey* three-pronged analysis of what constitutes an investment and its actions, and findings in the DAO report, concluded that Munchee's efforts constituted investment contracts that required registration with the SEC under the 1933 Act. It determined that the three-pronged requirements were met in that purchasers of the tokens would have a reasonable expectation of a future profit based on the efforts of others (Munchee) that included the app's revision and creation of the MUN "ecosystem" with the proceeds from sales of the tokens. The company complied with the Order by not delivering the tokens and returning the proceeds received for them.[31]

There were a number of commentators concerning the significance of the Munchee Order. The action highlights the position of the SEC in that offerings of blockchain-related tokens may be regulated as securities and are subject to registration and other Securities Acts requirements. The SEC stated that even if the tokens had a practical use, this did not preclude them from being a security. Characterizing the ICO as involving a "utility token" is not conclusory by its labelling but rather requires an assessment of the economic realities underlying the transaction. There were no findings or indications of fraud as is the usual basis in SEC rulings and no "bright-line" rules (clearly defined rules) expressed to guide future compliance of companies making similar offerings.[32] In addition to a lack of fraudulent conduct, there were no claims made by Munchee that investors would participate in the company's profits; rather, the "utility tokens" could be used to purchase goods and services once the company had raised sufficient capital to build the intended "ecosystem." Therefore, the case appears to symbolize the fact that the SEC will broaden its perspective concerning what constitutes a security under the *Howey* analysis and its intent to prosecute firms that fail to file registration requirements under the Securities Acts of 1933 and 1934.[33]

In another commentary, the lessons to be drawn are the need to consult counsel in making offerings which may draw SEC scrutiny where the emphasis, in addition to being a current utility, is that future development plans may materially enhance the value of the token; where the emphasis is on growth and profit or completion of a product rather than its utility; and where the marketing of the product or service is concentrated less on the utility and more on expansion. Thus, the offering should be strongly biased towards the existing practical application of the product, rather than the expectation of profit by future developments, to avoid SEC scrutiny.[34]

SEC Chairman's Commentary

Jay Clayton, the Chairman of the SEC, in a public statement on December 11, 2017 at the same time as the issuance of the Munchee Order, offered his personal views concerning cryptocurrency and ICOs. He commented on the legality of a cryptocurrency offering and persons making the offerings, the fairness of the trading markets to date including manipulation and attendant risks, market professionals and their impact, and related issues. He noted that the offerings present substantially less protection for the investor coupled with much greater opportunities and risks of fraud and manipulation. To date, no ICO has been registered with the SEC, nor has the SEC approved for listing and trading any exchange-traded products related to cryptocurrencies. Therefore, the public is warned about making investments and before doing so should consider a number of questions stated in the Public Statement and answered from those offering the ICOs. The list of questions suggested by the Commissioner is shown as Appendix 2. Among the risks faced by investors, and which the SEC has limited or no ability to assist with, are offerings that are trans-border with moneys paid deflected to foreign entities.[35]

Clayton cautioned market professionals, including their attorneys, accountants, and consultants, that a change in the structure of the offerings by recording through a blockchain ledger does not change the substance of the transaction, which may entail an offering of a security coupled with registration requirements. By calling a token a "utility" token does not remove it from consideration as a security. When the offered tokens incorporate features that place an emphasis on making profits through the managerial efforts and expertise of others, then the appropriate legislative and regulatory requirements are to be met. Those persons who sell securities ordinarily are required to be licensed. Excessive promotion of thinly traded securities may be an indication of *scalping* (recommendation of the sale of securities to investors while simultaneously selling them), *pump and dump* (artificial inflation of stock usually by heavy promotion and then selling the shares where cheaply purchased), and other possible fraudulent activities.

For offerings that allege they are currencies or concern currency-related products not subject to securities regulations, the persons making the offers should either be able to demonstrate that the product is not a security or that it complies with the applicable registration and filing requirements. Brokers and dealers permitting payments in cryptocurrencies or purchases of cryptocurrencies on margin, or who use them to facilitate securities transactions, should exercise caution in doing so, including assuring that the cryptocurrency activities do not violate anti-money laundering laws and "know-your-customer" obligations. They are to treat cryptocurrencies as cash obligations. Whether or not these currencies will be treated as securities will be dependent on the particular facts of each offering.[36]

SEC Warnings to Social Media

The enormous runup and partial collapse of Bitcoin had caused the SEC to issue warnings, particularly about celebrity endorsements that may sway unsophisticated investors to engage in high-risk involvement. In its Guidance Update of 2014, it noted that §206(4) of the Investment Advisers Act of 1940[37] generally prohibits an investment adviser from engaging in any act, practice, or course of business that is fraudulent, deceptive, or manipulative. It is a violation of the Act for an investment adviser to publish, circulate, or distribute any advertisement which refers, directly or indirectly, to any testimonial of any kind about the investment adviser or concerning any advice, analysis, report or other service rendered by such investment adviser. It is misleading to emphasize the positive aspects of the cryptocurrency and provide deceptive implication, or mistaken inference, while ignoring the known negative views. The prohibition covers not only investment advisers but also third parties with the endorsement of the adviser.[38]

With respect to virtual currencies, both the SEC and the Federal Trade Commission (FTC) have been critical of endorsements particularly those stated on online gambling services, and concerning cryptocurrencies. Paid celebrities, such as Floyd Mayweather, Paris Hilton, and Mike Tyson, have lent their names to tout Bitcoin and cryptocurrencies.[39] As a result, the SEC warned that celebrities and others using social media to encourage the public to purchase stocks and other investments may be acting unlawfully unless they disclose the nature, source, and amount of any compensation received. It further warned that any celebrity or other individual who promotes a virtual token or coin that is a security must disclose the compensation received. Failure to do so may violate the anti-touting provisions of the Securities Acts.[40] The FTC has similarly warned celebrities about false advertising that may be in violation of the Federal Trade Commission Act.[41] After reviewing numerous Instagram posts by celebrities, athletes, and other influencers, it sent out more than 90 letters reminding celebrities and their marketers that they should clearly and conspicuously disclose their relationships to brands when promoting or endorsing products through social media.[42]

SEC and Crypto Co.

SEC temporarily suspended trading of the shares of Crypto Co. until January 6, 2018 when its shares rose by 2700 percent in one month having gone public after its acquisition of a sport bra company. The SEC was concerned that the company's shares rose due to manipulative transactions in November, 2017. According to a former SEC chairperson, Harvey Pitt, the SEC and the Financial Industry Regulatory Authority (FINRA) are increasing their surveillance and enforcement rules with respect to cryptocurrencies and companies engaged in their use and exchange.[43]

SEC Disapproval of NYSE Proposed Rule Change

The New York Stock Exchange (NYSE) proposed a rule change to list and trade shares of SolidX Bitcoin Trust as Commodity-Based Trust Shares under the Exchange's Equities Rule which permits such listing of a security issued by a trust in a specified aggregate minimum number in return for a deposit of a quantity of the underlying commodity that could be redeemed at a holders' request by the Trust. The Trust would hold bitcoins as its primary asset together with smaller sums of cash which would be in the custody of and secured by the Trust's Bitcoin custodian, SolidX Management LLC, which is also the Sponsor. The Bank of New York Mellon would serve as the cash custodian and its administrator. Insurance would be procured to cover the potential loss of the Trust's bitcoins against loss or theft. The investment objective would be to track the price of bitcoins as measured by the TradeBlock XBX Index. The shares would be redeemable only in baskets of 100,000 shares and only to authorized participants.[44]

In summary, the SEC, disapproved the requested change stating that it did not find the proposal consistent with §6(b)(5)[45] of the Securities Exchange Act of 1934[46] which requires that the rules of a national securities exchange be designed to prevent fraudulent and manipulative acts and practices and to protect investors and the public interest. The reasons given are that the significant markets for bitcoins are unregulated and that the Exchange has not entered into or has been unable to enter into the type of surveillance-sharing agreement that addresses concerns about the potential for fraudulent or manipulative acts and practices in the markets for the shares.

Commodity Futures Trading Commission (CFTC)

The CFTC, which overseas and regulates all commodities and futures trading in accordance with the statutory requirements of the Commodity Exchange Act (CEA),[47] defines a *commodity* under §1a(9) quite broadly to include not only wheat, corn, other crops, livestock, and the like but also includes "all services, rights, and interests…in which contracts for future delivery are presently or in the future dealt in." It had determined in 2015 that Bitcoin and other virtual currencies are included under the definition. Its jurisdiction includes oversight of futures, options, and derivatives contracts and comes into play when a virtual currency is used in a derivatives contract or in cases of fraud or manipulation involving a virtual currency traded in interstate commerce.[48]

Prohibited Activities

The CFTC has indicated those activities that will call into play its enforcement. They include:

- Price manipulation of a virtual currency traded in interstate commerce;
- Pre-arranged or wash trading in an exchange-traded virtual currency swap or futures contract;
- A virtual currency futures or option contract or swap traded on a domestic platform or facility that has not registered with the CFTC as a SEF (Swap Execution Facility) or DCM (Designated Contract Markets);[49] and
- Certain schemes involving virtual currency marketed to retail customers such as off-exchange financed commodity transactions with persons who fail to register with the CFTC.[50]

In re Coinflip, Inc.

The seminal case wherein the CFTC *asserted* jurisdiction over Bitcoin trades is *In re Matter of Coinflip, Inc., d/b/a Derivabit*,[51] wherein the CFTC charged the company and its controlling person, Francisco Riordan, with violation of the provisions of the Commodity Exchange Act (CEA) by conducting activity related to commodity options and by operating a facility for the trading or processing of swaps without being registered as a swap execution facility or designated contract market. The company operated an online facility named Derivabit which offered to connect buyers and sellers of Bitcoin option contracts. It advertised itself as a "risk management platform…that connects buyers and sellers of standardized Bitcoin options and futures contracts." It designated numerous put and call options contracts as eligible for trading on the Derivabit platform, listed Bitcoin as the asset underlying the option, and denominated the strike and delivery prices in U.S. dollars. The customer would register as a user and deposit Bitcoin into an account in that particular user's name. The customer would receive premiums and payments of settlement of the options contracts payable using Bitcoin at a spot rate determined by a designated third-party Bitcoin currency exchange.

In a consent offer and order, the respondents were ordered to cease and desist from conducting the facility, and to comply with applicable rules and regulations including making any public statements denying the allegations in the consent order. The legal basis for the complaint is the violation of §4c(b) of the CEA which makes it unlawful for any person to "offer to enter into, enter into or confirm the execution of, any transaction involving any commodity…which is of the character of, or is commonly known to the trade as, an 'option'…, 'bid', 'offer', 'put', [or] 'call'…contrary to any rule, regulation, or order of the Commission prohibiting any such transaction." The company also violated §5h(a)(1) of the CEA forbidding such conduct without registration consisting of matching competitive bidding with a counterparty to execute a contract to exchange U.S. dollars for bitcoins at a predetermined price and date. The Commission noted that bitcoins are a commodity rather than a currency under §1a (9) of the Act which defines "commodity" to include, among other things, "all services, rights, and interests in which contracts for future delivery are presently or in the future dealt in."

CFTC v. Bitfinex

In a consent order, the CFTC fined BFXNA Inc. d/b/a/ BITFINEX, a Hong Kong company, the sum of $75,000. The order stated that the company operated an online platform for exchanging and trading cryptocurrencies, mainly bitcoins, which permitted ineligible contract participants or commercial entities to borrow funds from other users on the platform in order to trade bitcoins on a leveraged, margined, or financed basis. The company was not registered with the Commission. From April 2013 through August, 2015, it did not actually deliver bitcoins purchased on a leveraged, margined, or financed bases to the traders who purchased them but rather held them in an omnibus wallet account under its own private key for the customers who could not access the bitcoins until they were released by the company. The failure to "actually deliver" the commodity violated the CEA, notwithstanding that a book entry was noted on behalf of the customer.[52]

Section 4d(a) of the Act requires all persons acting as futures commission merchants to register with the Commission, which the company failed to do. Bitfinex accepted orders for retail commodity transactions and received funds from those customers in connection with retail commodity transactions. Bitfinex was not, however, registered with the Commission in any capacity which violated §4d(a) of the Act. Accordingly, the company was deemed to have engaged in illegal, off-exchange commodity transactions and failed to register as a futures commission merchant, in violation of §§4(a) and 4d of the Act, 7 U.S.C. §§6(a) and 6(d).[53]

CFTC v. LedgerX, LLC and TeraExchange

The CFTC has given recognition to cryptocurrency by its order granting LedgerX, LLC registration as a derivative clearing organization under the CEA.[54] It was granted an Order of Registration as a Swap Execution Facility on July 6, 2017 and authorized to provide clearing services for collateralized digital currency swaps.[55] It initially intends to clear Bitcoin options.[56] It is expected that swaps of other cryptocurrencies will follow.[57] The founder of Ledger X, Paul Chou, envisions a co-existence with fiat currencies, such as the U.S. dollar and the Euro, by the ease of transfer from one currency to the other irrespective of where a person resides and engages in financial transactions. Derivatives in these currencies will be required to manage the volatility attendant to the various currencies.[58] The CFTC had previously approved the registration of TeraExchange in May, 2016, which was the first facility to offer NDF (non-deliverable forward)[59] with underlying Bitcoin.[60] A year prior to the grant of registration, the

CFTC had sanctioned TeraExchange, which agreed to cease-and-desist without the imposition of a fine for having engaged in a Bitcoin swap that constituted *wash trading* (the same person sells and buys shares of the same security to simulate market activity) and pre-arranged trading in violation of its regulations.[61]

CME, CBOE, and Cantor Exchanges

On December 1, 2017, the CFTC gave recognition to three exchanges, namely, the Chicago Mercantile Exchange Inc. (CME) and the CBOE Futures Exchange (CFE) after both exchanges self-certified new contracts for Bitcoin futures products, and to the Cantor Exchange after it self-certified a new contract for Bitcoin binary options. The Chairman of the CFTC, J. Christopher Giancarlo, after noting the CFTC's limited statutory authority to oversee the cash market for Bitcoin, stated that the three exchanges agreed to significant enhancements to protect customers and maintain orderly markets. The major concerns are that of volatility and trading practices of participants and their potential impact on the futures contracts' price discovery process, including market manipulation and market dislocations due to flash rallies and crashes and trading outages.

Given the sudden increase of interest in the creation of new technological currencies, the Commission intends to participate in risk-monitoring activities including the monitoring and analysis of the size and development of the market, positions and changes in positions over time, open interest, initial margin requirements, variation margin payments, and stress testing positions. It will work closely with the National Futures Association (NFA) to conduct reviews of designated contract markets, derivatives clearing organizations, clearing firms, and individual traders involved in trading and clearing Bitcoin futures. If the Commission determines that the margins the Digital Clearing Organization (DCO) hold are inadequate, then it will require the margins held be increased.[62]

The recognition given to the exchanges has met opposition. In an open letter from President Walt (Walter) Lukken of the Futures Industry Association (FIA), on December 6, 2017 to the CFTC Chairman, Christopher Giancarlo,[63] he criticized the self-certification process of the exchanges commenting that the risks posed by cryptocurrency products require "a healthy dialogue between regulators, exchanges, clearinghouses and the clearing firms who will be absorbing the risk of these volatile, emerging instruments during a default. The one-day self-certification process and launch the following day, although adequate for standardized products, is highly inadequate because it does not align with the potential risks posed by the underlying trades. The fear is that clearing houses will bear a great risk associated with their guarantee fund contributions and assessment obligations. There should be a public discussion whether a separate guarantee fund for this product should be created and whether exchanges should increase their contributions to the clearing member guarantee fund. There should be a more thorough discussion among clearing member firms, clearinghouses, and exchanges to ascertain margin levels, trading limits, stress testing, and other protections and procedures in the event of excessive price movements."[64]

The Economist magazine was also critical of futures contracts in Bitcoin stating: "The CBOE's price is set by an auction on just one modestly size bitcoin exchange, Gemini," whereas the CME's price will be based on data compiled from four exchanges. Whereas most futures margins are from 5 to 15 percent, the margins for CBOE and CME are 44 percent and 47 percent respectively. It quoted the head of Interactive Brokers, Thomas Peterffy, who warned of the risk to clearing houses due to the high volatility of Bitcoin prices which could cause clients to be unable to meet margin calls thereby leaving brokers to bear the costs, resulting in their financial ruin and, in the end, leaving clearing houses to unwind the contracts.[65]

In contrast to the FIA letter, in a keynote address, Chairman Giancarlo gave his views concerning the future treatment of virtual currencies. In it he stated initially to do no harm and then proposed a five-step process: "(1) *Putting Our Best Foot Forward* – Financial regulators should designate dedicated, technology savvy teams to work collaboratively with FinTech companies – both new and established – to address issues of how existing regulatory frameworks apply to new, digital products, services and business models derived from innovative technologies, including DLT; (2) *Allowing Breathing Room* – Financial regulators should foster a regulatory environment that spurs innovation similar to the FCA's sandbox, where FinTech businesses, working collaboratively with regulators, have appropriate "space to breath" to develop and test innovative solutions without fear of enforcement action and regulatory fines; (3) *Getting Involved* – Financial regulators should participate directly in FinTech proof of concepts to advance regulatory understanding of technological innovation and determine how new innovations may help regulators do their jobs more efficiently and effectively; (4) *Listening and Learning* – Financial regulators should work closely with FinTech innovators to determine how rules and regulations should be adapted to enable 21st Century technologies and business models; and (5) *Collaborating Globally* – Financial regulators should provide a dedicated team to help FinTech firms navigate through the various state, federal and foreign regulators and regimes across domestic and international jurisdictions. In summary, the Chairman stated that he plans to make FinTech a priority."[66]

Authority Over Bitcoin Interpretation

On December 15, 2017, the CFTC announced a Proposed Interpretation concerning its authority over retail commodity transactions involving virtual currency such as Bitcoin. The proposed Interpretation provides for an exception that sets out the CFTC's view regarding the "actual delivery" exception that may apply to virtual currency transactions. Section 2(c)(2)(D) of the CEA grants the CFTC jurisdiction over *retail commodity transactions* which are defined as agreements, contracts or transactions in any commodity that are entered into with, or offered to, retail market participants on a leveraged or margined basis, or financed by the offeror, the counterparty, or a person acting in concert with the offeror or counterparty on a similar basis.

The exception to the exercise of jurisdictional authority is for contracts of sale that result in "actual delivery" within 28 days from the date of the transaction. The CFTC proposes that the exception will be granted for *actual delivery* of retail commodity transactions in virtual currency when: (1) a customer has the ability to: (i) take possession and control of the entire quantity of the commodity, whether it was purchased on margin, or using leverage, or any other financing arrangement, and (ii) use it freely in commerce (both within and away from any particular platform) no later than 28 days from the date of the transaction; and (2) the offeror and counterparty seller (including any of their respective affiliates or other persons acting in concert with the offeror or counterparty seller on a similar basis) does not retain any interest in or control over any of the commodity purchased on margin, leverage, or other financing arrangement at the expiration of 28 days from the date of the transaction.[67] The net import of the Proposed Interpretation is to exempt Bitcoin and other virtual currencies from heightened supervision although the CFTC will retain authority to investigate anti-fraud and manipulation in virtual currency cash markets as a commodity in interstate commerce.

CFTC Self-Certification Announcement

The CFTC, in an announcement dated January 4, 2018, discussed how it intends to extend its oversight over virtual currencies.[68] It asserted a five-pronged approach namely: "(1) *Consumer Education*—a greater understanding of the wild assertions, bold headlines, and extreme hyperbole; (2) *Assertion of Legal Authority*—over virtual currency derivatives to support its efforts to combat fraud and manipulation; (3) *Market Intelligence*—to gain the ability to monitor virtual currency derivatives markets and underlying reference rates by gathering trade information and counterparty data for regulatory and enforcement insights into those markets; (4) *Robust Enforcement*—police fraud and manipulation in cash or spot markets and enforce the law and prosecute fraud, abuse, manipulation, or false solicitation in markets for virtual currency derivatives and underlying spot trading; and (5) *Government-wide Coordination*—coordination with the SEC, FBI, Justice Department, the U.S. Treasury's Financial Stability Oversight Council (FSOC), state agencies, and with Congressional and executive policy-makers."

In accordance with Congressional and administrative authorizations to DCMs as a self-regulatory organization to certify new products and the CFTC's principle-based approach, the CME and CBOE as stated above, commencing on December 1, 2017, were permitted to and did self-certify, and the Cantor Exchange also self-certified, for Bitcoin binary options. The CFTC has few powers to stay a self-certification except for a false statement filing which did not occur with the above-stated self-certifications. Even if the CFTC was desirous of blocking self-certification of Bitcoin futures products, it would not have prevented the spectacular and volatile nature of Bitcoin and other virtual currencies. Its role is thus to continue regulatory surveillance to ensure that the virtual currency spot markets continue to operate lawfully. Currently, it has gained experience in virtual currency derivatives such as TeraExchange swaps, Nadex binary options, and LedgerX options. Additional issues raised included whether Bitcoin futures qualify as systemically important derivatives that would cause it to comply with the enhanced requirements of the Systemically Important Derivatives Clearing Organization (similar to the FSOC's powers over systemically important financial institutions) that are determined to materially affect the overall U.S. economy.

The CFTC has undertaken a heightened review of DCMs concerning the terms and conditions of Bitcoin futures products. The review will focus on the extensive visibility and monitoring of markets for virtual currency derivatives and their underlying settlement reference rates. The heightened reviews will enable the CFTC to have the means to police certain underlying spot markets for fraud and manipulation. The heightened review will consist of the following:

- DCMs setting a substantially high initial and maintenance margin for cash-settled Bitcoin futures;
- DCMs setting large trader reporting thresholds at 5 bitcoins or less;
- DCMs entering direct or indirect information-sharing agreements with spot market platforms to allow access to trade and trader data;
- DCM monitoring of data from cash markets with respect to price settlements and other Bitcoin prices more broadly, and identifying anomalies and disproportionate moves in the cash markets compared to the futures markets;
- DCMs agreeing to engage in inquiries, including at the trade settlement level when necessary;
- DCMs agreeing to regular coordination with CFTC surveillance staff on trade activities, including providing the CFTC surveillance team with trade settlement data upon request; and

- DCMs coordinating product launches so that the CFTC's market surveillance branch can carefully monitor minute-by-minute developments.[69]

The chairman of the CFTC, J. Christopher Giancarlo, indicated that the Commission's Market Risk Advisory Committee would hold a meeting at the end of January, 2018 to consider the process of self-certification of new products and operational rules by DCMs under the CEA and CFTC regulations, as well as the risks, challenges, and market developments of virtual currencies. Giancarlo recited the inherent risks of virtual currencies, in addition to the nascent stage of the technology itself. Risks associated with virtual currencies include: operational risks of unregulated and unsupervised trading platforms; cybersecurity risks of hackable trading platforms and virtual currency wallets; speculative risks of extremely volatile price moves; and fraud and manipulation risks through traditional market abuses of "pump and dump schemes," insider trading, false disclosure, Ponzi schemes, and other forms of investor fraud and market manipulation. He emphasized that responsible innovation and development are consistent with the Commission's role in preventing fraud and manipulation. The key is consumer education coupled with regulation and enforcement.[70]

Consumer Protection Resource Page

The CFTC has launched a virtual currency resource web page (cftc.gov/bitcoin) that will act as a repository for its resources concerning virtual currency. The resource is intended to educate and inform the public about the virtual currency commodities including potential risks, particularly when investing or speculating in them, especially Bitcoin futures and options. It also released a Customer Advisory "Understanding the Risks of Virtual Currency Trading" that highlights the risks.[71]

Financial Crimes Enforcement Network (FinCEN)

FinCEN's Guidance to Persons Administrating, Exchanging, or Using Virtual Currencies[72]

The U.S. Treasury Department's FinCEN has taken an active role in its guidance and administrative rulings particularly with respect to the application of regulations under the Bank Secrecy Act (BSA)[73] as they apply to virtual currencies with respect to persons who engage in their creation, acquisition, distribution, exchange, acceptance, or transmission.[74] In essence, the purpose of the Act is to ensure that banks have in place the necessary controls for access to law enforcement authorities to detect money laundering, terrorist financing, and other criminal acts.[75] Accordingly, there are record-keeping and registration requirements under the Act. In regulations pursuant to the Act, "money services businesses" (MSBs) are subject to the Act's requirements.[76]

The question that arises is whether users and dealers of convertible virtual currencies are subject to the Act's provisions and regulations. FinCEN states that persons obtaining such currencies are not subject to the registration, reporting, and record-keeping requirements for MSBs but administrators or exchanges who accept and transmit such currency or buy or sell it for any reason are money transmitters under the regulations.[77] The regulation does not differentiate between real and virtual currency but specifies that a *money transmitter* is one who provides money transmission services (acceptance of currency, funds, or other value as substitutes for them from one person and transmission to another) in the transfer of funds.[78]

In its Guidance, FinCEN defines persons who participate in generic virtual currency arrangements as follows: a *user* is a person who obtains virtual currency to purchase goods or services; an *exchanger* is a person engaged as a business in the exchange of virtual currency for real currency, funds, or other virtual currency; and an *administrator* is a person engaged as a business in issuing (putting into circulation) a virtual currency and who has the authority to redeem (to withdraw from circulation) such virtual currency The Guidance states that a user who obtains convertible virtual currency and uses it to purchase real or virtual goods or services is not an MSB under its regulations inasmuch as the said use, in and of itself, does not fit within the definition of "money transmission services."

It is unclear how to characterize a person who neither purchases goods nor services but rather makes a gift of the virtual currency. He or she does not appear to fall within the ambit of an exchanger because such use is not in pursuance to a business. On the other hand, an administrator or exchanger that (1) accepts and transmits a convertible virtual currency, or (2) buys or sells convertible virtual currency for any reason, is a money transmitter under the regulations unless a limitation to or exemption from the definition applies to the person. It is a money transmitter to the extent that it allows persons to transfer value to another or between one location to another location. It includes the allowance of payment to a third party for virtual goods and services.[79]

With respect to de-centralized convertible virtual currency (e.g., Bitcoin), a person who creates (mines) units of the currency to purchase real or virtual goods is not a transmitter but is characterized as a user and is thus exempt from the FinCEN regulations. On the other hand, if the said user who creates units of convertible virtual currency and sells them to another person for real money or equivalent, or accepts the said currency as part of the acceptance and transfer of funds, then he or she is considered to be a money transmitter engaged its transmission.[80] Money service businesses have additional requirements that include the maintenance of transaction records and, if a transaction is $3000 or more, the parties are to obtain information about the transmitter, the recipient, and the transaction between the parties, and relay the information to other intermediary financial institutions in subsequent fund transmissions. They are required to monitor transactions for any suspicious activity and report customer transactions involving cash of $10,000 or more.[81] This is one of the means by which anonymous Bitcoin and other virtual currencies may be investigated.

FinCEN's Ruling Concerning Virtual Currency Software Development January 30, 2014[82]

In a later opinion letter, FinCEN further elaborated upon its position *vis-à-vis* the application of its regulations to virtual currency development and virtual currency trading platforms. The following query was posed to FinCEN: the Company stated it intends to produce a piece of software that will facilitate the Company's purchase of a virtual currency from sellers by automating the collection of virtual currency and the payment of the equivalent in currency of legal tender. The potential sellers, using the Company's software interface, would initiate the process of offering virtual currency to the Company choosing among several options for receiving the equivalent in a currency of legal tender. The software remains private between the parties. The Company intends to invest in convertible virtual currency for its own account by buying the virtual currency from sellers and reselling the currency when it so chooses at a virtual currency exchange.

FinCEN's response is that based on the facts presented, and in accordance with its Final Rule of July 21, 2011 which defined a "money service business" as "a person wherever located doing business, whether or not on a regular basis or as an organized business concern, wholly or in substantial part within the United States, in one or more of the capacities listed [therein]…," so a "money transmitter" is one that provides money transmission services which includes the transmission of currency funds, or other value that substitutes for currency. The production of the Company's software does not in itself constitute acceptance and transmission of value making the Company a money transmitter; however, an administrator or exchanger of convertible virtual currencies that (1) accepts and transmits a convertible virtual currency, or (2) buys or sells convertible virtual currencies for any reason including acting as an intermediator between the user and a seller of goods or services the user is purchasing on the user's behalf, is a money transmitter under FinCEN's regulations. If the Company is buying and selling the said currency exclusively as investments for its own account it is not engaged in the exchange of the currency but if it provides services to others including investment-related or brokerage services that involves the acceptance and transmission of convertible virtual currencies, then it will come within the ambit of being a money transmitter requiring registration with FinCen and related obligations.[83]

FinCEN's Ruling Concerning Convertible Virtual Currency Trading and Booking Platform[84]

FinCEN issued a ruling as to whether a company's convertible virtual currency trading and booking platform caused it to be a money transmitter requiring compliance with registration requirements with the agency. The platform would consist of a trading system to match offers to buy and sell convertible virtual currency for currency of legal tender and a set of book accounts in which prospective buyers or sellers of one type of currency or the other can deposit funds to cover their exchanges. Each account would be segregated separately in U.S. dollars and a virtual wallet, and protected from seizure by the company's creditors. The customer submits an order with the company to purchase or sell the currency deposited at a given price. The platform to be created would automatically attempt to match each purchase order of one currency to one or more sell orders of the same currency. If the company finds a match, it will then purchase the virtual currency from the customer and sell it to the prospective buyer. If no match is found, the customer may either retain the funds in the company's account or have the funds returned to him or her.

   FinCEN ruled that, based on the given facts, the company would be a money transmitter. After reciting the definition of a money transmitter, it stated its disagreement with the company's position that that there is no money transmission when the instructions of the customers are issued subject to the condition of finding an offsetting match. The said definition does not contain any element of conditionality before it applies. A person that accepts currency, funds, or any value that substitutes for currency, with the intent and/or effect of transmitting currency, funds, or any value that substitutes for currency to another person or location, if a certain pre-determined condition established by the transmitter is met, is a money transmitter under FinCEN's regulations. The fact that the transmission is subject to finding a willing buyer, which may not occur, does not constitute an exception to the definition. Neither does a key feature of the Platform, that customers are never identified to each other, alter the ruling. Each trade conducted through the Platform results in two money transmission transactions, one between the company and the customer wishing to buy virtual currency, and another between the company and the customer wishing to sell such virtual currency at the same exchange rate.

FinCEN has concluded that the money transmission that takes place within the system does not qualify for the exemption as claimed by the company. FinCEN stated that there are three fundamental conditions that must be met for the exemption to apply: (1) the money transmission component must be part of the provision of goods or services distinct from money transmission itself; (2) the exemption can only be claimed by the person that is engaged in the provision of goods or services distinct from money transmission; and (3) the money transmission component must be integral (that is, necessary) for the provision of the goods or services. The company's intended platform facilitates the transfer of value, both real and virtual, between third parties. The money transmission is the sole purpose of the company's system, and is not a necessary part of another, non-money transmission service being provided by the company. Therefore, it must register as a money transmitter.[85]

FinCEN's Application of Money Transmission to Virtual Currency Mining[86]

FinCEN responded to an inquiry from a company which requested a ruling whether certain ways of disposing of the bitcoins mined by it would make it a money transmitter under the BSA. The company alleged that it mined bitcoins that have not yet been used or transferred but rather would be used in the future to purchase goods or services by converting the virtual currency into legal tender and using the legal tender currency to purchase goods and services, or to transfer the virtual currency to the owner of the company. FinCEN stated that it understands the mining of

Bitcoin imposes no obligation on a Bitcoin user to send the mined bitcoins to anyone or any place for the benefit of another but rather the user is free to use the mined currency for the user's own benefit to purchase real or virtual goods and services. Such use clearly does not cause the use to be a money transmission under the regulations because it is neither an "acceptance" nor a "transmission" within the meaning of the Rule.

Similarly, if the use is to pay debts incurred in the ordinary course of business or where a corporate user makes distributions to shareholders, these also do not come within the Rule. The key element is whether the person is engaging in the business of money transmission. Thus, if on occasion the person needs to convert the mined Bitcoin into real currency or other convertible virtual currency as, for example, where the person from whom goods or services are requested refuses to accept Bitcoin or where the user wishes to diversify currency holdings in anticipation of future needs for investment purposes, neither one is deemed to be a money transmission provided that the user is doing so for the user's own purposes and not as a business service for others. The said conversion of currencies does not, in itself, constitute a money transmission making the person a money transmitter.[87]

After reciting the regulations and definitions as stated in the Guidance above, FinCEN concluded that the company would be deemed a "user" of Bitcoin but is not a money service business to the extent that it uses bitcoins it has mined: (1) to pay for the purchase of goods or services, pay debts it has previously incurred (including debts to its owner(s)), or make distributions to owners; or (2) to purchase real currency or another convertible virtual currency, so long as the real currency or other convertible virtual currency is used solely in order to make payments or for the company's own investment purposes. In the event that the company were to engage in any transfer to third parties on behalf of sellers, creditors, owners, or counterparties, or should it engage in any other activity constituting acceptance and transmission of either currency of legal tender or virtual currency, then such activity should be carefully scrutinized inasmuch as the company may be engaged in money transmission activities that would be subject to the requirements of the BSA.

Requirements When Designated as a Money Services Business

Once a business has been designed as a "money services business" a panoply of requirements follows. Under the regulations issued pursuant to the BSA,[88] each money services business must develop, implement, and maintain an effective anti-money laundering program. As defined by the regulations, an effective anti-money laundering program is one that is reasonably designed to prevent the money services business from being used to facilitate money laundering and the financing of terrorist activities. The written program is to be commensurate with the risks posed by the location, size, nature, and volume of the financial services provided by the MSB. Copies of the program are to be made available to the Treasury Department upon request.

At a minimum, the program is to incorporate policies, procedures, and internal controls reasonably designed to assure compliance and shall include provisions: (1) verifying customer identification; (2) filing reports; (3) creating and retaining records; and (4) responding to law enforcement requests. The said business is to have an automated data processing system that integrates compliance procedures with such systems. It is to designate a person to assure day-to-day compliance with the program; that the money services business properly files reports and creates and retains records; provides appropriate training of appropriate personnel concerning their responsibilities under the program; includes training in the detection of suspicious transactions; and provides for independent review to monitor and maintain an adequate program.[89]

U.S. v. Lord

An example, in addition to other cases cited in the chapter on "Criminal Prosecutions and Civil Litigations Concerning Virtual Currencies" on the prosecution of crimes and civil offenses, is *U.S. v. Lord*.[90] Randall Lord, a chiropractor, and his son, Michael Lord, attempted to withdraw their plea of "Guilty" which plea was denied by the court. They began operating a business called localbitcoins.com in which they posted advertisements for Bitcoin exchange services wherein they exchanged cash, credit card payments, and other forms of payments for bitcoins. Interested persons would transfer money to the defendants' account and the defendants would then purchase bitcoins from Coinbase, which would then be transferred to the said interested persons less a commission for the services rendered. The defendants used a number of bank accounts for the transactions. Coinbase, an online Bitcoin broker, contacted the defendants after it noted the volume of their activity and told them that as Bitcoin exchanges they were required to register with FinCEN as per the Guidance of March 2013. The defendants stated to Coinbase that they were registered although they had not done so until months after the earlier transactions in which they had exchanged over $2.5 million for bitcoins for customers. Federal agents were made aware of the exchange when investigating Michael Lord for alleged drug dealing with a purchaser of bitcoins from the defendants. After an indictment of the defendants on various counts concerning the operation of the Bitcoin exchange business, Randall Lord pleaded guilty to Count 1 of the indictment which charged the defendants with conspiracy to operate and the actual operation of an unlicensed money service business. Michael Lord pleaded guilty to being a member of a drug conspiracy.

The court denied Michael Lord's request to withdraw his plea to the drug charge stating that he presented no arguments that constitute a "fair and just" reason for withdrawing his guilty plea on this count, and does not claim innocence of that count. With respect to the operation of a money transmission business without a license, the defendants had argued that a license was not required under Louisiana law, which the court agreed. Nevertheless, the court found the defendants were properly charged under federal law. The court noted that the statute sets forth two separate methods by which the government may prove that a defendant is an "unlicensed money transmitting business": (1) failure to obtain a state license where such a license is necessary (conceded by the government and not shown herein), or (2) failure to comply with separate federal registration requirements.

The court did find that the guilty plea for violation of the federal regulations regarding the unlicensed money transmission business appeared sufficiently to have a basis in fact and in law as presented by the prosecution. The court defined "money service business" and "money transmitter" and found there was sufficient evidence to so charge and permit the plea given to the violations. To allow a withdrawal of the pleas given the delay in doing so, the court applied a multi-factor test for making the determination whether to allow the withdrawal. The court examined each of the factors provided in the Federal Rules of Criminal Procedure and found, in essence, that the withdrawal would be highly inconvenient to the court and its resources which would have to try a 15-count indictment. The court had extensively questioned the defendants at the time of the pleas whether they were competent to enter a guilty plea and determined that the pleas were knowingly and voluntarily made with their free and voluntary waiver of their constitutional rights.[91]

Additional Agencies That May Regulate Virtual Currencies

Federal Reserve Board

The Governor and Vice-Chair for Supervision of the FED, Randal K. Quarles, stated that although digital currencies did not presently pose major concerns to the financial stability of the United States, nevertheless, issues may arise in the future if they attain wide-scale coverage. The problem is that if the central asset of the U.S. payment system cannot be predictably redeemed for the U.S. dollar at a stable exchange rate when the economy is faced with a financial crisis, the risk and potential liquidity resulting therein could raise fundamental concerns. Private-sector and non-banks can potentially face liquidity demands that cannot be attained which then may have significant spill-over effects on the entire economy.[92] Issues may be raised as to whether Bitcoin and/or other cryptocurrencies may come within the jurisdiction of the Financial Stability Oversight Council (FSOC), created under the Dodd-Frank Act, which oversees "systemically important" financial institutions whose demise or downturn may harm the entire U.S. economy. Under such circumstances, there may be instituted onerous rules and regulations that could hinder the development of the new technologies.[93]

The Federal Reserve Board has refrained from pursuing the regulation of virtual currencies. Janet Yellen, the former Chairperson of the Board of

Governors of the Federal Reserve System, stated that the Fed does not have the authority to supervise or regulate Bitcoin in any way and requested Congress for authority to enhance its supervision.[94]

Consumer Financial Protection Bureau (CFPB)

According to its website, the Bureau is responsible for making financial markets work for consumers, providers, and the economy as a whole, by affording protection from unfair, deceptive, or abusive tactics, and can initiate enforcement against violators of its provisions. Companies must ensure that consumers are made aware of the prices, risks, and terms of agreements so that they may make responsible financial decisions. Created under the Dodd-Frank Act,[95] the Bureau has become the proverbial whipping-boy of the political parties that began with the attempt by President Obama to name Elizabeth Warren as its first head but which was not consented to by the Senate thus leading her to successfully become elected as U.S. Senator for Massachusetts. With respect to virtual currency, the Bureau issued a consumer advisory alerting consumers to the risks associated with hackers, lack of protection that other fiat currencies possess, costs that may substantially exceed that of other currency transactions, and the scams that inevitably are attempted. It advised consumers to know whom they are dealing with and that, if using exchanges, they should consult the FinCEN website to ascertain whether the exchanges being dealt with are properly registered. It further warned of the use of Bitcoin kiosks which are unlike other ATMs and the protection afforded by the latter; the volatility of the price of bitcoins; the consequences of losing a private key (which may cause a total loss of the investment); and the lack of government insurance that is accorded to fiat bank and credit union deposits.[96]

Office of Comptroller of the Currency (OCC)

Although not directly addressing virtual currency, the OCC clearly is aware of the implications of the new technology. In accordance with recommendations for the implementation of innovative technologies, the

OCC created the Office of Innovation to Implement the Framework to address new and different consumer preferences for financial products and services. The rise in non-banks (shadow banks) and their increased importance rivaling that of traditional banks and, inferentially, the advent and greatly increased DLT, call for new banking models. Accordingly, the OCC commenced a study in 2015 focused on innovation in order to better understand the new, evolving, regulatory landscape. Accordingly, it arrived at a number of recommendations. The first is "responsible innovation" to meet the needs of consumers, businesses, and communities with sound risk management and aligned with the banks' business strategy. Its guiding principles are: support responsible innovation; foster an internal culture receptive to responsible innovation; leverage agency experience and expertise; encourage responsible innovation that provides fair access to financial services and fair treatment of consumers; further safe and sound operations through effective risk management; encourage banks of all sizes to integrate responsible innovation into their strategic planning; promote ongoing dialogue through formal outreach; and collaborate with other regulators.[97]

The newly created Office of Innovation would provide internal and external visibility whose functions would be: to serve as a central point of contact and facilitate responses to inquiries and requests; conduct outreach and provide technical assistance; enhance awareness, culture, and education; monitor the evolving financial services landscape; and collaborate with domestic and international regulators. The principles guiding the Office of Innovation are: ensure efficient and effective execution of core functions; leverage OCC expertise; preserve existing decision-making functions; develop resources on innovation for internal and external shareholders; and provide credible evidence to processes and decision-making.[98]

Federal Trade Commission (FTC)

The FTC was created under the Federal Trade Commission Act of 1914.[99] Originally, its mandate was to prevent unfair methods of competition in commerce and this was later amended to prevent unfair or deceptive acts or practices which, in effect, is to protect consumers. Its enforcement in

Bitcoin and blockchain activity has been negligible other than issuing warnings but it did participate in an action affecting consumers who purchased Bitcoin mining machines and services.

FTC v. BF Labs, Inc. In an action against BF Labs, Inc. d/b/a Butterfly Labs,[100] the FTC sought equitable relief consisting of injunctive relief, rescission or reformation of contracts, restitution, the refund of monies paid, and disgorgement of ill-gotten monies for alleged misrepresentations. It was alleged that the defendants operated Butterfly Labs, which sold Bitcoin mining machines and services that consumers purportedly could use to generate bitcoins. The defendants charged consumers upfront between $149 and $29,899 for the machines and services with the latter sum charged for the highest-powered machines. It was later alleged that, in many instances, consumers who purchased the machines or services, about 20,000 in number, were not able to use them to generate bitcoins because the machines and services were never provided. In other instances, the delivery of the machines was greatly delayed for up to a year, making them obsolete, or the machines were otherwise damaged or defective. Butterfly Labs' advertising on Facebook and elsewhere was allegedly misleading as well as its claim to provide mining services at a set upfront price. No refunds were made although at times promises of refunds were assured.

The action resulted in an agreed settlement whereby Butterfly Labs and two of its operators consented that they will be prohibited from misrepresenting to consumers whether a product or service can be used to generate bitcoins or any other virtual currency, on what date a consumer will receive the product or service, and whether the product is new or used. The company and a senior officer were prohibited from taking upfront payments for Bitcoin machines and other products used to mine for any virtual currency unless those products are available and will be delivered within 30 days. If the product is not actually delivered within 30 days, the defendants must provide a refund. Damaged or defective machines are to result in prompt refunds and lateness in delivery will require a consumer's permission to so deliver. The orders included partially suspended monetary judgments conditioned upon the surrender of the cash value of all bitcoins obtained for the machines.[101]

North American Securities Administrators Association (NASAA)

Non-governmental organizations also warn investors for reasons comparable to those previously stated. Thus, NASAA is particularly concerned about investors succumbing to the headlines and hype that has garnered so much attention with the seemingly extraordinary rise in value of cryptocurrencies. Joseph P. Borg, NASAA's President and Director of the Alabama Securities Commission, warned about the lack of a safety net via insurance or control by central banks and that cryptocurrencies cannot be exchanged for other commodities. NASAA's research shows that 94 percent of regulators believe there is a risk of fraud involving cryptocurrencies and were unanimous in their view that more regulation is needed to provide greater investor protection. It compared ICOs with IPOs whereby the latter sell shares of stock to raise capital but ICOs sell tokens which often have no value to fund a project. The concerns replicate those previously stated including common red flags of alleged guaranteed high investment returns, unsolicited offers, pressure to buy immediately, unlicensed sellers, and a "sounds too good to be true" fault line.[102]

In the chapter on "States' Regulation of Virtual Currencies," we will discuss how U.S. states, in addition to federal regulation, have begun to enter the fray inasmuch as their citizens' investments have been compromised by unscrupulous entrepreneurs who take advantage of people's lack of knowledge about the technical aspects of making transactions in cryptocurrencies. Each state, as a sovereign entity, adapts such regulations, if any, to its perceived best interests in protecting the public.

Notes

1. Sherisse Pham, *North Korea is trying to amass a Bitcoin war chest* (Sept. 12, 2017), CNN Tech, http://money.cnn.com/2017/09/12/technology/north-korea-hackers-Bitcoin/index.html. See also, Qin Chen, *Bitcoin 'mining': A new way for North Korea to generate funds for the regime* World Economy, Sept. 13, 2017, https://www.cnbc.com/2017/09/13/Bitcoin-mining-a-new-way-for-north-korea-to-generate-funds-for-the-regime.html

2. *North Korea's Political Elite is Not Isolated,* Insikt Group, July 25, 2017, https://go.recordedfuture.com/hubfs/north-korea-internet-activity.pdf
3. Jason Bloomberg, *Bitcoin: 'Blood Diamonds' of the Digital Era,* Forbes, Mar. 28, 2017, https://www.forbes.com/sites/jasonbloomberg/2017/03/28/Bitcoin-blood-diamonds-of-the-digital-era/#13d1abf6492a
4. Dan Boylan, *Military, intelligence agencies alarmed in surge of Bitcoin value in 'dark web' fight,* Washington Times, Aug. 10, 2017, https://www.washingtontimes.com/news/2017/aug/10/Bitcoin-value-surge-sign-of-criminal-activity/
5. Olivia McCoy, *Bitcoins for Bombs,* Council of Foreign Relations, Aug. 17, 2017, https://www.cfr.org/article/Bitcoin-bombs
6. Zachary K. Goldman, Ellie Maruyama, Elizabeth Rosenberg, Edoardo Saravalle, and Julia Solomon Strauss, *Terrorist Use of Virtual Currencies: Containing the Potential Threat,* CNAS, May, 2017, https://www.cnas.org/publications/reports/terrorist-use-of-virtual-currencies
7. Mike Orcutt, *Criminals Thought That Bitcoin Was the Perfect Hiding Place, But They Were Thought Wrong,* MIT Technology Review, Sept. 11, 2017, https://www.technologyreview.com/s/608763/criminals-thought-Bitcoin-was-the-perfect-hiding-place-they-thought-wrong/
8. Matthew J. Schwartz, *Tougher to Use Bitcoin for Crime? Why Anonymous Use of the Cryptocurrency May Prove Difficult,* Bank Info Security, Dec. 30, 2017, https://www.bankinfosecurity.com/tougher-to-use-Bitcoin-for-crime-a-7731
9. One of a number of sites that discuss the issue is by J. Dax Hansen and Joshua L. Boehm, *Treatment of Bitcoin Under U.S. Property Law,* Perkins Coie, Mar. 2017,, https://www.virtualcurrencyreport.com/wp-content/uploads/sites/13/2017/03/2016_ALL_Property-Law
10. U.S. Securities and Exchange Commission, *What We Do,* https://www.sec.gov/Article/whatwedo.html
11. U.S. Securities and Exchange Commission, *Initial Coin Offerings Investor Bulletin* (July 27, 2017), https://www.sec.gov/oiea/investor-alerts-and-bulletins/ib_coinofferings
12. U.S. Securities and Exchange Commission, *SEC Announces Enforcement Initiatives to Combat Cyber-Based Threats and Protect Retail Investors,* Press Release, Sept. 25, 2017, 2017–176, https://www.sec.gov/news/press-release/2017-176
13. The foregoing discussion stating some of the articles discussing the issue is found in J. Dax Hansen, Carla L. Reyes, and Josh Boehm,

Resources on Crypto-Tokens and Securities Law, June 5, 2017, Perkins Coie Virtual Currency Report, https://www.virtualcurrencyreport.com/2017/06/resources-on-crypto-tokens-and-securities-law/

14. For a commentary, see Richard M. Martinez, Mark W. Rasmussen, Stephen J. Obie, Harriet Territt, and Brendan Ballou, *Crackdown: SEC's New Cyber Unit Targets Blockchain and ICO Abuses* (Dec. 19, 2017), Mondaq, http://www.mondaq.com/unitedstates/x/657534/Securities/Crackdown+SECs+New+Cyber+Unit+Targets+Blockchain+And+ICO+Abuses

15. *SEC. v. REcoin Group Foundation, LLC.* No. 17 Civ.... (E.D., N.Y. Sept. 29, 2017), https://www.sec.gov/litigation/complaints/comp-pr2017-185.pdf.

16. David W. Adams and Edmund J. Zaharewicz, *SEC Files First ICO Enforcement Action,* Daily Journal, Oct. 6, 2017, cited by Carlton Fields, Mondaq, http://www.mondaq.com/unitedstates/x/643036/fin+tech/SEC+Files+First+ICO+Enforcement+Action

17. Steve Gatti, Megan Gordon, and Daniel Silver, *SEC Enforcement Against Initial Coin Offering*, Harvard L.S. On Corporate Governance and Financial Regulation, Oct. 30, 2017, https://corpgov.law.harvard.edu/2017/10/30/sec-enforcement-against-initial-coin-offering/

18. Herbert F. Koslov, Karl S. Larsen, Michael Selig and Matthew H. Kita, *United States: SEC Enforcement Action Involving Coin Offering Muddles Jurisdictional Waters*, Reed Smith, Oct. 4, 2017, https://www.reed-smith.com/en/perspectives/2017/10/sec-enforcement-action-involving-initial-coin-offering

19. Pub.L. 73–22, 48 Stat. 74 (1933).

20. Pub.L 112–106, 126 Stat. 306 (2012).

21. U.S. Federal Register, *Crowdfunding,* 80 F.R. 71387. https://www.federalregister.gov/documents/2015/11/16/2015-28220/crowdfunding

22. U.S. Securities and Exchange Commission, *Report of Investigation Pursuant to Section 21(a) of the Securities Exchange Act of 1934*, Release No. 81207 (July 25, 2017), https://www.sec.gov/litigation/investreport/34-81207.pdf.

23. *Id.* at 11–15.

24. Citing 15 U.S.C. §77b(a)(4).

25. Citing *Doran v. Petroleum Mgmt. Corp.,* 545 F.2d 893, 909 (5th Cir. 1977).

26. U.S. Securities and Exchange Commission, *supra,* note 15 at 15–17.

27. *Id.* at 5–8.
28. U.S. Securities and Exchange Commission, *SEC Issues Investigative Report Concluding DAO Tokens, a Digital Asset, Were Securities,* Press Release, No. 2017-131, https://www.sec.gov/news/press-release/2017-131
29. Klint Finley, *A $50 Million Dollar Hack Just Showed That The DAO Was All Too Human,* WIRED, June 18, 2016, https://www.wired.com/2016/06/50-million-hack-just-showed-dao-human/
30. Matthew Leising, *The Ether Thief,* BLOOMBERG, June 13, 2017, https://www.bloomberg.com/features/2017-the-ether-thief/
31. *Munchee Inc.,* SEC Adm. Proc. No. 3-18304 (2017), https://www.sec.gov/litigation/admin/2017/33-10445.pdf
32. Adam T. Ettinger, *When Does Software Become Securities,* Lexology, Dec. 12, 2017, (https://www.lexology.com/library/detail.aspx?g=87cce8ca-e51f-4b7e-8769-c67c63bd1455
33. Jeffrey L. Robins, *SEC Issues Cease and Desist Order Shutting Down ICO,* Cadwalader News and Headlines, Dec. 11, 2017, https://www.findknowdo.com/news/12/11/2017/sec-issues-cease-and-desist-order-shutting-down-ico
34. *SEC Takes Aim at Initial Coin Offerings Again,* Perkins Coie LLP, Jan, 11, 2018, https://www.perkinscoie.com/en/news-insights/sec-takes-aim-at-initial-coin-offerings-again.html
35. Jay Clayton, *Statement on Cryptocurrencies and Initial Coin Offerings,* Public Statement, Dec. 11, 2017, https://www.sec.gov/news/public-statement/statement-clayton-2017-12-11
36. *Id.*
37. Codified at 15 U.S.C. §80b-1 through 15 U.S.C. §80b-21.
38. U.S. Securities and Exchange Commission, *IM Guidance Update,* No. 2014-04, Mar. 2014, https://www.sec.gov/investment/im-guidance-2014-04.pdf
39. Emmie Martin, *Jamie Foxx, Floyd Mayweather and other celebrities Who are hyping cryptocurrencies,* CNBC, Dec. 20, 2017, https://www.cnbc.com/2017/12/20/celebrities-who-have-endorsed-or-invested-in-cryptocurrency.html
40. U.S. Securities and Exchange Commission, Div. of Enforcement, *Statement on Potentially of Unlawful Initial Coin Offerings and Other Investments by Celebrities and Others,* Public Statement, Nov. 1, 2017, https://www.sec.gov/news/public-statement/statement-potentially-unlawful-promotion-icos

41. 15 U.S.C. §§41–58, as amended.
42. U.S. Federal Trade Commission, *FTC Staff Reminds Influencers and Brands to Clearly Disclose Relationship,* Press Release, Apr. 19, 2017, https://www.ftc.gov/news-events/press-releases/2017/04/ftc-staff-reminds-influencers-brands-clearly-disclose
43. Michael Sheetz, *The SEC's crackdown on cryptocurrencies is about to get serious, former chairman says,* Yahoo Finance, Dec. 21, 2017, https://finance.yahoo.com/news/sec-apos-crackdown-cryptocurrencies-serious-233456948.html
44. U.S. Securities and Exchange Commission, Release No. 34-80319, File No. SR-NYSEArca-2016-101, at 23–24, https://www.sec.gov/rules/sro/nysearca/2017/34-80319.pdf
45. §6(b)(5) states: "(5) The rules of the exchange are designed to prevent fraudulent and manipulative acts and practices, to promote just and equitable principles of trade, to foster cooperation and coordination with persons engaged in regulating, clearing, settling, processing information with respect to, and facilitating transactions in securities, to remove impediments to and perfect the mechanism of a free and open market and a national market system, and, in general, to protect investors and the public interest; and are not designed to permit unfair discrimination between customers, issuers, brokers, or dealers, or to regulate by virtue of any authority conferred by this title matters not related to the purposes of this title or the administration of the exchange."
46. Securities Exchange Act of 1934, Pub.L. 73–291, 48 Stat. 881, (1934), codified at 15 U.S.C. §78a et seq.).
47. Commodity Exchange Act, Ch. 545, 49 Stat. 1491 as amended, (1936).
48. Stan Higgins, *CFTC Aligns With SEC: ICO Token Can Be Commodities,* CoinDesk, Oct. 17, 2017, https://www.coindesk.com/cftc-no-inconsistency-sec-cryptocurrency-regulation/
49. "DCMs" (Designated Contract Markets) are trades or exchanges that operates under the authority of the CFTC. They are like traditional futures exchanges, which may allow access to their facilities by all types of traders, including retail customers. They may list for trading futures or option contracts based on any underlying commodity, index, or instrument. *Designated Contract Markets,* U.S. Commodity Futures Trading Commission, http://www.cftc.gov/IndustryOversight/Trading Organizations/DCMs/index.htm

50. LabCFTC, *A CFTC Primer on Virtual Currencies*, Oct. 17, 2017, http://www.cftc.gov/idc/groups/public/documents/file/labcftc_primercurrencies100417.pdf

51. *Coinflip, Inc. d/b/a/ Derivavit*, CFTC Docket No. 15-29, Sept. 17, 2015, http://www.cftc.gov/idc/groups/public/@lrenforcementactions/documents/legalpleading/enfcoinfliprorder09172015.pdf

52. §2(c)(2)(D) provides that such an agreement, contract, or transaction shall be subject to Sections 4(a), 4(b), and 4b of the Act "as if the agreement, contract, or transaction was a contract of sale of a commodity for future delivery." 7 U.S.C. §2(c)(2)(D)(iii).

53. *In re BFXNA Inc. d/b/a BITFINEX*, CFTC Docket 16-19, June 2, 2016, http://www.cftc.gov/idc/groups/public/@lrenforcementactions/documents/legalpleading/enfbfxnaorder060216.pdf

54. Ch. 545, 49 Stat. 1491

55. U.S. Commodity Futures Trading Commission, *Order of Registration of LedgerX, LLC*, July 24, 2017, http://www.cftc.gov/idc/groups/public/@otherif/documents/ifdocs/ledgerxdcoregorder72417.pdf

56. U.S. Commodity Futures Trading Commission, *CFTC Grants DCO Registration to LedgerX LLC*, July 24, 2017, http://www.cftc.gov/PressRoom/PressReleases/pr7592-17

57. Camila Russo, *Bitcoin Options Will Be Available This Fall*, Bloomberg, July 24, 2017, https://www.bloomberg.com/news/articles/2017-07-24/Bitcoin-options-to-become-available-in-fall-after-cftc-approval

58. About Ledger X, Ledger X, https://ledgerx.com/about-ledgerx/

59. A NDF (non-deliverable forward) is a foreign exchange hedging strategy pertaining to the settlement of a profit or loss usually prior to the settlement date with respect to a foreign currency futures contract. Generally, it involves a thinly traded currency in emerging markets settled in major foreign currencies in offshore financial centers. Investopedia, http://www.investopedia.com/video/play/nondeliverable-forward-ndf/

60. U.S. Commodity Futures Trading Commission, *CFTC Grants Registration to 3 Swap Execution Facilities*, May 26, 2016, http://www.cftc.gov/PressRoom/PressReleases/pr7375-16

61. *In re TeraExchange LLC*, CFTC Docket No. 15-33 (Sept. 24, 2015), http://www.cftc.gov/idc/groups/public/@lrenforcementactions/documents/legalpleading/enfteraexchangeorder92415.pdf

62. U.S. Commdity Futures Trading Commission, *CFTC Statement on Self-Certification of Bitcoin Products by CME, CFE, and Cantor Exchange*,

Press Release pr7654-17, Dec. 1, 2017. http://www.cftc.gov/
PressRoom/PressReleases/pr7654-17

63. The Futures Industry Association, founded in New York in 1955 under
the then name of the Association of Commodity Exchange Firms, now
encompasses offices through the globe, particularly in Europe and Asia,
with its mission to "support open, transparent, and competitive markets; protect and enhance the integrity of the financial system, and promote high standards of professional conduct," *About FIA,* https://fia.
org/about-O

64. Walt Lukken, *Open letter to CFTC chairman Giancarlo regarding the
listing of cryptocurrency derivatives,* Futures Industry Association, Dec.
7, 2017, https://fia.org/articles/open-letter-cftc-chairman-giancarlo-
regarding-listing-cryptocurrency-derivatives

65. *Blooming futures?* The Economist, Dec. 16, 2017, at 67.

66. Commissioner J. Christopher Giancarlo, *Keynote Address J. Christopher
Giancarlo Before SEFCON VII,* Jan. 18, 2017, http://www.cftc.gov/
PressRoom/SpeechesTestimony/opagiancarlo-19

67. U.S. Commodity Futures Trading Commission, C*FTC Issues Proposed
Interpretation on Virtual Currency "Actual Delivery" in Retail Transactions,*
Dec. 15, 2017, Release No. Pr7664-17, http://www.cftc.gov/
PressRoom/PressReleases/pr7664-17

68. U.S. Commodity Futures Trading Commission, *CFTC Backgrounder
on Oversight of and Approach to Virtual Currency Futures Markets,* Jan. 4,
2018, http://www.cftc.gov/idc/groups/public/@newsroom/docu-
ments/file/backgrounder_virtualcurrency01.pdf

69. *Id.*

70. U.S. Commodity Futures Trading Commission, *Chairman Giancarlo
Statement on Virtual Currencies,* January 4, 2018, http://www.cftc.gov/
PressRoom/SpeechesTestimony/giancarlostatement010418

71. U.S. Commodity Futures Trading Commission, *CFTC Launches
Virtual Currency Resource Web Page,* Dec. 15, 2017, Release No. pr7665-
17, http://www.cftc.gov/PressRoom/PressReleases/pr7665-17

72. U.S. Treasury Department, Financial Crimes Enforcement Network,
Guidance, Mar. 18, 2013, FIN 2013-G001, https://www.fincen.gov/
sites/default/files/shared/FIN-2013-G001.pdf

73. An Act to amend the Federal Deposit Insurance Act to require insured
banks to maintain certain records, to require that certain transactions

in U.S. currency be reported to the Department of the Treasury, and for other purposes. Bank Secrecy Act, Pub.L. 91-508, 84 Stat. 1114-2.

74. U.S. Department of the Treasury, Financial Crimes Enforcement Network, *Application of FinCEN's Regulation to Persons Administering, Exchanging, or Using Virtual Currencies,* FIN-2013-G001, Mar. 18, 2013, https://www.fincen.gov/resources/statutes-regulations/guidance/application-fincens-regulations-persons-administering. A discussion of regulatory enactments of virtual currencies may be found in Latham & Watkins, *The Other Side of the Coin: Bitcoin, Blockchain, Regulation & Enforcement,* Mar. 24, 2016, https://lc.fia.org/events/other-side-coin-Bitcoin-blockchain-regulation-and-enforcement

75. U.S. Office of the Comptroller of the Currency, *Bank Secrecy Act,* https://www.occ.treas.gov/topics/compliance-bsa/bsa/index-bsa.html

76. The Act defines an "MSB" as "a person wherever located doing business, whether or not on a regular basis or as an organized or licensed business concern, wholly or in substantial part within the United States, in one or more of the capacities…" as stated in the Rule including any agent, agency, or branch or office in the United States. 31 CFR §1010.100(f).

77. 31 CFR§1010.100(ff)(1-7) and 31 CFR§1010.100(ff)(5)(i)(A). See *supra,* note 48 at 2–3.

78. *Id.,* 31 CFR §1010.100(ff)(5)(i)(A).

79. *Supra, Id.,* note 198.

80. *Id.*

81. *Supra,* note 165 at 13–14.

82. U.S. Department of the Treasury, Financial Crimes Enforcement Network, *Application of FinCEN's Regulation to Virtual Currency Software Development and Certain Investment Activity,* Jan. 30, 2014, FIN-2014-R002, https://www.fincen.gov/resources/statutes-regulations/administrative-rulings/application-fincens-regulations-virtual/

83. *Id.*

84. U.S. Department of the Treasury, Financial Crimes Enforcement Network, *Request for Administrative Ruling on the Application of FinCEN's Regulations to a Virtual Currency Trading Platform,* Oct. 27, 2014, FIN-2014-R011.

85. *Id.*

86. U.S. Department of the Treasury, Financial Crimes Enforcement Network Financial Crimes Enforcement Network, *Application*

of FinCEN's Regulations to Virtual Currency Mining Operations, Jan. 30, 2014, FIN-2014-R001, https://www.fincen.gov/resources/statutes-regulations/administrative-rulings/application-fincens-regulations-virtual-0

87. *Id.*
88. 31 U.S.C. §5318(h)(1)(D). The regulation is §103.125, Anti-money laundering programs for money services businesses, https://www.gpo.gov/fdsys/pkg/CFR-2004-title31-vol1/pdf/CFR-2004-title31-vol1-sec103-125.pdf
89. For an excellent discussion of the regulation in connection with virtual currencies, see Peter Van Valkenburgh, *The Bank Secrecy Act, Cryptocurrencies, and New Tokens: What is Known and What Remains Ambiguous,* Coin Center, May, 2017, https://coincenter.org/entry/aml-kyc-tokens
90. *U.S. v. Lord,* Cr. No. 15-00240-01/02 (W.D.La, Apr. 20, 2017), https://scholar.google.com/scholar_case?case=4687444852356921249
91. *Id.*
92. Randal K. Quarles, *Thoughts on Prudent Innovation in the Payment System* (Nov. 30, 2017), Speech, U.S. Board of Governors of the Federal Reserve, https://www.federalreserve.gov/newsevents/speech/quarles20171130a.htm
93. For a lengthy discussion of the Council and the ramifications attendant to a finding of "systemically important" financial firm, see Roy J. Girasa, *The Rise, Risks, and Rewards of Non-Bank Financial Services,* (2016), Palgrave Macmillan.
94. Katie Little, *Fed lacks authority to regulate Bitcoin: Janet Yellen,* CNBC, Feb. 27, 2014, https://www.cnbc.com/2014/02/27/fed-chain-janet-yellen-discusses-Bitcoin-regulation.html?view=story&%24DEVICE%24=native-android-tablet
95. Dodd-Frank Wall Street Reform and Consumer Protection Act, Pub.L 111-203, H.R. 4173, enacted into law, July 21, 2010.
96. U.S. Consumer Financial Protection Bureau, *Risks to consumers posed by virtual currencies* consumer advocacy, Aug. 2014, http://files.consumerfinance.gov/f/201408_cfpb_consumer-advisory_virtual-currencies.pdf
97. U.S. Office of the Comptroller of the Currency, *Recommendations and Decisions for Implementing a Responsible Innovation Framework,* Oct. 2016, https://www.occ.gov/topics/responsible-innovation/comments/

recommendations-decisions-for-implementing-a-responsible-innovation-framework.pdf
98. *Id.,* at 4.
99. Federal Trade Commission Act, 15 U.S.C. §§41–58 as amended.
100. *Federal Trade Commission v. BF Labs, Inc.,* No. 4:14-cv-00815-BCW (D.C. Mo. filed Sept. 14, 2014), https://www.ftc.gov/system/files/documents/cases/140923utterflylabscmpt.pdf
101. U.S. Federal Trade Commission, *Operators of Bitcoin Mining Operation Butterfly Labs Agree to Settle FTC Charges They Deceived Consumers,* Press Release, Feb. 16, 2016, https://www.ftc.gov/news-events/press-releases/2016/02/operators-bitcoin-mining-operation-butterfly-labs-agree-settle
102. North American Securities Administrators Association, *NASAA Reminds Investors to Approach Cryptocurrencies, Initial Coin Offerings and Other Cryptocurrency-Related Investment Products with Caution,* Jan. 4, 2018, http://www.nasaa.org/44073/nasaa-reminds-investors-approach-cryptocurrencies-initial-coin-offerings-cryptocurrency-related-investment-products-caution/

States' Regulation of Virtual Currencies

The federal government, acting slowly in promulgating regulations concerning cryptocurrencies, has to date ceded to the states the enactment of legislation or guidance concerning their use within their jurisdictions. The problem is that there is no model uniform legislation which states find acceptable to promulgate but instead have adopted a variety of statutes and regulations. States that have enacted legislation concerning virtual currencies generally adopt one of several regimes, namely: that of requiring a license for the transmission of currencies; make reference to virtual currencies with respect to other statutory requirements such as money laundering; or post warnings about the risks of virtual currencies.[1] All states except Montana, New Mexico, and South Carolina have money transmission legislation generally requiring registration and/or licensing to engage in the exchange services for the transmission of currencies.[2] A review of the pertinent states and their laws follows below, particularly the money transmitter legislation based on a 50-state examination.[3]

© The Author(s) 2018
R. Girasa, *Regulation of Cryptocurrencies and Blockchain Technologies*, Palgrave Studies in Financial Services Technology, https://doi.org/10.1007/978-3-319-78509-7_5

States Requiring Licenses for Virtual Currency Businesses

Alabama

Alabama requires a license for persons engaged in money transmission business including use of virtual currencies. The legislation, as newly amended, includes virtual currency within the definition of monetary value for the purposes of transmission.[4]

California

California initially repealed a statute in June, 2014 that prohibited the circulation of any money other than lawful money of the United States. Under its Money Transmission Act, a person is prohibited from advertising, soliciting, or holding him/herself out as providing money transmission in this state unless the person is licensed by the Commissioner of Business Oversight or is exempt from licensure under the Act. Under current legislation known as the Virtual Currency Act,[5] proposed by the California Assembly, the bill would prohibit a person from engaging in any virtual currency business as defined in the state unless the person is licensed by the said Commissioner or is otherwise exempt from the licensure requirement.

The bill would require applicants for licensure to pay the applicable fee; provide detailed information about the business of virtual currency and prior virtual currency services provided by the applicant; submit a sample form of receipt for transactions involving the business of virtual currency; and furnish specified financial statements. This bill would require each licensee to maintain at all times sufficient capital as the Commissioner determines, subject to specified factors, to ensure the safety and soundness of the licensee, its ongoing operations, and the maintenance of consumer protection. The bill would also require each licensee to possess a bond or trust account in U.S. dollars for the benefit of its consumers in the form and amount as specified by the Commissioner. There are civil penalties and other judicial relief for non-compliance.[6]

Connecticut

Connecticut amended its Money Transmission Act which provides for the licensing of persons engaged in the business of transmitting monetary value in the form of virtual currency as mandated by the Commissioner of Banking unless the issuance thereof may pose an undue risk of financial loss to consumers. *Virtual currency businesses* refer to "any type of digital unit that is used as a medium of exchange or a form of digitally stored value or that is incorporated into payment system technology." Excluded are online gaming and virtual currency that are part of a customer rewards program not convertible into fiat currency. The Commissioner may require the posting of a surety bond for such services.[7]

Georgia

Georgia had initially issued a guidance in 2014 to consumers concerning virtual currency.[8] Thereafter, the state legislature enacted a bill in 2016, signed into law by the Governor, that granted its Department of Banking and Finance the power to enact rules and regulations concerning money transmission to include virtual currency and requiring all money transmitters to apply and possess a license for their transactions.[9]

Idaho

Under Idaho's Money Transmission Act, a money transmitter must acquire a license from the state's Finance Department including *virtual currency exchangers*, i.e., those that act as "a virtual/digital currency exchanger and accept legal tender (e.g., government backed/issued 'fiat' currencies) for later delivery to a third party in association with the purchase of a virtual currency...."[10]

Nevada

Nevada, in its recognition of blockchain technology, requires a certificate, license, or permit to use a blockchain, or any other requirement of blockchain use.[11] It became the first state to ban taxes on the use of blockchain technology by prohibiting any county commissioner from imposing any taxes on the licensing of blockchain and smart contracts.[12]

New York

New York was the first state to set forth regulations governing digital currency businesses.[13] By regulations issued on June 3, 2015 by the N.Y.S. Department of Financial Services, a person engaged in any *virtual currency business activity* is required to be licensed by the Superintendent of Banking (a BitLicense). Such activity is defined as a New York resident or involves such a resident receiving or transmitting virtual currency except when undertaken for non-financial purposes or is nominal in value; storing, holding, or maintaining custody or control of virtual currency; buying and selling virtual currency as a customer business; performing exchange services as a customer business; or controlling, administering, or issuing virtual currency.[14] Excluded from licensing requirements are online gaming. A recitation of the pertinent parts of the regulation are provided here because they were emulated in part by the National Conference of Commissioners on Uniform State Laws in its suggested model code for states, the Uniform Regulation of Virtual Currency Business Act, which is summarized below.

BitLicense

The licensing requirements provide that anyone engaged in virtual currency business activity must first obtain a license. The application, together with the payment of a $5000 fee, must include (1) the exact name of the applicant, including any doing business as name…; (2) a list of all the applicant's affiliates and an organization chart illustrating [their] relationship [to] the applicant…; (3) a list of… each individual applicant and each director…including such individual's name, physical and mailing addresses, and information and documentation regarding such individual's personal history, experience, and qualification, which shall be accompanied by a form of authority, executed by such individual, to release information to the Department; (4) a background report prepared by an independent investigatory agency acceptable to the superintendent for each individual applicant, and each principal officer, principal stockholder, and principal beneficiary of the applicant, as applicable; (5) for each individual applicant…and for all individuals to be employed by the applicant who have access to any customer funds, whether denominated in fiat currency or virtual currency, a set of fingerprints and photographs; (6) an organization chart of the applicant and its management structure …; (7) a current financial statement for the applicant and each principal officer, principal stockholder, and principal beneficiary of the applicant, as applicable, and a projected balance sheet and income statement for the following year of the applicant's operation; (8) a description of the proposed, current, and historical business of the applicant…; (9) details of all banking arrangements; (10) all written policies and procedures required…; (11) an affidavit describing any pending or threatened actions or proceedings of any kind; (12) verification from the New York State Department of Taxation and Finance that the applicant is compliant with all…tax obligations …; (13)…a copy of any insurance policies maintained for the benefit of the applicant, its directors or officers, or its customers; (14) an explanation of the methodology used to calculate the value of virtual currency in fiat currency.

There are provisions for requiring mandatory compliance with anti-money laundering rules, the maintenance of adequate books and records, and the obligation to allow the Superintendent to inspect such records, minimum capitalization requirements, and the obligation to protect its customers' assets in several enumerated respects.[15]

The first trust company charter to receive a license issued under the regulations was the Bitcoin exchange, itBit Trust Company, LLC on May 7, 2015.[16] The first BitLicense granted to a virtual currency firm was issued on September, 2015 to Circle Internet Financial.[17] Litigation was commenced by an individual, Theo Chino and his firm, China Ltd., in an Article 78 proceeding (a proceeding to challenge an administrative regulation in New York courts) contesting the validity of the regulation. The Department filed a motion to dismiss the lawsuit which was granted based on lack of standing.[18] A subsequent case concerning the same parties was also dismissed on the same basis. The plaintiffs-petitioners sought nullification of the BitLicense alleging the regulation was arbitrary and capricious; and that implementation of the regulation violated federal law that pre-empted the regulation. They sought an order setting aside the regulation as being made in violation of law in that the Department of Financial Services exceeded its jurisdiction, and other relief.

To date few BitLicenses have been issued in addition to the ones stated above. Additional BitLicenses were granted to Ripple in July, 2016, and to Coinbase in January, 2017.[19] All other applications have been denied. When the requirements for a BitLicense was first promulgated, many existing and potential Bitcoin startups left or commenced their platforms outside of New York State. It remains to be seen whether the exodus or extensions to New York State of blockchain startups will continue due to the alleged onerous requirements.[20]

North Carolina

North Carolina requires all persons, unless exempted, engaged in the business of money transmission to obtain a license from the Commissioner of Banks. Such engagement is defined as "a person who solicits or advertises money transmission services from a Web site that North Carolina citizens may access in order to enter into those transactions by electronic means." A surety bond is required the size of which is dependent on the sums transmitted.[21]

Texas

Texas may require a license as stated in a 2014 Supervisory Memorandum from the Texas Department of Banking.[22] In a detailed discussion of virtual currencies the Banking Commissioner stated that exchanging virtual currency for sovereign (fiat) currency is not deemed to be a currency exchange under the Texas Finance Code inasmuch as it defines *currency* for the purposes of currency exchange as "the coin and paper money of the United States or any country that is designated as legal tender and circulates and is customarily used and accepted as a medium of exchange in the country of issuance." Therefore, no currency exchange license is required in Texas to conduct any type of transaction exchanging virtual with sovereign currencies.

With respect to *money transmission* defined as "the receipt of money or monetary value by any means in exchange for a promise to make the money or monetary value available at a later time or different location," the Commissioner noted that cryptocurrency is not currency in that a unit of cryptocurrency is not a claim, does not entitle its owner to anything, and creates no duties or obligations in a person who gives, sells, or transfers it; and no entity must honor the value of a cryptocurrency, or exchange any given unit of a cryptocurrency for sovereign currency. Thus, it is not money under the Money Services Act[23] and receiving it in exchange for a promise to make it available at a later time or different location is not a money transmission. When a cryptocurrency transaction includes sovereign currency, it may be a money transmission depending on how the sovereign currency is handled. A license is not needed if the exchange is between two parties but if a third party exchanger is utilized then it would constitute money transmission requiring the third party to comply with licensing requirements. A Bitcoin ATM, on the other hand, may or may not be money transmission dependent on whether it acts as a third party facilitating the transaction between the seller and the buyer. If the ATM is configured to be a direct transaction between the user and the ATM, then it is not a money transmitter under Texas law.

Vermont

Vermont statutory legislation provides that a digital record electronically registered in a blockchain shall be self-authenticating under its rules of evidence if accompanied by a written declaration of a qualified person under oath of the date and time the record entered into and received from the blockchain; that the record was maintained in the blockchain as a regularly conducted activity; and that the record was made by the regularly conducted activity as a regular practice. It will be presumed as a matter of law that the fact or record, the date and time, and the persons involved in the transmission are authentic, and the parties have agreed to the blockchain format as a means of authentication. The presumptions of authentication apply to contractual parties, ownership of property, identification of the parties, the authenticity of a record, and related issues.[24] It further requires licenses of persons engaged in the money transmission business that includes exchange of virtual currency.[25]

Virginia

Virginia has stated that the Virginia Bureau of Financial Institutions does not regulate virtual currencies. If the virtual currency transaction involves fiat currency then it may be subject to the requirements of its money transmission provisions that require a license for such transmission.[26]

Washington

Washington enacted a statute comparable to that of North Carolina whereby a license is required for a person to engage in money transmission, advertising, solicitation, or hold oneself out as providing money transmission. Section 7 of the Act provides that each online currency exchanger licensee shall maintain a surety bond in an amount based on the previous year's currency exchange dollar volume for the benefit of the state and any person who suffers loss by reason of a licensee's violation of the Act.[27]

Wyoming

Wyoming requires a license for those engaged in money transmission which includes virtual currencies. The added requirement of *permissive investments* has caused virtual currency companies to avoid operations within the state. The provision states that "each licensee shall at all times possess permissible investments having an aggregate market value calculated in accordance with generally accepted accounting principles, of not less than the aggregate face amount of all outstanding payment instruments and stored value issued or sold by the licensee in the United States. This requirement may be waived by the commissioner if the dollar volume of a licensee's outstanding payment instruments and stored value does not exceed the bond or other security devices posted by the licensee. Permissible investments are to be held in trust for the benefit of the purchasers and holders of the licensee's outstanding payment instruments in the event of the bankruptcy of the licensee."[28]

Miscellaneous States Giving Recognition to Virtual Currencies

Arizona

Arizona joined other states in its recognition of blockchain technology by requiring that a signature that is secured, as well as a record or contract though the technology, is considered to be in an electronic signature, form, and record. *Smart contracts*, defined as "an event driven program that runs on a distributed, decentralized, shared and replicated ledger and can take custody over and instruct transfer of assets on that ledger," are to be given validity, legal effect, and enforceability.[29]

Delaware

Delaware gave recognition to distributed ledgers or a blockchain by the passage of legislation signed into law on July 21, 2017.[30] The provisions thereof provide Delaware corporations with statutory authority to use networks of electronic databases (distributed ledgers or blockchain) to create and maintain corporate records including stock ledgers in order to prepare lists of stockholders, record transfers of stock, and to give notices to holders of uncertified shares. The effect of the legislation in a state that is home to two-thirds of the Fortune 500 companies, is to give recognition that the new technology needs to maintain lists of shareholders on a blockchain rather than the more conventional method of Excel spreadsheets or a SQL database.[31]

Florida

Due in great part to the adverse decision whereby a Florida judge dismissed a money laundering case against an individual, Mitchell Espinosa, for money laundering because virtual currency was not considered to be money, the law was amended as suggested by the said judge who believed she had no choice, absent clarification by the legislature. Accordingly, Florida added to its Money Laundering Act prohibitions to include "virtual currency."[32]

Hawaii

The state of Hawaii initially was one of the first states to enact legislation concerning digital currency (blockchain) which establish a working group consisting of representatives from public and private sectors to examine, educate, and promote best practices for enabling blockchain technology designed to defend against cyber-attacks and encourage economic growth. It noted that blockchain's structure is naturally cyber-resilient, redundant, immutable, and verifiable. Beyond Bitcoin, the legislation seeks to adapt the technology for cybersecurity, disaster recovery, clearance and settlement, supply chain transparency, title registries, communications, and document verification. Other areas for its adaptation include health care; legal services by verification of contracts and other uses; financial services to save billions in overheads and fees; manufacturing to provide accountability and transparency including the reduction of counterfeit products and improve competitiveness for local businesses; and tourism by making it easier for Asians and other to gain access.[33]

It appears, however, that after its initial welcoming foray into digital currency accommodation, the state caused concern among virtual currency exchanges owing to a proposal requiring a license under its Money Transmission Act which includes the need to possess "permissible investments." The said investments are to have an aggregate market value of not less than the aggregate amount of all outstanding payment obligations. The exchanges are to post a bond or other security devices or possess like-kind virtual currency of the same volume as the outstanding payment obligations to be completed in virtual currency pursuant to the contract with the licensee. The Commissioner is given the power to determine the applicable levels and types of permissible investments to be maintained by the exchanges.[34] The result of the legislation to be enacted is that Coinbase, which operates in most of the U.S. states and abroad, has decided to leave Hawaii because of the onerous restrictions.[35]

Illinois

Illinois's Money Transmitters of Money Act[36] states that a *money transmitter*, defined as one located in Illinois or doing business therein who engages in the business of selling or issuing payment, instruments, transmitting money, or exchanging money for compensation must be licensed unless otherwise exempted therefrom. The exchange of virtual currencies comes within the definition of money and the transmission thereof.[37]

Massachusetts

Although Massachusetts does have licensing requirements for money transmitters, it is unclear as of this writing whether virtual currencies and their transmission fall within the statute. The Massachusetts Securities Division indicated that it will conduct an examination to ascertain compliance with state law. The Secretary of the Commonwealth, William Galvin, on December 15, 2017, opined that ICOs involving the purchase and sale of digital coins are securities which require registration with the state unless otherwise exempt.[38]

In its first action against a cryptocurrency ICO, the Massachusetts Securities Division Enforcement Section filed a complaint against Caviar, a Cayman Islands corporation, and its founder Kirill Bensonoff, a resident of Massachusetts, for violation of its securities laws.[39] It was alleged that Caviar tokens would be issued that represented interests in diverse assets including real estate and blockchain assets to be managed by Caviar. The firm raised over $3.1 million and its investors were advised of their ownership through DLT. The cost of each token was $0.10. The respondents intended to distribute a total of 375 million Caviar tokens. The respondent Bensonoff allegedly represented to investors that the proceeds received in the ICO would be pooled and used to finance short-term "flips" of residential real estate properties. Investors were to receive quarterly dividends equal to their pro rata share of 75 percent of the combined profit from the pooled investment fund Although the website indicated that U.S., including Massachusetts, residents were not eligible to participate in the offering, nevertheless, the complaint alleges that Caviar failed to prevent the sale of tokens to residents by its lack of reasonable requirements of customer identification.

The complaint further alleged that the respondents' procedures to prevent the sale to U.S. residents were inadequate; that they promoted the Caviar ICO through general solicitations; that the caviar tokens are securities; that the purchasers of caviar tokens reasonably expected to profit from their investments; and that profit was through the efforts of others whose investments were not registered with Massachusetts as required under its statute (Mass. Gen. Laws Ch. 110A. §201 and §301). Accordingly, the Commonwealth sought an immediate cease and desist order, rescission with respect to the state's residents, disgorgement of profits, an accounting and administrative fine, and other relief.[40]

New Jersey

It appears to date that New Jersey has not adopted legislation regarding virtual currencies but has taken note of them for tax purposes. The state choose the position that convertible virtual currency, such as Bitcoin, of equivalent value in real currency may be used by taxpayers to pay for goods and services. Accordingly, the state tax authorities assumed the position that conforms to the federal tax treatment of convertible virtual currency (discussed in the chapter on "Crowdfunding and the Taxation of Virtual Currencies"). Transactions using virtual currency must be reported in U.S. dollars for federal tax purposes whereby taxpayers are required to determine the fair market value of the convertible virtual currency in U.S. dollars as of the date of payment or receipt. New Jersey imposes sales or use tax on receipts from the retail sale of tangible personal property, specified digital products, and enumerated services, unless a valid exemption exists. The said currency is treated as intangible property and, as such, the purchase or use of the currency in a transaction is not subject to sales tax. The sales or use tax applies when a person transfers convertible virtual currency for taxable goods or services. Any seller and/or retailer of taxable goods or services that accepts convertible virtual currency as payment must determine the fair market value of the currency in U.S. dollars as of the date of payment and charge the purchaser sales tax on the underlying transaction.[41]

West Virginia

West Virginia gave recognition to virtual currency by adding it to the definition of transmissions prohibited for any person to conduct or attempt to conduct a financial transaction involving the proceeds of criminal activity knowing that the property involved in the financial transaction represents the proceeds of, or is derived directly or indirectly from the proceeds of, criminal activity.[42]

States That Have Not to Date Enacted Legislation Concerning Virtual Currencies

A number of states have failed to enact legislation either requiring registration or requiring licenses for their transactions, albeit most are in the early stages of considering laws and regulations governing their exchange. Generally, these states post warnings about the risks of purchasing virtual currencies but no clearly defined laws or regulations have been set forth. Of course, criminal penalties still apply for fraud and other malfeasance. The states where licenses or registration are not required include Alaska, Arkansas, Colorado, Indiana, Iowa, Kansas, Kentucky, Louisiana, Maine, Maryland, Michigan, Minnesota, Mississippi, Missouri, New Mexico, Missouri, Montana, Nebraska, North Dakota, Ohio, Oklahoma, Oregon, Rhode Island, South Dakota, Tennessee, West Virginia, and Wisconsin.

Kansas has issued a guidance concerning virtual currency and the state's Money Transmission Act. The guidance states that the action of a two-party currency exchange by itself is not covered by the statute unless a third-party is involved in the transaction; however, the presence of a third party involved in a currency exchange transaction will likely subject the transaction to the Act. The guidance specifically states that it does not address money transmission activities involving the various centralized virtual currencies in existence. It notes that many of the virtual currency schemes are complicated and nuanced, and cannot be addressed adequately to cover all the possible types. It takes the view that, unlike the U.S. dollar, virtual currency has no intrinsic value and has no claim as a commodity. The Money Transmission statute concerns "money," therefore begging the question whether virtual currency is money. The guidance continued by stating that inasmuch as the value of a unit of cryptocurrency is only what a buyer is willing to pay for it and what a seller is willing to accept in order to part with it, there is no intrinsic or set value for a unit of cryptocurrency. Therefore, because cryptocurrencies as currently in existence are not considered "money" or "monetary value" they are not covered by the Money Transmission Act. Nevertheless, should the transmission of virtual currency include the involvement of sovereign currency in a transaction, it may be considered a money transmission depending on how such a transaction is organized.[43]

Maryland has not enacted legislation as indicated to require licensing or registration of virtual currency. A court in a Maryland case dismissed charges that a virtual currency casino engaged in unlawful gambling stating that under the firm's term of service, the virtual goods and services could not be redeemed for "real money," goods or other items having monetary value. It involved virtual gold and not dollars and was being used for entertainment purposes. There was no ability to "cash out" of the game and, thus, this resembled purchasing tickets for a movie or amusement park.[44] Similarly, a California court dismissed a class action lawsuit commenced against Machine Zone Inc. alleging that it violated the California Penal Code that criminalize the manufacture, ownership, or possession of a slot machine or device. The court ruled that the machine was a game of skill and not chance and, in any event, the plaintiffs had no standing and had neither established injury under the California Unfair Competition statute, nor established the claim of unjust enrichment.[45]

Although Missouri does not have licensing or registration requirements pertaining to virtual currency, it has previously issued a cease and desist order under its securities laws against Virtual Mining Corp., Kenneth E. Slaughter, and related firms with respect to the use of an online forum known as "Bitcointalk" to solicit funds from investors for the purpose of developing, manufacturing, and selling Bitcoin mining equipment. The moneys would be given to the Virtual Mining Corp. and Active Mining Corp., which Slaughter controlled, for which investment investors could expect to receive a two-year return up to 2812 percent and 100 percent profit. The scheme brought in $200,000 of investment in bitcoins. The defendants failed to advise investors of the risks, the volatility of the value of bitcoins, the lack of government backing of the bitcoins, and other pertinent data. The action took place in 2014 before the Bitcoin frenzy.[46]

Montana has no provision governing licensing or money transmission but does provide specifically a complaint mechanism with the Montana Department of Administration, Banking & Financial Institutions with respect to virtual currencies.[47] New Hampshire specifically exempts by statute persons using virtual currencies from registering as money transmitters.[48] Ohio has no restrictions concerning licensing or use as evidenced by the opening of Bitcoin ATMs in the state.[49]

Proposed Uniform Virtual Currency Codes

Uniform Regulation of Virtual-Currency Business Act

The Uniform Law Commission[50] recommended and approved for enactment by all the states a proposed Uniform Regulation of Virtual-Currency Business Act.[51] In essence, the proposal would require that businesses whose products and services include the exchange of such currencies for cash, bank deposits, or other virtual currencies, or their transfer between customers, or provide custodial or fiduciary services, be licensed and be subject to regulations to protect customers. It states that the proposed regulation is modeled on the Uniform Money Services Act and conforms to FinCEN's guidance as well as the Framework issued by the Conference of State Bank Supervisors discussed below.[52] The closest statute and regulations from which the Model Act is framed is that of New York's "BitLicense" regulation discussed previously.

Among the "novel" features of the proposed Act that differ from state "money services" or "money transmitter" statutes are the provisions: (a) for a three-tier system for determining whether a provider is to be deemed exempt from the Act—(1) persons engaged only in minor activity; (2) an intermediate registration status modeled as an "on-ramp" or "regulatory sandbox" that has simpler regulatory requirements so as to facilitate virtual currency innovations; and (3) a full-fledged licensure system for providers with a designated volume of business; (b) provisions requiring that the virtual currency business with "control" over virtual currency held by state residents must maintain a specified type of virtual currency sufficient to satisfy the requirements of each type of virtual currency for the benefit of the states' residents together and to favor the interests of the said persons place control under the said control over the interests of creditors of the licensee; (c) heightened emphasis of cross-state reciprocal licensure to lower regulatory costs of the providers; and (d) more flexible provisions on net worth and reserve requirements than are currently found in states' money transmitter statutes where the provider with control over virtual currency customers' accounts has complied with custodial arrangement as stated in (b) above.[53]

To date, no state has enacted the Uniform Regulation but rather has generally taken the approaches of licensing firms engaged in the exchange of virtual currencies (somewhat comparable to the suggested Model Code), requiring registration of firms so engaged, or simply posting warnings concerning the potential risks to consumers who trade in the currencies. The Uniform Regulation was opposed vigorously by the Bitcoin Foundation which stated that its adoption "would discourage inclusive financial innovation arising out of blockchain technology and cryptocurrencies like Bitcoin."[54] The Executive Director of the Foundation, Llew Claasen, alleged that the proposed regulation, modeled on New York's regulation, has caused small businesses in the financial technology business to be driven out of the state by its alleged onerous licensing and compliance requirements.[55] Claasen's position is that it may be premature to regulate cryptocurrencies due to the variety of types being created whereby some may be akin to use as a commodity, others as a store of value, and some as a medium of exchange. He would assume a wait-and-see attitude that initially permits startups to develop their new creations which could, at a later date, be subject to regulations appropriately suited to the particular outcome.[56]

Conference of State Bank Supervisors: Model Framework (CSBS)

The Conference of State Bank Supervisors (CSBS) had formed the CSBS Emerging Payments Task Force to examine the intersection between state supervisors, state law, and payments in order to determine which regulatory approaches to adopt with respect to virtual currencies and the participants thereof. In summary, it concluded that states should enact licensing requirements and provide supervision with respect to centralized (third-party) virtual currencies.[57] Excluded from the recommendations are merchants and consumers who use virtual currencies solely for the purchase of goods and services; non-financial activities such as the use of blockchain technology for bookkeeping activities that concern units of value issued as rewards which are not redeemable for fiat or virtual currencies; and activities that are solely for online gaming.

CSBS stated that state laws applicable to activities involving fiat currencies should also be made applicable to virtual currencies. At a minimum, states should provide in their laws, regulations, and interpretations that cover the transmission, exchange of virtual currencies for fiat currencies and vice versa, and services that facilitate third-party exchange, storage, and/or transmission of virtual currency either through the use of wallets, vaults, payment processors or by other related means, Licensing requirements should include details of the firm's business plan, how risk is determined, and consumer protection. Regulators should be enabled to share information in real time and attempt to streamline the technical aspects of licensing. Concerning investment reserves required of companies engaged in the transmission of virtual currencies, the Conference suggested alternative possibilities for state regulators dependent on the business model. The investment reserves may be in the form of cash, virtual currency, or high-quality, high-liquid, investment-grade assets.[58]

There should be consumer protection requirements in the form of disclosures and notices, complaint resolution procedures, and receipt requirements. Audits of the firm should be performed by a competent third party including that of cybersecurity and encouragement of cybersecurity insurance. A Customer Identification Program should be required to detect and prevent fraud and other illegal activity. Companies should be required to have periodic reporting to the relevant state agency and these requirements should be standardized. Compliance was an issue concerning the quantum of information that had to be rendered. The CSBS urged flexibility dependent on the company, usefulness of the information, and feasibility of efficiently transferring the information. It further urged that there be a strength and stability component in place to protect customer access in the event of failure of the company. It should cover, at a minimum, policies and procedures regarding how private keys are transferred or recovered in such an event. Another concern is access to the banking sector by virtual companies. The recommendation is for banks to evaluate the existing and potential customer relationships with the particular customer to include whether the customer is acting in accordance with state laws and regulations.

Lastly, there should be appropriate training of state personnel to understand cryptocurrency and how it is created, managed, and valued.[59]

In the chapter on "Criminal Prosecutions and Civil Litigations Concerning Virtual Currencies", we will discuss how the federal government has commenced prosecution and civil litigation to thwart the errant behavior of persons and firms who take advantage of the lack of public knowledge of the new technologies.

Notes

1. For an excellent summary of the laws and regulations pertaining to virtual currencies or the lack thereof, see Carlton Fields, Matthew Kohen, and Justin Wales, *State Regulations On Virtual Currencies and Blockchain Technologies,* Nov. 10, 2017, https://www.jdsupra.com/legalnews/state-regulations-on-virtual-currency-14945/

2. *State Survey on the Treatment of Virtual Currency,* https://advance.lexis. com/open/document/lpadocument/?pdmfid=1000522&crid=13 b9c497-adf7-4e02-b764-76be211e569b&pddocfullpath=%2Fshared% 2Fdocument%2Fforms%2Furn%3AcontentItem%3A5FV2-K6T1- JFSV-G1GF-00000-00&pddocid=urn%3AcontentItem%3A5FV2- K6T1-JFSV-G1GF-00000-00&pdcontentcomponentid=102984&pdt easerkey=sr0&ecomp=5vkg&earg=sr0&prid=66adc 6fe-f905-4247-96b9-525fa86b58a6

3. The review relies heavily on the analysis of Thomas Brown, *50-STATE- SURVEY: Money Transmitter Licensing Requirements,* http://abnk.assem- bly.ca.gov/sites/abnk.assembly.ca.gov/files/50%20State%20Survey%20 -%20MTL%20Licensing%20Requirements%2872986803_4%29.pdf and Latham & Watkins' *The Other Side of the Coin: Bitcoin, Blockchain, Regulation & Enforcement,* FIA, Mar. 24, 2016, https://lc.fia.org/sites/ default/files/LW_2016%20FIA%20Bitcoin%20Webinar%20 Presentation.pdf

4. Alabama Money Transmission Act, H.B. 215, 2017 Leg., Reg. Sess. (Ala. 2017) §8-7A-2(8).

5. Cal. Stat. §320.6.

6. Cal. Assembly Bill AB-1123, Virtual Currency: Regulation (Feb. 17, 2017), https://leginfo.legislature.ca.gov/faces/billTextClient.xhtml?bill_ id=201720180AB1123

7. Conn. Pub. Act 15-53, An act Concerning Mortgage Correspondent Lenders, The Small Act, Virtual Currencies and Security Freezes on Consumer Credit Reports, Sec. 7(7)(c)((d), https://www.cga.ct. gov/2015/ACT/PA/2015PA-00053-R00HB-06800-PA.htm

8. Georgia Department of Banking and Finance, *Consumer and Investor Guidance on Virtual Currency,* April 30, 2014, https://dbf.georgia.gov/ sites/dbf.georgia.gov/files/related_files/document/consumer-advisory- virtual-currencies.pdf

9. Ga. Code Ann. §7-1-680(26), discussed in Justin S. Wales and Matthew E. Kohen, *State Regulations on Virtual Currency And Blockchain Technologies,* Oct. 17, 2017, https://www.carltonfields.com/state-regula- tions-on-virtual-currency-and-blockchain-technologies-10-17-2017/. This article was also used as a source for discussion of the laws and regu- lations governing virtual currencies among the 50 states.

10. Idaho Department of Finance, Idaho Money Transmitters Section, http://www.finance.idaho.gov/MoneyTransmitter/MoneyTransmitter.aspx

11. An Act relating to electronic transactions; recognizing blockchain technology as a type of electronic record for the purposes of the Uniform Electronic Transactions Act; prohibiting a local government from taxing or imposing restrictions upon the use of a blockchain; and providing other matters properly relating thereto. SB 398, June 5, 2017, https://www.leg.state.nv.us/App/NELIS/REL/79th2017/Bill/5463/Overview

12. Stan Higgins, *Nevada Becomes First US State to Ban Blockchain Taxes*, CoinDesk, June 6, 2017, https://www.coindesk.com/nevada-first-us-state-ban-blockchain-taxes/

13. New York Statutes. Title 23, Ch. 1, Part 200, Virtual Currencies, http://www.dfs.ny.gov/legal/regulations/adoptions/dfsp200t.pdf

14. *Id.* Part 200.2(q).

15. Taken from the recitation by the court in *Chino v. New York Dept. of Financial Services*, 2017 NY Slip Op 51908, NY: Supreme Court 2017, https://scholar.google.com/scholar_case?case=15872102065273065030. The regulation is 23 NYCRR §§200.7–200.22.

16. New York State Department of Financial Services, *NYDFS Grand First Charter to a New York Virtual Currency Company* (May 7, 2017), Press Release, http://www.dfs.ny.gov/about/press/pr1505071.htm

17. New York State Department of Financial Services, *NYDFC Announces Approval of First BitLicense Application From a Virtual Currency Firm*, Sept. 22, 2015, Press Release, http://www.dfs.ny.gov/about/press/pr1509221.htm

18. *Chino v. Dept. of Financial Services,* Claim No. 124835, Index No. 101880-15 (NY Ct. Cl., 2015), http://vertumnus.courts.state.ny.us/claims/html/2015-049-021.html

19. Michael del Castillio, *Bitcoin Exchange Coinbase Received New York BitLicense*, Coindesk, Jan. 17, 2017, https://www.coindesk.com/bitcoin-exchange-coinbase-receives-bitlicense/

20. Daniel Roberts, *Behind the "exodus" of bitcoin startups from New York,* Aug. 14, 2015, Fortune, http://fortune.com/2015/08/14/bitcoin-startups-leave-new-york-bitlicense/

21. The North Carolina Money Transmitters Act, N.C. Gen. Stat. §53-208.1, et seq. §53-208.43 and §53-208.47, https://www.nccob.org/Public/financialinstitutions/mt/mtrules.aspx

22. Texas Department of Banking, *Supervisory Memorandum – 1037*, April 3, 2014, http://www.dob.texas.gov/public/uploads/files/consumer-information/sm1037.pdf

23. Texas Money Services Act, Ch. 1099 (H.B. 2218), Sec. 1, eff. September 1, 2005.

24. Vermont statutes, Title 12, Ch. 081, §1913.

25. Josh Garcia, *Vermont changes money transmitter law to formally include virtual currency*, Cooley Fintech, May 8, 2017, https://fintech.cooley.com/2017/05/08/vermont-changes-money-transmitter-law-to-formally-include-virtual-currency/

26. Virginia State Corporation Commission, *Notice to Virginia Resident Regarding Virtual Currencies*, https://www.scc.virginia.gov/bfi/files/virtcur.pdf, citing Chapter 19 of Title 6.2 of the Code of Virginia (Money Order Sellers and Money Transmitters), §6.2-1900, et seq.

27. *An Act Addressing licensing and enforcement provisions applicable to money transmitters and currency exchanges under the uniform money services act*, §3, Wa SB 531, eff. July 31, 2017, https://legiscan.com/WA/drafts/SB5031/2017

28. Wy Stat §40-22-107 (1997 through Reg Sess), https://law.justia.com/codes/wyoming/2011/title40/chapter22/section40-22-107/

29. An Act amending Section 44-7003, Arizona Revised Statutes by amending Article 5 relating to electronic transactions, HB2417, signed into law March 29, 2017, https://legiscan.com/AZ/text/HB2417/id/1497439

30. An Act to Amend Title 8 of the Delaware Code Relating to the General Corporation Law, signed into law on July 21, 2017, https://legis.delaware.gov/BillDetail/25730

31. John Roberts, *Companies Can Put Shareholders on a Blockchain Starting Today*, Fortune, Aug. 1, 2017, http://fortune.com/2017/08/01/blockchain-shareholders-law/

32. Florida Money Laundering Act, Fl. Stat. §896.101(j), http://www.leg.state.fl.us/Statutes/index.cfm?App_mode=Display_Statute&URL=0800-0899/0896/0896.html

33. Hawaii-2017, https://legiscan.com/HI/text/HB1481/2017

34. Hawaii Sen. Bill No. 3082, eff. July 1, 2018, https://www.capitol.hawaii.gov/session2018/bills/SB3082_.HTM

35. Jamie Redman, *Hawaii's New Money Transmitters Act Will Require Virtual Currency Licenses*, bitcoin.com Jan. 31, 2018, https://news.bitcoin.com/hawaiis-new-money-transmitters-act-will-

require-virtual-currency-licenses/, and Kevin Helms, *Coinbase Exits as Hawaii Requires Bitcoin Companies to Hold Fiat Reserves,* bitcoin.com, (Feb. 28, 2017), https://news.bitcoin.com/coinbase-exits-as-hawaii-requires-money-transmitter-license/

36. Illinois *Transmitters of Money Act,* 205, ILC§6571, http://www.ilga.gov/legislation/ilcs/ilcs3.asp?ActID=1201&ChapterID=20

37. *Id.,* 205 ILCS 605/10, P.A. 88-643, eff. 1-1-95.

38. Justin Marble, *Massachusetts Announces ICO Sweep* (Dec. 18, 2017), Foley Hoag, http://www.foleyhoag.com/our-firm/technology-and-entrepreneurship/insights/2017/massachusetts-announces-ico-sweep

39. *In re Caviar and Kirill Bensonoff,* Docket No. E-2017-0120 (Ma. Adm. Proceeding, Jan. 17, 2018).

40. *Id.*

41. State of New Jersey, Convertible Virtual Currency, TAM-2015-1(R), July 28, 2015, http://www.state.nj.us/treasury/taxation/pdf/pubs/tams/tam-2015-1.pdf

42. W. Va. Code §61-15-1-4 (2017).

43. Kansas Office of the State Bank Commissioner Guidance Document, *Regulatory Treatment of Virtual Currencies Under the Kansas Money Transmission Act,* MT-2014-01, https://www.scribd.com/document/233896435/Kansas-Virtual-Currency-Guidance-June-2014

44. James G. Gatto, *Maryland Court Rules Virtual Currency Casino Not Illegal Gambling Despite Secondary Market,* National Law Review, Nov. 15, 2016, https://www.natlawreview.com/article/maryland-court-rules-virtual-currency-casino-not-illegal-gambling-despite-secondary

45. Angie Jin, *Virtual Casino Doesn't Violate California's Gambling Laws-Mason v. Machine Zone,* Technology and Marketing Law Blog, Jan. 12, 2016, http://blog.ericgoldman.org/archives/2016/01/virtual-casino-doesnt-violate-californias-gambling-law-mason-v-machine-zone-guest-blog-post.htm

46. *In re Virtual Mining, Corporation,* Mo. Sec. State, Case No. AP-14-09, June 2, 2014, https://www.sos.mo.gov/cmsimages/securities/orders/AP-14-09.pdf

47. Department of Administration, Department of Financial Institutions, http://banking.mt.gov/Complaints

48. N.H. 436, 2017 165th Sess. (N.H. 2017), https://legiscan.com/NH/bill/HB436/2017

49. Amanda Garrett, *First Bitcoin ATM Arrives in Akron as virtual currency challenges the real thing,* Akron Beacon Journal, April 30, 2016, https://www.ohio.com/akron/business/first-bitcoin-atm-arrives-in-akron-as-virtual-currency-challenges-the-real-thing

50. The Uniform Law Commission, also known as the National Conference of Commissioners on Uniform State Laws, was established in 1892 whose mission is "provide states with non-partisan, well-conceived and well-drafted legislation that brings clarity and stability to critical areas of state statutory law," http://www.uniformlaws.org/Narrative.aspx?title=About the ULC

51. National Conference of Commissioners on Uniform State Laws, *Uniform Regulation of Virtual-Currency Businesses Act,* July 14–20, 2017. http://www.uniformlaws.org/shared/docs/regulation%20of%20virtual%20currencies/2017AM_URVCBA_AsApproved.pdf

52. *Id.* at 2.

53. *Id.*

54. *State Legislators: Reject the "Uniform Regulation of Virtual Currency Business Act,"* The Bitcoin Foundation, July 19, 2017, https://bitcoinfoundation.org/reject-uniform-regulation-virtual-currency-businesses-act/

55. Citing Daniel Roberts, *Behind the "exodus" of bitcoin startups from New York,* Fortune, Aug. 14, 2017, http://fortune.com/2015/08/14/bitcoin-startups-leave-new-york-bitlicense/

56. Llew Claasens, *Letter to the National Conference of Commissioners on Uniform State Laws,* The Bitcoin Foundation, Inc., July 14, 2017, https://bitcoinfoundation.org/wp-content/uploads/2017/07/ULC-Virtual-Currencies_Jul142017-final.pdf

57. Conference of State Bank Supervisors, *CSBS Policy on State Virtual Currency Regulation,* Sept.15, 2017, https://www.csbs.org/model-regulatory-framework-virtual-currencies

58. Conference of State Bank Supervisors, *State Regulatory Requirements for Virtual Currency Activities: CSBS Model Regulatory Framework* (Sept. 15, 2015), https://www.csbs.org/sites/default/files/2017-11/CSBS-Model-Regulatory-Framework%28September%2015%202015%29.pdf

59. *Id.*

Criminal Prosecutions and Civil Litigation Concerning Virtual Currencies

Statutory Prohibitions

There are numerous federal and state statutes that may come into play that concern virtual currencies. The following are the major federal statutes to date that have led to prosecutions and convictions[1]:

Violation	Statute	Maximum penalty
Operation of an unlicensed money service business	18 U.S.C. §1960[a]	5 years' imprisonment
Conspiracy to commit money laundering	18 U.S.C. §1956(h)[b]	20 years' imprisonment and a $500,000 fine or twice the value of the property involved in the transaction
Money laundering	18 U.S.C. §1956(a)(1)[c]	20 years' imprisonment and a $500,000 fine or twice the value of the property involved in the transaction (each count)
Engaging in unlawful monetary transactions	18 U.S.C. §1957[d]	10 years' imprisonment and a $500,000 fine or twice the value of the property involved in the transaction (each count)

(continued)

© The Author(s) 2018
R. Girasa, *Regulation of Cryptocurrencies and Blockchain Technologies*, Palgrave Studies in Financial Services Technology, https://doi.org/10.1007/978-3-319-78509-7_6

(continued)

Violation	Statute	Maximum penalty
Requirement of registration of money transmission business	31 U.S.C. §5330[e]	Civil penalty of $5000 per violation
Securities laws violation	15 U.S.C. §§77a et. seq. and 78a et. seq.[f]	Up to 20 years' imprisonment, fines, and forfeiture of assets attributable thereof[g]
Wire fraud	18 U.S.C. §1343[h]	Up to 30 years' imprisonment and up to $1 million fine
Mail fraud	18 U.S.C. §1341[i]	5 years' imprisonment and up to 30 years if financial institution involved plus fines of $250,000 or $1 million

[a]18 U.S.C. §1960 (a) Whoever knowingly conducts, controls, manages, supervises, directs, or owns all or part of an unlicensed money transmitting business, shall be fined in accordance with this title or imprisoned not more than 5 years, or both.
(b) As used in this section—
(1) the term "unlicensed money transmitting business" means a money transmitting business which affects interstate or foreign commerce in any manner or degree and—
(A) is operated without an appropriate money transmitting license in a State [includes U.S. possessions, Puerto Rico] where such operation is punishable as a misdemeanor or a felony under State law, whether or not the defendant knew that the operation was required to be licensed or that the operation was so punishable;
(B) fails to comply with the money transmitting business registration requirements under section 5330 of title 31, United States Code, or regulations prescribed under such section; or
(C) otherwise involves the transportation or transmission of funds that are known to the defendant to have been derived from a criminal offense or are intended to be used to promote or support unlawful activity;
(2) the term "money transmitting" includes transferring funds on behalf of the public by any and all means including but not limited to transfers within this country or to locations abroad by wire, check, draft, facsimile, or courier;...
[b]18 U.S.C. §1956(h). *Laundering of money instruments.*
(h) Any person who conspires to commit any offense defined in this section or section 1957 shall be subject to the same penalties as those prescribed for the offense the commission of which was the object of the conspiracy.
[c]18 U.S.C. §1956(a), Laundering of money instruments
(a) (1) Whoever, knowing that the property involved in a financial transaction represents the proceeds of some form of unlawful activity, conducts or attempts to conduct such a financial transaction which in fact involves the proceeds of specified unlawful activity—

(A) (i) with the intent to promote the carrying on of specified unlawful activity; or **(ii)** with intent to engage in conduct constituting a violation of section 7201 or 7206 of the Internal Revenue Code of 1986; or

(B) knowing that the transaction is designed in whole or in part— **(i)** to conceal or disguise the nature, the location, the source, the ownership, or the control of the proceeds of specified unlawful activity; or **(ii)** to avoid a transaction reporting requirement under State or Federal law, shall be sentenced to a fine of not more than $500,000 or twice the value of the property involved in the transaction, whichever is greater, or imprisonment for not more than twenty years, or both. For purposes of this paragraph, a financial transaction shall be considered to be one involving the proceeds of specified unlawful activity if it is part of a set of parallel or dependent transactions, any one of which involves the proceeds of specified unlawful activity, and all of which are part of a single plan or arrangement.

d18 U.S.C. §1957. Engaging in monetary transactions in property derived from specified unlawful activities:

(a) Whoever, in any of the circumstances set forth in subsection (d), knowingly engages or attempts to engage in a monetary transaction in criminally derived property of a value greater than $10,000 and is derived from specified unlawful activity, shall be punished as provided in subsection (b).

(b) (1) Except as provided in paragraph (2), the punishment for an offense under this section is a fine under title 18, United States Code, or imprisonment for not more than ten years or both. If the offense involves a pre-retail medical product (as defined in section 670) the punishment for the offense shall be the same as the punishment for an offense under section 670 unless the punishment under this subsection is greater...

e31 U.S.C.§5330.Registration of money transmitting businesses provides in part:

(a) Registration with Secretary of the Treasury Required.—

(1)In general.—Any person who owns or controls a money transmitting business shall register the business (whether or not the business is licensed as a money transmitting business in any State) with the Secretary of the Treasury not later than the end of the 180-day period beginning on the later of—

(A) the date of enactment of the Money Laundering Suppression Act of 1994; or

(B) the date on which the business is established....

f15 U.S.C. §77a et seq. is a lengthy statute that states securities, unless exempted, require registration with the SEC. coupled with civil and criminal penalties for violations thereof under the Securities Act of 1933 and 78a states registration requirements for securities exchanges under the Securities Exchange Act of 1934 as well as the creation of the Securities and Exchange Commission.

g18 U.S.C. §1963.

h18 U.S. §1343, Fraud by wire, radio, or television, states:

Whoever, having devised or intending to devise any scheme or artifice to defraud, or for obtaining money or property by means of false or fraudulent pretenses, representations, or promises, transmits or causes to be transmitted by means of wire, radio, or television communication in interstate or foreign

commerce, any writings, signs, signals, pictures, or sounds for the purpose of executing such scheme or artifice, shall be fined under this title or imprisoned not more than 20 years, or both. If the violation occurs in relation to, or involving any benefit authorized, transported, transmitted, transferred, disbursed, or paid in connection with, a presidentially declared major disaster or emergency... or affects a financial institution, such person shall be fined not more than $1,000,000 or imprisoned not more than 30 years, or both.
[i]18 U.S.C. §1341, Frauds and swindles, states:
Whoever, having devised or intending to devise any scheme or artifice to defraud, or for obtaining money or property by means of false or fraudulent pretenses, representations, or promises, or to sell, dispose of, loan, exchange, alter, give away, distribute, supply, or furnish or procure for unlawful use any counterfeit or spurious coin, obligation, security, or other article, or anything represented to be or intimated or held out to be such counterfeit or spurious article, for the purpose of executing such scheme or artifice or attempting so to do, places in any post office or authorized depository for mail matter, any matter or thing whatever to be sent or delivered by the Postal Service, or deposits or causes to be deposited any matter or thing whatever to be sent or delivered by any private or commercial interstate carrier, or takes or receives therefrom, any such matter or thing, or knowingly causes to be delivered by mail or such carrier according to the direction thereon, or at the place at which it is directed to be delivered by the person to whom it is addressed, any such matter or thing, shall be fined under this title or imprisoned not more than 20 years, or both. If the violation occurs in relation to, or involving any benefit authorized, transported, transmitted, transferred, disbursed, or paid in connection with, a presidentially declared major disaster or emergency...or affects a financial institution, such person shall be fined not more than $1,000,000 or imprisoned not more than 30 years, or both.

Additional statutes that may be applicable in future cases include the possible violation of counterfeiting and forging of U.S. and foreign coins, currency, and obligations.[2] Although there is a paucity of prosecutions under federal statutes, nevertheless, inevitably, there may be charges relating to fake digital or virtual coins that ensnare unsuspecting investors. States may also enter the fray for violations of law either emanating within the states or affecting residents of the states.[3] There is a possibility of civil enforcement both under the securities laws and also under the Federal Trade Commission Act that prohibits unfair methods of competition and unfair or deceptive practices affecting commerce.[4] The latter provision of the Act was used as the basis of a civil complaint that resulted in a consent order made against Butterfly Labs, discussed previously, which had charged thousands of dollars for its Bitcoin mining machines which were either never delivered or were delivered so late as to be rendered useless to the purchasers.[5]

Criminal Prosecutions

U.S. v. Murgio

The federal government has begun prosecuting alleged offenses concerning virtual currency and, in particular, operating unlawful Bitcoin exchanges. In a sealed indictment, in *United States v. Murgio*,[6] the defendants, Anthony R. Murgio, Yuri Lebedev, and unidentified co-conspirators were charged with operating Coin.mx, a Florida-based Bitcoin exchange service on the Internet in which millions of dollars were exchanged in cash for bitcoins on behalf of customers for which the exchange service received fees for its services. To avoid registration and reporting requirements, the defendants engaged in violation of money-laundering laws and regulations by operating through a fake front company and website. They also opened bank accounts in New York and falsely represented that the firm was a members-only association of collectibles called "Collectibles Club." They told customers to lie about the nature of the transactions; conspired to conduct an unlicensed money transmission business; paid bribes to bank officials; conspired and engaged in wire fraud; and participated in money laundering. The defendant, Murgio, was given half of the sentence recommended by prosecutors, to wit, five and a half years in a federal prison.[7]

U.S. v. BTC-e

An international investigation led to the indictment of BTC-e and Alexander Vinnik[8] charging them with the operation of an unlicensed money transmission business, conspiracy to commit money laundering, and engaging in unlawful money transactions. It was alleged that from 2011 to 2017, the defendants operated one of the world's largest digital currency exchanges through shell companies and affiliates processing billions of dollars of money exchanges for some 700,000 customers including in U.S. dollars, euros, and rubles, which exchanges were allegedly directed and supervised by Alexander Vannik. The said exchanges allegedly acted as money laundering operations in the United

States, Cyprus, the Seychelles, France, and elsewhere through which cyber criminals laundered the proceeds from their criminal activities, exchanging fiat moneys for bitcoins and other currencies. The said criminal activity enabled by BTC-e included acting as a conduit for proceeds from ransomware, which was an international malicious download of encryption software affecting computers worldwide; theft of hundreds of millions of dollars of bitcoins from U.S. customers; theft of 530,000 bitcoins from the Mt. Gox, a Japanese exchange, causing its collapse; and numerous other alleged violations of law. Vinnik, a Russian national, claiming innocence, was arrested in Greece and is awaiting extradition to the United States.[9]

"Darknet" Prosecutions

Darknet, in the context of this book, is the use of blockchain and related technologies for criminal purposes such as money laundering, credit card fraud, identity theft, and other internet crimes. It accomplishes the activity by use of identity-concealing aspects to prevent detection and prosecution. Although it appears that criminal elements have engendered significant profits in taking advantage of the technological capabilities, nevertheless, there have been major prosecutions of persons detected by the use of alternative sources of discovery. The following are a sample of the prosecutions that have been instituted.

U.S. v. Budovsky (Liberty Reserve)

Prosecution took place against one of the largest digital currency company operations whereby the company, Liberty Reserve, processed over 55 million illegal transactions on behalf of at least one million users in 17 countries including the Netherlands, Spain, Morocco, Sweden, Switzerland, Cyprus, Australia, China, Norway, Latvia, Luxembourg, the U.K., Russia, Canada, and over 200,000 users in the United States. The complaint alleged the firm laundered more than $6 billion in suspected proceeds of crimes that included credit card fraud, identity theft, investment fraud, computer hacking, child pornography, and narcotics trafficking. A number of defendants were arrested abroad including one, Arthur Budovsky, the principal founder of Liberty Reserve, and Vladimir Kats, a co-founder. Federal agents seized five domain names, four exchanger websites, 45 bank accounts, and other assets. A civil forfeiture action was commenced against 35 exchangers whose domain names were the subject of the litigation.[10]

The defendants were accused of willfully creating, structuring, and opening Liberty Reserve as a criminal business venture designed to enable criminals to conduct criminal operations and launder the proceeds from their crimes. It attracted criminal persons by making financial activity anonymous and untraceable. When learning of federal investigation, the company and its principal parties created shell corporations in diverse countries to conceal the said proceeds of the alleged crimes. After the dismemberment of its prior company, E-Gold, Liberty Reserve was created to continue the unlawful activities and, in fact, became the largest criminal money laundering operation globally. Although it required users to state their names and other identifying information, it did not require users to validate the information given. Once registered with Liberty, the users were able to use Liberty Reserve to transmit their funds effectively and without fear of personal identification or other personal data being identified. The company used a number of "pre-approved" exchangers that worked in conjunction with the company and its operations.[11] As a result of the arrest of Budovsky, who was previously convicted of operating an unlicensed currency transmission business and who was extradited from Spain in October, 2014, he pleaded guilty to one count of conspiring to commit money laundering on January 29, 2016 and was sentenced to 20 years in federal prison.[12]

U.S. v. Cazes (AlphaBay)

An alleged "darknet" site, known as AlphaBay, used for the distribution of fentanyl and heroin leading to numerous deaths and unlawful use by thousands of people globally, was shut down by the Department of Justice in July, 2017. In collaboration with foreign governmental entities, a seizure was made of millions of dollars of cryptocurrencies representing the proceeds of the site's illegal activities involving some 200,000 users and 40,000 vendors. A civil forfeiture complaint was made against Alexandre Cazes and his wife for seizure of substantial assets located worldwide. Allegedly, there were over 60,000 listings of illegal drugs and toxic chemicals on AlphaBay and over 100,000 listings of stolen and fraudulent identification documents and access devices, counterfeit goods, malware, and other computer hacking tools, firearms, and fraudulent services. AlphaBay was the largest underground marketplace of the dark net used by criminals to conduct business anonymously.[13]

Immigration and Customs Enforcement (ICE)

ICC v. Hubbard (PDXBlack)

ICE commenced its "Operation Denial" investigation following the fentanyl overdose death of an 18-year old individual from Grand Forks, North Dakota on January 3, 2015. It then discovered that there were four other individuals who had suffered from an overdose of fentanyl, one of whom died. The sale of the controlled substance was found to be linked to the darknet market site, Evolution, and a fentanyl vendor, later identified as Brandon Hubbard from Portland, Oregon, whose user name was PDXBlack, and who later claimed he was the largest supplier in the United States having sold approximately $1.5 million of the substance. He had procured the drug from international sources, mainly from a Colombian national who purchased the drug from Chinese suppliers. The value of the wholesale purchases was estimated at $9 million which was paid for by both fiat and bitcoins over a two-year period. The sales on the darknet market were accomplished by use of bitcoins to compensate for the drug purchases. The sales and purchases were also linked to other darknet markets such as Silk Road and Agora. Upon a plea of guilty to three criminal offenses, Hubbard was sentenced to a life term in federal prison.[14]

"Silk Road" Prosecutions

The Tor Project, Inc.

The "Silk Road" generically refers to the trade routes that have existed since ancient times between Asia and the countries of the Mediterranean Sea including European and northern African countries. When used in the context of this study, it is a type of darknet that was started about February, 2011 by Ross William Ulbricht and which was shut down by the U.S. federal government. Ulbricht utilized the TOR anonymity network that was created by a group of computer scientists as a non-profit Massachusetts corporation, legally known as the Tor Project, Inc. According to the Tor website, it is a group of volunteer-operated servers that maintains the privacy and security of users of the Internet by use of a network that is connected through a series of virtual tunnels that allows users to share information over public networks while simultaneously protecting their privacy. It exists ostensibly to prevent governmental censorship by allowing users to connect to blocked destinations or content, link up to new sites, and permit instant messaging services. It conceals IP addresses using the ".onion" algorithm. As with almost all newly innovative technologies, its use may be for beneficial as well as harmful and illegal purposes. It has been praised by organizations such as the Electronic Frontier Foundation as protecting individual liberties, by corporations as protecting their trade secrets, and even by the U.S. Navy for open source gathering.[15]

U.S. v. Ulbricht (Computer Hardware Bitcoins)

Ross William Ulbricht was initially charged with four crimes, later amended to one of seven crimes, including narcotics trafficking and distribution, conspiracy to aid and abet computer hacking, continuing criminal enterprise, trafficking in false identity documents, and money laundering conspiracy. He was also charged with threatening to release the identities of users of the site and the offer of $500,000 to murder certain persons associated with a user.[16] Ulbricht created Silk Road in

January 2011 and used and operated the website until October, 2013 when the government shut it down. The site served as a black market bazaar for the sale of unlawful goods and services which was exploited by several thousand drug dealers to distribute large quantities of illegal drugs and to obtain and launder hundreds of millions of dollars.

Ulbricht operated the website under the name "Dread Pirate Roberts" deliberately for the unlawful purposes operating on the Tor Network (the Onion Router) described above, which enabled the concealment globally of the true IP addresses of the computers on the network thereby enabling anonymous distribution. It included a Bitcoin-payment system to facilitate the transactions taking place on the site which had 13,000 listings of controlled substances that included heroin, cocaine, cannabis, ecstasy, and other controlled drugs that were sold to users in the United States, Germany, Canada, the Netherlands, the U.K. and other western European countries. Services offered included computer hacking, forgeries, pirated media content, credit card statements, and other forms of identification documents. Ulbricht received commissions of many millions of dollars for the site and solicited six murders-for-hire, although there was no evidence of their actual occurrence. The government seized over 173,000 bitcoins from servers that ran the Silk Road connection and from Ulbricht's hardware. In addition, an indictment was also filed in the federal District Court in Manhattan charging a number of other individuals in connection with the Ulbricht enterprise. The U.S. Attorney for the Southern District gave credit to the foreign law enforcement agencies of Australia, Ireland, Iceland, and France for their co-operation in ending the operations.[17] Ulbricht received a life sentence without parole on May 29, 2015.

In an earlier proceeding, the U.S. Marshals Service publicly offered and sold over 44,000 bitcoins that were held in wallet files on a computer belonging to Ulbricht who also owned Computer Hardware Bitcoins that was involved in money laundering. The court order that was consented to by the United States and Ulbricht decreed that all or any portion of the Computer Hardware Bitcoins would be held and deposited to the account of the U.S. Marshals Service.[18]

U.S. v. Benthall

According to a complaint filed by the U.S. Attorney for the Southern District of New York, Blake Benthall sought to revive the Silk Road network by conspiring to distribute narcotics operating under the pseudonym "Defcon" from November 2013 through October, 2014, when he was arrested. Other charges included computer hacking and use of false identification documents, He allegedly operated an underground website known as "Silk Road 2.0" for the purpose of distributing unlawful substances to over 150,000 purchasers globally, generating $8 million monthly. Like Ulbricht, Benthall used the Tor network almost immediately after the government had shut down the Silk Road network created by Ulbricht. Whereas the original website stated that the site had been seized, Benthal's website contained the words, "This Hidden Site has Arisen Again."

The site was an almost identical repeat of the Ulbricht website and offered drugs for sale to prospective purchasers. It used a Bitcoin-based payment system whereby the purchaser transferred bitcoins to the Benthall site to purchase unlawful substances. Silk Road uses a "tumbler" (mixer) that conceals the identities of the parties by passing the bitcoins through numerous dummy transactions on the blockchain. With the assistance of foreign law enforcement authorities, Defcon and its connection with the defendant Benthall were established and the arrest made. The complaint is noteworthy because of its detailed description of the connection between bitcoins and the Tor network and their use for unlawful purposes.[19] It is unclear what transpired in the case thereafter, although an alleged staff member of Silk Road 2.0, Brian Farrell, was sentenced to eight years in prison.[20]

U.S. v. Shrem and Faiella

In a sealed complaint, *United States v. Shrem*, the defendants Charlie Shrem and Robert Faiella, were charged with operating an unlicensed money transmission business known as "Silk Road" that traded bitcoins of over $1 million over a two-year period in violation of 15 U.S.C.

§5330[21] which activity was intended to support narcotics trafficking. Additional charges made included money laundering, conspiracy, and related charges. It was alleged that the defendants knowingly conducted, controlled, and owned the website under the username of "BTCKing" without having registered the business as required by law that engaged in the transmission both within and outside the United States. Shrem was charged with failing to report suspicious activity with respect to numerous Bitcoin purchases from 2011 to 2013 which activity violated anti-money laundering laws. He hosted an online black market bazaar and acted as an exchanger for virtual currency used in large part for unlawful narcotics trafficking.[22] The charges resulted in a guilty plea by Shrem to the reduced charge of aiding and abetting an unlicensed money transmission service and he was sentenced to two years in prison.[23]

U.S. v. Force[24] and U.S. v. Bridges[25]

In a Silk Road related case, two former federal agents of the U.S. Drug Enforcement Administration and the U.S. Secret Service respectively, Carl M. Force and Shaun W. Bridges, who had investigated the Silk Road criminal network, were themselves charged in March, 2015, with money laundering and wire fraud for stealing bitcoins during their investigations. Force allegedly diverted bitcoins uncovered to his own personal account and Bridges, a computer forensics expert, was charged also with diverting some $800,000 of bitcoins to his control while investigating Ulbricht and others in the then Silk Road connection. Force, using the pseudonym Nob, communicated with Dread Pirate Roberts, a pseudonym for Ulbricht, to extort moneys from him by providing insider government investigation information for which he was given the then $50,000 in value of bitcoins, later converted to nearly $800,000 in value, to his personal account.[26] Bridges pleaded guilty to money laundering and obstruction of justice and received a 71-month prison sentence. The day before he was to commence his prison sentence, he was arrested anew for stealing another 1600 bitcoins which added another two years to his sentence after pleading to a count of money laundering.[27] Carl M. Force was sentenced to 78 months in prison and additionally ordered to pay monetary restitution to two individuals.[28]

Bitcoin as Money

After an initial slow hesitancy to act, the SEC has aggressively pursued enforcement against persons who fail to observe registration requirements for ICOs as possible securities and possible fraudulent offerings and misrepresentations. There appears to be much confusion concerning whether Bitcoin is money, which may be highly relevant with respect to charges made under federal and state criminal statutes. As stated later, the IRS treats bitcoins and other virtual currencies as property. On the one hand, as stated in *U.S. v. Murgio* cited above, the court determined that Bitcoin was money and thus came within the purview of the statute requiring that money transmission exchanges be registered. The court refused to dismiss two charges requested by defendant's counsel concerning Murgio's use of Coin.mx as an unlicensed exchange. The court stated that virtual currency came within the definition of "funds" under the statute requiring money transmission businesses be licensed.[29]

Alternatively, a Florida state court judge ruled that Bitcoin is not money and the defendant thereby did not violate a money laundering statute in a case brought against a Florida developer. The developer was charged with money laundering and acting as an unauthorized money transmitter when he allegedly sold $31,000 worth of bitcoins to undercover police officers through a Bitcoin-selling website. The court noted that the value of bitcoins varies wildly due to insufficient liquidity, uncertainty of future value, and a lack of a stabilization mechanism.[30] As a result of the said case, a bill to amend the state's statute to include virtual currency as "monetary instruments" and making it a felony to knowingly engage in its unauthorized transmission for unlawful purposes, was enacted into law and made effective on July 1, 2017. "Virtual currency" is defined in the amended statute to mean: "a medium of exchange in electronic or digital format that is not a coin or currency of the United States or of any other country."[31]

Law Enforcement Prosecution Difficulties

The challenges faced by law enforcement officers are well documented owing to the decentralized nature and concealment of users of virtual currencies.[32] According to an FBI report, among the challenges are: regulatory compliance disparities found in many countries that have weak or non-existent anti-money laundering and customer identification programs causing criminals to reside therein and making prosecution very challenging; transaction obfuscation and anonymity that greatly complicates investigations of users; and the systems' global nature whereby, even in vigilant countries, it makes it difficult time-wise to identify and prosecute criminal transactions. Bitcoin-related crimes include "stolen wallets," "botnet mining," "ransomware," and a multitude of criminal uses of Bitcoin to finance drug and other illegal operations. Bitcoin wallets are stolen by obtaining the user's private key by infecting the victim's computer with malware or hacking into the wallet-service provider or exchanger. Thereafter, criminal elements use a "tumbler" or "mixing" service to conceal their identities and the transactions by routing and redistributing them. Investigative methods include standard cyber investigative techniques in theft cases; imaging the victim's computer system and obtaining the internet service provider's logs; and acquiring the victim's public key to determine the address to which the virtual currency was sent.[33]

The time-honored technique of "follow the money" has led to a number of prosecutions. Often, when arrests are made, information is received that assists in the identification of criminal networks and their activities in the use of virtual currencies. Bitcoin, while protecting privacy, does leave footprints by generating much data that investigators use in attempting to make the connection between the publicly recorded transactions and sales to online drug markets and thence to the sellers. It becomes much easier to trace if exchanges or other third-parties are used. In the Ulbricht cases above, investigators were able to investigate and convict Ulbricht not because they cracked the privacy aspects of Bitcoin but owing to the carelessness of the defendant who used the same pseudonym he adopted for years that the FBI was able to track down to a San Francisco internet café.[34]

SEC Civil Enforcement

After a rather slow commencement of litigation against persons acting in violation of securities laws, the SEC is now aggressively acting to cease the operations of firms in violation of securities laws. In criminal matters, reference is made to the Attorney General's Office for investigation and prosecution. Because of the added burden of proof beyond a reasonable doubt standard in such cases, the preferred method is to commence civil litigation with its fair preponderance of proof burden.

SEC v. PlexCorps

In an emergency action, the SEC filed a civil complaint for violations of U.S. securities laws against Dominic Lacroix and his partner, Sabrina Paradis-Rogers of Quebec, Canada, who raised the sum of approximately $15 million from thousands of investors through alleged fraudulent and unregistered offers and sales in an ICO of securities called "PlexCoin" or "PlexCoin Tokens" from August 2107 through to the commencement of the action on December 1, 2017. They allegedly made false and misleading statements including the promise of returns of 1354 percent n 29 days. Previously, they had been enjoined by a Quebec tribunal from engaging in this same conduct that later occurred in the United States. The purpose of the ICO was to obtain tokenized currency based on blockchain technology to permit investors to "take control" of their money. The promised returns were to emanate from the appreciation in value investments from the use of the tokens and the managerial efforts of "FlexCorps" which allegedly was composed of a team of experts, Thus, the SEC sought a preliminary and permanent injunction to cease such sales together with other relief including the freezing of assets, payment of civil penalties, and prohibiting the defendants from acting as officers in a securities firm and participating in any offering of digital securities.[35] Lacroix was later sentenced to prison on December 8, 2017 for two months and fined Canadian $110,000 by the Quebec Superior Court.[36]

In a commentary on the case by a Canadian counsel, she indicated that the outcome of the case should not be a surprise to Canadians inasmuch as the Canadian Securities Administrators issued CSA Staff Notice 46-307 concerning Cryptocurrency Offerings that stated their marketing as software products does not preclude their being subject to Canadian securities laws. The Administrators will look to substance over form in making a determination whether securities laws are applicable to particular ICOs. Canada's viewpoint is almost identical to that of the Chairman of the U.S. SEC, Jay Clayton, in holding that each offering must be examined on a case-by-case basis rather than to set a bright-line rule in making a determination as to the application of securities law enforcement. The author noted that the Ontario Securities Commission approval of the ICO of Token Funder Inc. on October 17, 2017 illustrates the government's acceptance of cryptocurrency offerings provided the issuers play by the rules.[37]

SEC v. Voorhees

In an administrative proceeding, on June 3, 2014, the SEC charged Erik T. Voorhees, a co-owner of two Bitcoin-related websites, with offering shares in the websites beginning in May, 2012 without registering them in violation of §§5(a) and 5(c) and regulations thereto under the Securities Act of 1933, which resulted in a consent order. Voorhees published prospectuses on the Internet and solicited investors to buy shares in SatoshiDICE and FeedZeBirds, who paid for them by using bitcoins. Voorhees received a profit of almost $16,000 which he agreed to disgorge, consented to a fine of $35,000, as well as agreeing not to participate in any issuance of any security in an unregistered transaction in exchange for any virtual currency including Bitcoin for a period of five years. Voorhees had raised 2600 bitcoins through the sale of 30,000 shares in FeedZeBirds, which promised to pay bitcoins to Twitter users who forward its sponsored text messages. In two other offerings from August 2012 to February 2013, SatoshiDICE sold 13 million shares and raised 50,600 bitcoins that were worth approximately $722,659 at the time.[38]

SEC v. Sand Hill Exchange

In a cease-and-desist action brought against Sand Hill Exchange, Gerritt Hall, and Elaine Ou, which the parties settled and that resulted in an Order by the SEC, the parties were charged with violation of §8 of the of the Securities Act of 1933 (registration requirements) and §21C of the 1934 Act (commencement of cease-and-desist proceedings) in that beginning in mid-February 2015, Hall and Ou began to buy and sell agreements that were linked to liquidity events, such as mergers, initial public offerings, and dissolutions. They solicited people, mainly friends and acquaintances, to fund accounts at Sand Hill using dollars or bitcoins. Investors bought and sold contracts linked to liquidity events and to the value of the companies and their securities. The claimed violations were Dodd-Frank provisions amending the Securities Act which limited transactions in security-based swaps with persons who were not eligible contract participants. They also allegedly exaggerated Sand Hill's trading, operations, controls, and financial backing. They immediately ceased operations and were ordered to pay a relatively small financial penalty.[39]

SEC v. Willner

In a pending action, the SEC charged Joseph P. Willner with having engaged in an illegal brokerage account takeover and unauthorized trading scheme with a second unidentified person from September 2014 through August, 2016 by accessing secretly without authorization approximately 100 brokerage accounts to place securities trades in order to artificially affect the stock prices of a number of public companies, He was charged with violation of §17a of the Securities Act of 1933 (use of interstate commerce for the purpose of fraud or deceit), §10b of the Securities Exchange Act of 1934 (fraudulent transaction of securities), and money laundering. Allegedly, to mask payments he transferred proceeds of profitable trades to a digital currency company that converted U.S. dollars to bitcoins which were then transferred to the said unidentified second party with whom he had a profit-sharing arrangement. Accordingly, the SEC sought a court order for a permanent injunction barring the defendants from engaging in the unlawful transactions in violation of securities laws, for disgorgement of profits received, and civil financial penalties.[40]

SEC v. UBI Blockchain Internet, Ltd.

In a continuing effort to compel compliance by companies engaged in cryptocurrencies and blockchain technology, the SEC reminds firms to strictly comply with the statutory and regulatory provisions of the Securities Acts. On January 5, 2018, it temporarily suspended trading of securities of UBI Blockchain Internet, Ltd. (UBIA) of Hong Kong, PRC, effective January 8, 2018 and ending on January 22, 2018 because it questioned the accuracy of assertions in the company's filings with the SEC regarding the company's business operations and concerns about recent, unusual, and unexplained market activity in the company's Class A common stock from November, 2017 to date.[41] The SEC has the authority under §12(k) of the Securities Act of 1934, to suspend, alter, and restrict the sale of securities when there is uncertainty about the impact on the equities and options markets due to a major market disturbance characterized by a sudden and excessive fluctuations of securities prices generally, or a substantial threat thereof, that threatens fair and orderly markets.[42]

SEC v. Arisebank

The SEC filed a complaint against Arisebank in January, 2018 that sought and received a court order against the defendants, Arisebank, Jared Rice Sr., and Stanley Ford to immediately cease an alleged ICO offering that promoted itself as the world's first "decentralized bank." The complaint alleged that the Dallas, Texas-based bank offered and sold unregistered investments in "AriseCoin" cryptocurrency that could be used for banking products and services using more than 700 different virtual currencies. It used social media, celebrity endorsements, and other means to promote the venture based on an algorithmic trading application that automatically trades in the diverse cryptocurrencies. It further alleged that some $600 million of moneys were raised towards its goal of $1 billion in two months. Other alleged false statements and omissions included that Arisebank purchased an FDIC-insured bank that would offer investors FDIC monetary protection; an Arisebank Visa credit card could be used to make purchases; and the omission of the criminal backgrounds of key executives, all of which constituted an alleged scam upon the investors.

The court ordered an emergency asset freeze over the defendants and appointed a receiver to take over the bank and its digital assets. The public sale of the bank's offerings, prior to the court order, was scheduled for December 26, 2017 to conclude on January 27, 2018. In addition to the cessation order, the SEC requested disgorgement of all unlawful gains, including interest and penalties, a permanent bar of the individual defendants from serving as officers or directors of a public company, and a bar from offering digital securities in the future. Among the cryptocurrencies secured by the court were Bitcoin, Litecoin, Bitshares, Dogecoin, and BitUSD.[43]

CFTC Civil Enforcement

In addition to SEC enforcement, the CFTC that regulates commodities has also actively pursued wrongdoing by unscrupulous individuals. Among the actions commenced are those that follow herein.

CFTC v. Gelfman

In a civil complaint demanding an injunction and monetary penalties against Nicholas Gelfman and Gelfman Blueprint, Inc., the CFTC alleged in its complaint filed in the New York federal district court[44] that from January 2014 through January, 2016, the defendants, Gelfman Blueprint, Inc. and its CEO, Nicholas Gelfman, allegedly operated a Bitcoin Ponzi scheme in which they fraudulently solicited participation in a pooled fund that purportedly employed a high-frequency, algorithmic trading strategy, executed by the defendants' computer program called "Jigsaw," to trade the virtual currency Bitcoin which the CFTC designated as a commodity in interstate commerce. The defendants allegedly obtained approximately $600,000 from at least 80 investors through these fraudulent solicitations.

The complaint further stated that the strategy was fake, that the purported performance reports were false and akin to all other Ponzi schemes, and that the payouts of supposed profits to customers in actuality consisted of other customers' misappropriated funds. They allegedly made false and misleading claims and omissions about the performance and reliability of Jigsaw and attempted to conceal their scheme through issuance of false reports, misrepresentation of the percentage of monthly increases of Bitcoin balances, the company's assets and performance, fake trading results, and a fake hacking. The moneys received were diverted to the defendants own personal accounts.

The CFTC demanded that that the court issue an order declaring the defendants in violation of §6(c)(1) the CEA and regulations pursuant thereto, a permanent injunction, monetary penalties, disgorgement of all moneys received, full restitution to the company's customers, and other related relief. The statute makes it unlawful for any person, directly or indirectly, to use or employ, or attempt to use or employ, in connection with any swap, or a contract of sale of any commodity in interstate commerce, or for future delivery on or subject to the rules of any registered entity, any manipulative or deceptive device or contrivance, in contravention of the Commission's such rules and regulations. The outcome of the case is pending awaiting a trial by jury.[45]

CFTC v. McDonnell

The CFTC commenced two civil filings in a federal court in New York on January 18, 2018 alleging fraud by various defendants. In the first case against Patrick K. McDonnell and Cabbagetech, Corp. d.b.a. Coin Drop Markets, it was alleged that McDonnell operated a deceptive and fraudulent virtual currency scheme to induce customers to send money and virtual currencies to defendants in exchange for virtual currency trading advice concerning the trading of virtual currencies, including Bitcoin and Litecoin, and for virtual currency purchases and trading on behalf of customers under McDonnell's direction. The Commission alleged that the said solicitations were deceptive and fraudulent, and soon after obtaining the funds, the defendants stopped communicating with their customers who lost their funds due to their misappropriation by the defendants. The deceptions were by use of social media, advertisements, and promotional materials. They were thus charged like the *Gelfman* case above with violation of §6(c)(1) of the Commodity Exchange Act of 1934. Relief sought was a permanent injunction, civil penalties, disgorgement of all benefits received, restitution, an accounting of all moneys received, and other related relief.[46]

CFTC v. Dean

In the second action filed on the same day and venue, the CFTC brought a civil action against Dillon Michael Dean and the Entrepreneurship Headquarters Limited (TEH), alleging that the defendant, Dean, through his company TEH, commencing April 2017, solicited at least $1.1 million worth of Bitcoin from some 600 members of the public to participate in a pooled investment vehicle for trading commodity securities. Instead of converting customer funds from Bitcoin to fiat currency, Dean and the company allegedly misappropriated the funds in a Ponzi-type scheme and lied to customers about their account balances. They made material misstatements and omissions in solicitations to pool participants, including misrepresenting Dean's experience and track record, and misrepresenting that 40 percent of the customers' funds would be pooled and invested in, among other things, binary options for the customers' benefit, moneys kept in reserve in Bitcoin to fund customer withdrawals. There were no such trades and electronic account statements purportedly reflecting customers' accounts were fraudulent. In addition, the defendants failed to register with the Commission as a commodity pool operator. Relief requested of the court was comparable to the *McDonnell* case.[47]

CFTC v. My Big Coin Pay, Inc.

The CFTC requested the federal court in Massachusetts in January 2018 for an order granting numerous forms of relief with respect to My Big Pay, Inc. (MBP) and multiple other defendants.[48] The allegations were that the defendant company and Randall Crater and Mark Gillespie, through its website and through numerous solicitation materials and exchanges, from approximately January 2014 through June 2017, received about $6 million by making false and misleading claims and omissions about the value, usage, and trade status for at least 28 customers through fraudulent solicitations. The company claimed that MBP was backed by gold, misrepresented in reports the daily trading price when no price actually existed, and payouts made were from other MBC customers through an elaborate Ponzi scheme. When customers raised questions about their accounts, the defendants attempted to conceal their fraud by providing additional coins to them and falsely represented that they had secured a deal with another exchange to trade MBC. They also requested customers to refrain from redeeming their holdings until they became active on a new exchange. They then misappropriated almost all of the $6 million received by purchasing jewelry, luxury goods, furniture, and other personal items and services.

Accordingly, the defendants were charged with making false and misleading statements and material omissions that were spelled out in substantial detail in violation of §6(c)(1) of the CEA and regulations pursuant thereto and misappropriation of funds. Relief requested included a permanent injunction enjoining the defendants from engaging in the wrongful conduct, trading on any exchange, entering into any commodity transaction, applying for registration of the company, payment of a monetary penalty, disgorgement of moneys received, full restitution, and other related relief. The court granted a temporary injunction pending a hearing and further determination.[49]

It thus appears that aggressive enforcement actions have been commenced on two major governmental fronts, the SEC and the CFTC, each asserting jurisdictions based on the securities laws and regulations by the SEC and the CEA and regulations by the CFTC. It is anticipated that as virtual currencies become disseminated, these agencies will be at the forefront of preventing and prosecuting wrongdoing by individuals and their companies who appear to believe they can commit unlawful acts without fear of criminal prosecution and civil litigation.

Private Litigation

Ripple Labs and R3

Due to the nature of blockchain-based technologies, there is a paucity of private civil cases that have arisen to date. A significant case that involved litigants based in New York was litigated between R3 LRC LLC and Ripple Labs Inc., both of which are funded by major banks. Litigation had been commenced in the Delaware Chancery Court whereby the New York-based R3 sued a rival company, Ripple Labs, relating to the alleged right of R3 to purchase 5 billion XRPs, a virtual currency traded against the U.S. dollar on cryptocurrency exchanges, at the purchase price of $0.0085 per unit up to the timeframe of September, 2019. The chief executive of Ripple Labs sought to terminate the options contract which R3 claims it had a legal right to its enforcement. The action sought was for a judicial determination whether such an option contract is enforceable. A possible alleged basis for Ripple's refusal is that the value of an XRP had dramatically escalated to $0.21 per unit making the value of the option over $1 billion.[50]

Ripple Labs also commenced litigation against R3 in the Superior Court in San Francisco on September 8, 2017 claiming that R3 misled Ripple Labs into signing multiple agreements and then breached the said agreements.[51] The alleged misrepresentations consisted of R3's representations that it was a large consortium of banks with whom Ripple could partner and promote its technology. After R3's alleged failure to follow up on its promises, Ripple thereafter cancelled the agreements. It further claimed a fraudulent concealment, negligent misrepresentation, breach of contract, breach of implied covenant of good faith and other allegations. A third action also commenced by R3 against Ripple in the Supreme Court (a trial court), New York County, also asserted claims made in the Delaware litigation.[52] The outcomes of the cases await further determination. Conflicting claims have been made concerning the outcome of the Delaware litigation, one claiming dismissal based on lack of jurisdiction and a return to the San Francisco court, while another observer stated that both the New York and San Francisco courts may exercise jurisdiction.[53]

It would appear that the actions should be consolidated and determined by a federal court based on diversity of the parties. It should be noted that the President's Council of Advisers on Science and Technology (PCAST) refers to R3 as the world's largest distributed ledger consortium of banks with 50 leading banks partaking.[54]

In the chapter on "Crowdfunding and the Taxation of Virtual Currencies", we discuss the taxation of virtual currencies that has created much comment and controversy concerning: how to report tax transactions; the tax basis to be used; whether to treat them as property or currency; the difficulty of ascertaining the parties engaged in their dealings; issues of privacy; foreign tax considerations; and other tax-related issues. We will highlight the issues and the latest governmental guidance and actions.

Notes

1. The table, in part, was taken from the U.S. Department of Justice press release concerning the prosecution of *U.S. v. Vinnik*, U.S. Dept. of Justice, Northern District Ca., *Russian National and Bitcoin Exchange Charged in 21-Count Indictment for Operating Alleged International Money Laundering Scheme and Alleged Laundering From Hack of Mt. Gox*, News Release, July 26, 2017, https://www.justice.gov/usao-ndca/pr/russian-national-and-bitcoin-exchange-charged-21-count-indictment-operating-alleged

2. 18 U.S.C. §§470–477 which criminalize counterfeiting acts both domestically and internationally including uttering, dealing, possession of plates, stones, or analog, or electronic images for counterfeiting obligations securities, and §§485–489 concerning making or possession or making impressions of dies or tokens or paper used as money.

3. For an excellent review of federal and state statutes and regulations governing counterfeiting including that of virtual currencies, see Ralph E. McKinney, R. E., Shao, L. P., Shao, D. H., Rosenlieb Jr., *The evolution of financial instruments and the legal protection against counterfeiting: a look at coin, paper, and virtual currencies,* Journal of Law, Technology, & Policy, 2015(2), 273–313, http://mds.marshall.edu/cgi/viewcontent.cgi?article=1146&context=mgmt_faculty

4. 15 U.S.C. §45(a)(1).

5. U.S. Federal Trade Commission, *Operators of Bitcoin Mining Operation Butterfly Labs Agree to settle FTC Charges They Deceived Customers* (Feb. 18, 2016), Press Release, https://www.ftc.gov/news-events/press-releases/2016/02/operators-bitcoin-mining-operation-butterfly-labs-agree-settle

6. Sealed Complaint, *U.S. v. Murgio*, No. 15-MAG-2508 (S.D.N.Y., July 17, 2015), https://www.justice.gov/usao-sdny/file/830616/download

7. Jonathan Stempel, *UPDATE 1-Bitcoin exchange operator tied to hacks gets 5-1/2 years U.S. prison* (July 27, 2017) Reuters, https://www.reuters.com/article/cyber-jpmorgan-murgio/update-1-bitcoin-exchange-operator-tied-to-hacks-gets-5-1-2-years-u-s-prison-idUSL1N1JO1BH. For a discussion of actions pertaining to electronic payments including Bitcoin, see Sarah Jane Hughes, Stephen T. Middlebrook, and Tom Kierner, *Developments in the Law Affecting Electronic Payments and Financial Services* (2107), at 259–261, *Articles by Maurer Faculty*, 2445, http://www.repository.law.indiana.edu/cgi/viewcontent.cgi?article=-3445&context=facpub

8. *U.S. v. BTC-e*, No. CR 16-00227-SI (N.D. Ca., Jan. 17, 2017), sealed indictment, https://www.justice.gov/usao-ndca/press-release/file/984661/download

9. Nikhilesh De, *Alleged BTC-e Operator Claims Innocence in New Interview*, CoinDesk, Sept. 11, 2017, https://www.coindesk.com/alleged-btc-e-administrator-i-do-not-consider-myself-guilty/

10. U.S. Department of Justice, *Manhattan U.S Attorney Announces Charges Against Liberty Reserve, One of the World's Largest Digital Companies, and Seven of Its Principal Employees For Allegedly Running a $6 Billion Money Laundering Scheme* (May 28, 2013), Press Release, https://www.justice.gov/usao-sdny/pr/manhattan-us-attorney-announces-charges-against-liberty-reserve-one-world-s-largest

11. Sealed indictment, *United States v. Liberty Reserve*, No. 13cr368 (DLC) (D.C. N.Y. Sept. 23, 2015), https://www.justice.gov/sites/default/files/usao-sdny/legacy/2015/03/25/Liberty%20Reserve%2C%20et%20al.%20Indictment%20-%20Redacted.pdf
12. U.S. Department of Justice, *Liberty Reserve Founder Arthur Budovsky Sentenced In Manhattan Federal Court to 20 Years for Laundering Hundreds of Millions of Dollars Through His Global Digital Currency Business*, Press Release, May 6, 2016, https://www.justice.gov/usao-sdny/pr/liberty-reserve-founder-arthur-budovsky-sentenced-manhattan-federal-court-20-years
13. *U.S. v. Cazes*, No. 1:17-at-00597 (N.D. Ca., July 17, 2017), https://www.justice.gov/opa/press-release/file/982821/download. *See, also, commentary by the Department of Justice, AlphaBay, the Largest Online 'Dark Market' Shut Down, Justice News, July 20, 2017,* https://www.justice.gov/opa/pr/alphabay-largest-online-dark-market-shut-down
14. The three offenses Hubbard pled guilty to were 21 U.S.C. §841(b)(1)(E), *Conspiracy to Distribute Controlled Substances Resulting in Serious Bodily Injury and Death*; 21 U.S.C. §841(b)(1)(E), *Distribution of a Controlled Substance Resulting in Death*, and 18 U.S.C. §1956, *Money* Laundering Conspiracy, https://www.ice.gov/sites/default/files/documents/Report/2017/CSReport-13-2.pdf
15. TOR, *Tor Overview*, https://www.torproject.org/about/overview.html.en
16. *United States v. Ulbricht*, 14-cr-68 (KBF) (S.D.N.Y., Sept. 27, 2013).
17. U.S. Bureau of Investigation, *Manhattan U.S. Attorney Announces the Indictment of Ross Ulbricht, the Creator and Owner of the Silk Road Website*, Press Release, Feb. 4, 2014, https://archives.fbi.gov/archives/newyork/press-releases/2014/manhattan-u.s.-attorney-announces-the-indictment-of-ross-ulbricht-the-creator-and-owner-of-the-silk-road-website
18. *United States v. Ulbricht*, 1-13 06919-JPO Civ. (D.C.N.Y. Jan. 27, 2014), https://www.usmarshals.gov/assets/2015/dpr-bitcoins/sale-order.pdf
19. *U.S. v. Benthall*, 14 MAG 2427 (S.D.N.Y. 2016), http://documents.latimes.com/united-states-america-vs-blake-benthall/
20. Nate Raymond, *An alleged staff member of Silk Road 2.0 was sentenced to 8 years in prison*, Reuters, cited in Business Insider, June 4, 2016, http://www.businessinsider.com/r-key-player-in-silk-road-successor-site-gets-eight-years-in-us-prison-2016-6

21. 31 U.S.C.§5330. *Registration of money transmitting businesses* provides in part:

   (a) Registration with Secretary of the Treasury Required.—
   (1) In general.—Any person who owns or controls a money transmitting business shall register the business (whether or not the business is licensed as a money transmitting business in any State) with the Secretary of the Treasury not later than the end of the 180-day period beginning on the later of—
   (A) the date of enactment of the Money Laundering Suppression Act of 1994; or
   (B) the date on which the business is established....

22. *U.S. v. Faiella*, No. 14 MAG 0164 (S.D.N.Y., Jan. 24, 2013), https://www.justice.gov/sites/default/files/usao-sdny/legacy/2015/03/25/Faiella%2C%20Robert%20M.%20and%20Charlie%20Shrem%20Complaint.pdf

23. *U.S. v. Ulbricht*, 15-1815 (2d Cir. Mar 31, 2017), http://caselaw.findlaw.com/us-2nd-circuit/1862572.html

24. *U.S. v. Force*, No. 3:15-cr-01319-RS-2 (N.D. Ca., Oct. 20, 2015).

25. *U.S. v. Bridges*, No. 1:15-mj-02125-BPG (D.C.Md., Oct. 17, 2016).

26. Benjamin Weiser and Matt Apuzzo, *Inquiry of Silk Road Website Spurred Agents' Own Illegal Acts, Officials Say*, New York Times, March 30, 2015, https://www.nytimes.com/2015/03/31/nyregion/silk-road-case-federal-agents-charges.html

27. Andrew Blake, *Ex Secret Service agent sentenced again for stealing from the government*, The Washington Times, Nov. 8, 2017, https://www.washingtontimes.com/news/2017/nov/8/shaun-bridges-ex-secret-service-agent-sentenced-ag/

28. Stan Higgins, *Rogue Silk Road Agent Carl Force Jailed for 78 Months*, Coindesk, Oct. 19, 2015, https://www.coindesk.com/rogue-silk-road-agent-carl-force-jailed-for-78-months/

29. CNBC, *Bitcoin is money, US judge says in case tied to JPMorgan hack*, Reuters, Sept. 20, 2016, https://www.cnbc.com/2016/09/20/bitcoin-is-money-us-judge-says-in-case-tied-to-jpmorgan-hack.html

30. Rob Price, *Bitcoin isn't money, a Florida judge rules*, Business Insider, July 26, 2016, http://hp.myway.com/flightsearch/ttab02/index.html?n=7839260D&p=%5EC73%5Exdm007%5ETTAB02%5Eus&ptb=C444429A-0C1B-499B-8321-E6C4D6EF256B&si=CIO_kYacvdECFZmK-swodM-4Gcw&coid=52bafe06493b4978be01745e48707b39

31. Florida Money Laundering Act, Ch. 2017-155, §896. 101 as amended, eff. July 1, 2017, https://www.flsenate.gov/Session/Bill/2017/1379/BillText/er/PDF

32. For an earlier report exhibited much frustration about the FBI in investigating crimes involving virtual currency, see *(U) Bitcoin Virtual Currency: Unique Features Present Distinct Challenges for Deterring Illicit Activity* (April 24, 2012), FBI Intelligence Assessment, http://www.sciencemag.org/news/2016/03/why-criminals-cant-hide-behind-bitcoin

33. Bret Nigh and C. Alden Pelker, *Virtual Currency: Investigative Challenges and Opportunities*, U.S. Bureau Of Investigation, Sept. 8, 2015, https://leb.fbi.gov/articles/featured-articles/virtual-currency-investigative-challenges-and-opportunities

34. John Bohannon, *Why criminals can't hide behind Bitcoin*, Science Magazine, Mar. 9, 2016, http://www.sciencemag.org/news/2016/03/why-criminals-cant-hide-behind-bitcoin

35. *SEC v. PlexCorps*, 17-Civ-7007 (E.D.N.Y., Dec. 1, 2017), https://www.sec.gov/litigation/complaints/2017/comp-pr2017-219.pdf

36. Autorite Des Marches Financiers, Dossier PlexCoin, Dominic Lacroix condamne a la prison, https://lautorite.qc.ca/grand-public/salle-de-presse/actualite/fiche-dactualite/dominic-lacroix-condamne-a-la-prison/

37. Lisa R. Lifshitz, *Cracking Down on a Bad Coin Offering*, Canadian Lawyer, Dec. 11, 2017, http://www.canadianlawyermag.com/author/lisa-r-lifshitz/cracking-down-on-a-bad-coin-offering-15064/

38. Voorhees, SEC 3-15902, (2014). See, also, U.S. Securities and Exchange Commission, *SEC Charges Bitcoin Entrepreneurs with Offering Unregistered Securities*, Press Release, 2014-111, https://www.sec.gov/news/press-release/2014-111

39. *In re Sand Hill Exchange*, SEC 3-16598 (2015), https://www.sec.gov/litigation/admin/2015/33-9809.pdf

40. *SEC v. Willner*, 1:17-cv-06305 (E.D.N.Y., Oct. 30, 2017), https://www.sec.gov/litigation/complaints/2017/comp-pr2017-202.pdf

41. Securities and Exchange Commission, Release No. 82452, Jan. 5, 2018, https://www.sec.gov/litigation/suspensions/2018/34-82452.pdf

42. Securities and Exchange Commission, Release No. 44791, Sept. 14, 2001.

43. *SEC v. Arisebank, No.-cv-* (N.D.Tx, filed Jan. 2018). A summary of the case may be viewed in Securities and Exchange Commission, *SEC Halts Alleged Initial Coin Offering Scam*, Press Release, Jan. 20, 2018, https://

www.sec.gov/news/press-release/2018-8. A copy of the complaint can be found at https://www.sec.gov/litigation/complaints/2018/comp-pr2018-8.pdf

44. *CFTC v. Gelfman Blueprint, Inc.*, No. 1-17-cv-07181 (S.D.N.Y., filed Sept. 21, 2017).
45. *Id.*
46. *CFTC v. McDonnell*, No. 18-cv-0361 (E.D.N.Y., Jan. 18, 2018), http://www.cftc.gov/ide/groups/public/@lrenforcementactions/documents/legalpleading/enfcdmcomplaint011818.pdf
47. *CFTC v. Dean*, No. 18-cv-00345 (E.D.N.Y., Jan. 18, 2018).
48. *CFTC v. My Big Pay, Inc.*, No. 18-cv-10077-RWZ (D.C. Ma. Jan. 16, 2018), http://www.cftc.gov/idc/groups/public/@lrenforcementactions/documents/legalpleading/enfmybigcoinpaycomplt011618.pdf
49. *Order Granting Plaintiff's Motion, for an Ex Parte Temporary Restraining Order*, Jan. 16, 2018, http://www.cftc.gov/idc/groups/public/@lrenforcementactions/documents/legalpleading/enfmybigcoinpayorder011618.pdf
50. Reuters, *Blockchain Startup R3 Sues Rival Ripple Labs*, Fortune, Sept. 8, 2017, http://fortune.com/2017/09/08/blockchain-r3-sues-ripple-labs/
51. *Ripple Labs Inc. v. R3 LRC LLC*, No. CGC 17-561205 (Sup. Ct. San Fran. Sept. 8, 2017). For a copy of the complaint and other court documents, see XRP Chat, *Ripple Labs v. R3 (actual court documents)* (Sept. 19, 2017), https://www.xrpchat.com/topic/9857-ripple-labs%C2%A0v-r3-actual-court-documents/
52. *R3 Holdco LLC v. Ripple Labs, Inc.*, No.655781/17 (Sup. Ct. N.Y. Cty). A copy of the documents filed may be found at https://www.xrpchat.com/topic/9857-ripple-labs%C2%A0v-r3-actual-court-documents/
53. Jeff John Roberts, *Ripple Claims Early Victory in Court fight with Blockchain Rival R3*, Fortune, Oct. 13, 2017, http://fortune.com/2017/10/13/blockchain-ripple-r3/
54. President's Council of Advisers on Science and Technology, *R3 and Distributed Ledger Technology*, May 2016, https://obamawhitehouse.archives.gov/sites/default/files/microsites/ostp/PCAST/10.40%20D%20Gran.pdf

Crowdfunding and the Taxation of Virtual Currencies

Due to the inherent nature of Distributed Ledger Technology (DLT) tax authorities understandably are concerned about the difficulty of ascertaining the taxable consequences of DLT transactions. This is reminiscent of the jurisdictional issues arising in the cyberlaw context wherein the center of gravity giving rise to judicial authority was often in question.[1] Because of its anonymity and its peer-to-peer (P2P) transactions, which may occur cross-border, determining who, when, and how to tax such transactions understandably remain critical issues for governmental authorities which may differ in their analysis of taxable events. As noted by the International Monetary Fund (IMF), the issues presented to national entities include whether to treat virtual currencies as a form of non-monetary property or as a form of currency; the tax treatment of newly created virtual currencies from mining; and the value added tax and sales tax treatment of transactions. It further noted that tax authorities' recordkeeping requirements and their complexity may reduce the attractiveness of virtual currencies for day-to-day business transactions.[2]

© The Author(s) 2018
R. Girasa, *Regulation of Cryptocurrencies and Blockchain Technologies*, Palgrave Studies in Financial Services Technology, https://doi.org/10.1007/978-3-319-78509-7_7

Crowdfunding and Virtual Currency[3]

We begin with a discussion of crowdfunding because it is a new and unique source of capital that has become the source of many of the cryptocurrencies that have arisen. Included among the virtual currencies that emanated from crowdfunding is Ethereum.[4] Crowdfunding refers to investments, other than by more traditional means of raising capital, by a substantial number of persons with respect to particular, mostly new, projects. In past years such funding most often occurred by investments by venture capitalists who assumed substantial risks in the hope of attaining more substantial financial rewards with respect to innovative ideas that appear to have financial merit. Although venture capital funding continues to be an important source of capital for newly arising business ventures, crowdfunding has now overtaken venture capital as a major source of financing. Statistically, crowdfunding rose from $6.1 billion in 2013 to $16.2 billion in 2014, and projected to be $34.3 billion in 2015. Venture capital investments constituted approximately $30 billion in the comparable timeframe although the sum had substantially increased by 2017 (some $70 billion).[5] *Having Forbes Magazine* estimated growth to reach $300 billion by 2025.[6]

Crowdfunding constitutes an investment of capital in order to seek a profit through the efforts of other persons and thus comes within the parameters of the *Howey* test, requiring, unless exempted, registration with the SEC.[7] The exemption of crowdfunding from such registration requirements arose from the enactment in 2012 of the Jumpstart Our Business Startups Act.[8] The Act is composed of seven titles, with "Crowdfunding" constituting Title III.[9] In essence, the Act permits an exemption from the substantial filing requirements with the SEC mandated under §4 of the Securities Act of 1933.[10]

Section 302 of Title III amended §4 of the Securities Act of 1933, to provide an additional exemption from registration by adding a sixth exemption to §4(a)[11] as follows:

(6) transactions involving the offer or sale of securities by an issuer (including all entities controlled by or under common control with the issuer), provided that—

(A) the aggregate amount sold to all investors by the issuer, including any amount sold in reliance on the exemption provided under this paragraph during the 12-month period preceding the date of such transaction, is not more than $1,000,000;

(B) the aggregate amount sold to any investor by an issuer, including any amount sold in reliance on the exemption provided under this paragraph during the 12-month period preceding the date of such transaction, does not exceed—

(i) the greater of $2,000 or 5 percent of the annual income or net worth of such investor, as applicable, if either the annual income or the net worth of the investor is less than $100,000; and

(ii) 10 percent of the annual income or net worth of such investor, as applicable, not to exceed a maximum aggregate amount sold of $100,000, if either the annual income or net worth of the investor is equal to or more than $100,000.[12]

Thus, Congress limited financial exposure and possible losses by: (1) limiting the amount raised by a startup to $1 million over a 12-month period; (2) restricting individual investments over a 12-month period to either the greater of $2000 or 5 percent of the annual net worth of the individual investor if the investor's income is less than $100,000 annually so as to protect less sophisticated investors; or (3) the greater of 10 percent of the investor's annual income if such income is $100,000 or more but not to exceed the an amount sold to investors of $100,000.

SEC Final Rule

Pursuant to the crowdfunding amendment to the 1933 Act, the SEC issued a Final Rule effective May 16, 2016 with 685 pages of the rule and commentaries detailing the requirements for issuers, intermediaries, and other requirements in an endeavor to the limit exposure of unsophisticated investors and provide a framework for the registration which registered funding portals and broker-dealers are required to use as intermediaries.[13]

Limitations on Investments

The question arises concerning how an intermediary is to determine the net worth of the investor. The final rule provides that the person's annual income and net worth are to be calculated in accordance with the values calculated for determining accredited investor status (in essence, net worth exceeding $1 million and annual income exceeding $200,000)[14]. The issuer may rely on the efforts of the intermediary to ensure that the appropriate limits on investments have been adhered to.[15] The exemption applies only to transactions involving the sale or offering of securities that are organized within the United States, not by an investment company, and the issuer is not otherwise ineligible to sell securities.

Requirements Relating to Issuers

The definition of an *issuer* varies dependent upon the context in which it is used. In the context of crowdfunding, it is defined under §2(4) of the Securities Act of 1934 as "every person who issues or proposes to issue any security" with a number of exceptions not applicable in this context. Title III of the Jobs Act requires an issuer that offers or sells securities to file with the Commission, and provide investors and the relevant broker or funding portal, and make available to potential investors, detailed information concerning the issuer's name, legal status, physical and website addresses, names of directors, officers, and persons holding 20 percent or more of the issuer's shares. Additional requirements include a description of the business and business plan; material factors concerning risk or speculation; the financial condition certified by the chief executive officer of the issuer for the preceding 12-month period for target offering amounts of $100,000 or less including tax returns, and if over $100,000 and under $500,000, financial statements by an independent public accountant, and audited statements if over $500,000; a description of the purpose and intended use of the proceeds; the price of the offerings to the public; a description if the ownership and capital structure of the issuer; and numerous other details concerning the price structure, return of funds if an investment is cancelled, rights of principal shareholders, and other pertinent data. Thus, the degree of information to be filed and given to investors and intermediaries increases exponentially as the target investment increases.[16]

Issuers offering or selling securities have to file an offering statement with the Commission as well as any amendments, progress updates, and an annual report.[17] Advertising by prospective issuers is strictly limited to directing the potential investor to the intermediary's platform and includes a statement of the offering, name of the intermediary, terms of the offering, factual information about the proposed business and location, and how to communicate with the intermediary.[18] Compensation from the issuer to the promoter is permitted but the extent of compensation is to be disclosed through the intermediary.[19] The final rule has an appendix displaying the forms required under the rule, to wit, forms for the offering statement, progress updates, amendments to the offering statement, annual report and amendment, and termination of reporting.

Requirements Relating to Intermediaries (Brokers and Funding Portals)

Investors generally act through intermediaries respecting the sale or purchase of securities. These persons must register with the SEC as either a *broker* defined as "any person engaged in the business of effecting transactions in securities for the account of others"[20] or as a *funding portal* defined as "any person acting as an intermediary in a transaction involving the offer or sale of securities for the account of others but does not offer investment advice, solicits purchase or sales of securities or holds or manages such securities."[21] Such person or entity must also register with any applicable self-regulatory organization[22] (generally, FINRA) and provide disclosures to investors of risks and other educational materials as the Commission may require to ensure that each investor reviews the relevant information about the crowdfunding offering, affirms an understanding that he or she understands the risks associated with the investment, including that of a total loss of the investment, and understands the level of risk applicable to the investment and an understanding of the risk of illiquidity.[23]

Before accepting any investment commitment and additional commitment, the intermediary must have a reasonable belief that the investor satisfies the investor limitations cited above although the intermediary may rely on the investor's representations such as his or her annual income, net worth, and the amount of the investor's other investments unless the intermediary has reasons to question the reliability of the representations. The intermediary is required to obtain from the investor a representation that the investor has read the intermediary's educational materials, understands that the entire amount invested may be lost, and that the investor is in a financial position to absorb the loss. Other data to be received from the investor includes a questionnaire completed by the investor that demonstrates his or her understanding of restrictions on cancelling a commitment to invest or difficulty in reselling the said securities, and the risk of loss that is otherwise not affordable.[24]

Additional provisions relating to intermediaries include the requirement that the Commission take measures to reduce fraud by mandating a background check and regulatory history with respect to each officer, director, and persons holding more than 20 percent of the outstanding equity of every issuer whose securities are being offered under the Jobs Act; provide that all proceeds from the offer may be given and used by the issuer only when the target offering amount is reached and allow investors to withdraw their proceeds if such a target is not met; information collected from investors; and protection relating to promotors, finders, or lead generators.[25] Any director, officer, or partner of the intermediary may not have a financial interest in the *issuer* (defined as "a direct or indirect ownership of, or economic interest in, any class of the issuer's securities") including compensation for services rendered to the intermediary. The intermediary may also not have a financial interest in the issuer unless it receives compensation for services provided respecting the sale or offer for sale of the particular class of crowdfunded securities.[26]

The regulations require that an intermediary takes measures to reduce the risk of fraud. The intermediary must have a reasonable basis for believing that the issuer has complied with the requirements of the crowdfunding statute; that the issuer has established means to keep accurate records of the holders of the securities it would offer and sell through the intermediary's platform; and deny access to its platform to an issuer when it has a reasonable basis for believing that the issuer (or officers thereof) is subject to a disqualification.[27] The intermediary must assure that the investor has opened an account with the intermediary with consent for electronic delivery and provide all information on its platform and to the investor that is required by the intermediary including: educational materials that explain the process of the offer, risks, types of securities offered, restrictions on resale, limitations on amounts that may be invested and other relevant information; whether promoters have been utilized and compensation thereof; and disclosure of compensation of the intermediary.[28]

The intermediary must provide communication channels on its platform to enable persons to communicate with each other and with representatives of the issuer unless the intermediary is a funding platform that does not participate in communication other than to provide guidelines for communication and remove abusive or potential fraudulent communication; permits public access to view discussions in the communication channels; restricts posting of comments to those who have opened an account with the intermediary on its platform; and requires that persons posting comments clearly state whether they are a founder or employee of the issuer engaged in promotional activities or are otherwise compensated for the comments.[29] When an investor receives an investment commitment from an issuer the intermediary must promptly provide the investor with the dollar amount of the investment commitment; the price of the securities, if known; the name of the issuer; and the date and time by which the investor may cancel the commitment.[30]

An intermediary that is a registered broker must comply with regulations governing the transmission or maintenance of payments in connections with underwritings. The regulations provide that it is a "fraudulent, deceptive, or manipulative act or practice" under the Securities Act for any broker or dealer participating in any distribution of securities to accept any part of the sale price of any security being distributed unless: (a) the money or other consideration received is promptly transmitted to the entitled persons; or (b) if not to be payable to the person on whose behalf the distribution is made, then the money or other consideration received is promptly deposited in a separate bank account, as agent or trustee or in escrow for the persons who have the beneficial interests.[31]

An intermediary that is a funding portal must direct investors to transmit the money or other consideration to a qualified third party (registered broker or dealer holding such funds or an insured bank or credit union) which has agreed in writing to hold the funds on behalf of the persons entitled to them. The funds are to be transmitted to the issuer when the aggregate amount of investment commitment achieves the target amount of the offering but no sooner than 21 days after the date on which the intermediary makes publicly available the required information on its platform. If the investment commitment has been cancelled, then the funds are to be returned to the investor upon failure to complete the offering. Investors are to receive a confirmation from the intermediary that discloses the date of the transaction, type of security purchased, identity, price and number of securities, and other related information.[32]

Special Rules for Registered Funding Portals

As stated above, a funding portal is required to be registered with the Commission and become a member of a national securities association (e.g., FINRA). It is exempt from broker registration requirements in connection with its activities as a funding portal.[33] When acting as a crowdfunding intermediary with respect to the offer or sale of securities it may not offer investment advice or recommendations; solicit purchases, sales, or offers to buy the offered securities displayed on its platform; or compensate other persons for such solicitation. It may not hold, manage, possess, or otherwise handle investor funds or securities. It may, however:

- Determine what terms to allow an issuer to offer and sell securities under its platform;
- Apply objective criteria to highlight offerings on its platform that are reasonably designed to highlight the issuers' offering;
- Provide search functions or other tools investors can use to examine the offerings available through the funding portal's platform;
- Provide communication channels by which investors can communicate with each other and with representatives of the issuer concerning the offerings;
- Advise an issuer about the structure or content of the issuer's offering, including assistance in the preparation of the offering documentation;
- Compensate a third party for referring a person to the funding portal provided the third party does not provide the portal with personally

identifiable information of any potential investor and the compensation is not based on the purchase or sale of a crowdfunding security except for compensation paid to a registered broker;

- Pay compensation to a registered broker or dealer in connection with the offer or sale of crowdfunding securities pursuant to a written agreement, and such services and compensation comply with the rules of the registered national securities association of which the funding portal is a member;
- Receive compensation from a broker or dealer for services performed by the portal for sale or offer of the said securities;
- Advertise the existence of the funding portal and identify one or more issuers or offerings available in accordance with certain designated criteria;
- Deny access to its platform or cancel an offering of an issuer where it believes there may be fraud or it concerns investor protection;
- Accept on behalf of an issuer an investment commitment for the offered crowdfunding securities;
- Direct investors where to transmit funds and remit payments in connection with the said securities; and
- Direct a third party to release proceeds to an issuer upon completion of the crowdfunding offering.[34]

Non-resident Funding Portal Requirements

A *non-resident funding portal* is defined as a funding portal incorporated in or organized outside the United States or having its principal place of business beyond U.S. borders. Registration by a non-resident funding portal is conditional upon information-sharing arrangement between the Commission and the competent regulator in the non-resident portal's jurisdiction. The portal must have a designated U.S. agent upon whom any service of process, pleadings, or other papers may be served. The portal must maintain books and records, including a written consent and power of attorney appointing the U.S. agent for a period of three years after the agreement with the agent is terminated. All books and records are to be accessible to the Commission regarding the portal and an opinion of counsel that the portal is legally able to provide access to such records as a matter of law within the foreign jurisdiction.

Completion of Offerings and Cancellations

An investor may cancel an investment commitment for any reason up to 48 hours before the deadline identified in the issuer's offering materials. If there is a material change to the terms of the offering or with respect to the information provided by the issuer, then the intermediary is to notify the investor of such change and that the investment commitment is being cancelled unless the investor reconfirms the commitment within five business days of receipt of the notice.[35] If the target offering amount is reached prior to the deadline identified in the offering, the issuer may close the offering before the deadline date provided certain requirements are met, to wit: the offering must remain open for 21 days; notice is given to potential investors of the new deadline, the right to cancel the investment up to 48 hours before the new deadline offering; and whether any additional investment commitments will be permitted within 48 hours of the deadline.[36]

Miscellaneous Provisions Applicable to Funding Portals

Funding g portals are subject to inspections and examinations by the Commission and by registered national securities organizations. Records are to be kept for a period of five years (two years in an easily accessible place) concerning an investor's purchase or attempts to purchase crowdfunding securities; records relating to issuers for such offerings; communications regarding the platform; records relating to the promotion of issuer's securities that uses communication channels; notices to issuers and investors; written agreements relating to the offerings; all daily, monthly, and quarterly summaries of transactions effected; organizational documents; and financial record-keeping and reporting of currency and foreign transactions.[37]

Restriction on Resales and Disqualification Provisions

Securities issued under the crowdfunding exemption may not be transferred by any purchaser for one-year commencing when the securities were issued unless the securities are transferred to the issuer; to an accredited investor; as part of an offering with the Commission; or to a family member of the purchaser.[38] The crowdfunding exemption is not available to the issuer if it or its predecessor, officers, director, general partner, or managing member, or any beneficial owner of 20 percent or more of the issuer's outstanding voting equity securities has been convicted within 10 years before the offering statement of any felony or misdemeanor in connection with the sale or purchase of any security. or made any false filing with the Commission. or has been enjoined by any court of competent jurisdiction in connection with the purchase or sale of securities. The prohibition also applies to persons who have been suspended or had a registration revoked, or subject to other bars by the Commission.[39]

Crowdfunding Platforms

There are many hundreds of crowdfunding platforms[40] or methodologies (models) that may be used by people seeking funding which to date have raised more than $65 billion for startup companies resulting in the creation of over 270,000 jobs by the statutory enactment.[41] The major models of which the first two models are the primary types, may be summarized as follows:

Rewards-Based Model

The rewards-based crowdfunding model offers certain perks to non-accredited investors such as t-shirts, movie passes, free software, and other perks at little cost to investors but without receipt of any ownership in the company.

Equity-Based Model

The equity-based model gives accredited investors an opportunity to invest in new companies that have unique offerings with potentially sizeable future monetary returns.

The best known example of the equity model is that of Kickstarter. com. Kickstarter was launched in Brooklyn, New York on April 28, 2009 by three individuals and teakes the form of a public benefit corporation.[42] The company, which has raised over $2.1 billion dollars 10 million people has funded almost 100,000 projects. Its stated mission is to help bring creative projects to life.[43] Among the projects launched include the arts, fashion, music, food, publishing, film, theater, and other noteworthy areas. Other platforms have raised some $10 billion for comparable projects.[44]

Charity-Based Model

This model offers investors moral satisfaction rather than monetary or other such rewards by donations to worthy non-profits seeking to promote social enterprises. An example of charitable crowdfunding is the website at the author's university whereby donors are encouraged to contribute donations for a multitude of students' projects and endeavors including an undergraduate students' research travel fund, internships in non-profits and social enterprises, and environmental studies in Cuba.[45]

Debt Model (Peer-to-Peer)

In the crowdfunding debt-model investors pool money into a fund that lends unsecured money online to potential borrowers based on their credit-risk portfolios, permitting investors to receive interest. The model offers alternatives to borrowers particularly when money from banks or mortgage companies becomes unavailable.

Litigation Model

The litigation model of crowdfunding provides money for the purpose of commencing or continuing litigation against companies for perceived wrongdoings and other related alleged malfeasances. Investors receive a stake in the potential final result of the litigation. An example of this model is LexShares where, according to its website, the raised capital may be utilized for litigation expenses such as attorneys' fees, expert witnesses, trial exhibits, and court fees; working capital for rent, supplies, and other business-related expenses; personal expenses for the litigants; and serves as a means of acquiring high-quality legal talent that lessens the perceived need to settle cases for less money than the desired outcome.[46]

Product Pre-Order Model

The product pre-order model enables investors to receive products being manufactured before they become available to the public, at a discount price.[47] It has some degree of similarity to the rewards-based model (http://backersmanual.com/2014/03/01/crowdfunding-is-not-a-pre-order).

Enforcement

Inevitably, whenever there are monetary investments, there are abuses emanating from negligent conduct or criminal enterprise. The first enforcement action with respect to crowdfunding was commenced by the Federal Trade Commission (FTC) in June 2015 in *Federal Trade Commission v. Erik Chevalier*[48] wherein the FTC sought to obtain a permanent injunction and other relief against the defendant for violating §5(a) of the FTC Act[49] which prohibits "unfair or deceptive acts or practices in or affecting commerce" by charging commission for a product not delivered in connection with the individual's crowdfunding campaign. Specifically, the defendant, doing business as the Forking Path, Co., is accused of raising money with respect to a purported board game.

The defendant allegedly represented that the investing consumers would receive certain reward deliverables, such as a copy of the board game and certain figurines, if the crowdfunding goal of $35,000 was attained. The defendant raised some $122,000 from 1246 investors and then informed the consumer-investors that the game would not be produced and that refunds would be issued. Few, if any, of the investors received back any monetary contribution.[50]

The action resulted in a settlement agreement and court order whereby Chevalier was prohibited from making misrepresentations about any crowdfunding campaign, and had failed to honor the refund policies stated in the offering. The defendant was barred from disclosing or otherwise benefiting from customers' personal information, and had failed to dispose of such information properly. A fine and judgment of $111,793.71 was also imposed but was suspended because of Chevalier's alleged inability to pay but would be reinstated if it is determined that the defendant had misrepresented his financial condition.[51]

Crowdfunding has been a major contributor to the growth of virtual currency. The U.S. Internal Revenue Service (IRS) clarified its position concerning the tax treatment of crowdfunding and, more specifically, the income tax consequences of a crowdfunding effort to purchase a company through contributions for which the contributors receive constructive receipt of the contributed funds before the funds are used to purchase the company. In its guidance letter, the IRS stated that §61(a) of the Internal Revenue Code mandates that gross income includes all income from whatever source derived whether received in cash, property, or other economic benefit. Exceptions from inclusion in gross income are crowdfunding revenues that are not: (1) loans that must be repaid; (2) capital contributed to an entity in exchange or for an equity interest in the entity; or (3) gifts without any "quid pro quo." Crowdfunding revenues must generally be included in income to the extent they are received for services rendered or are gains from the sale of property. Under §1.451-2 of IRS Regulations, constructive income is includible if constructively received by the taxpayer in the taxable year during which the income is credited to his or her account or if made available for drawing on his or her account.[52]

Virtual Currency as Property for Tax Purposes

The IRS, in its Guidance concerning virtual currency, has taken the position that the sale or exchange of convertible virtual currency or use thereof for goods or services has tax consequences that may result in a tax liability. It is not considered as a currency that could generate a foreign currency gain or loss for U.S. tax purposes; rather it is treated as "property" with all of the taxable consequences as other forms of property. It has a determinable value which may be exchanged for fiat currency or other assets. Thus, a taxpayer receiving virtual currency for goods or services must include the fair market value of the virtual currency in computing gross income. The basis for tax purposes is the fair market value of the virtual currency in U.S. dollars as of the date of payment or receipt and, if listed on an exchange, then it is determined by converting the virtual currency into U.S. dollars at the exchange rate. A taxable gain or loss is dependent on the fair market value of the property received. Gain or loss may be dependent on whether the virtual currency is a capital asset or whether the virtual currency exchange concerns stocks, bonds, or other investment property. There is a $600 threshold for trade or business payments to taxable recipients.[53] On the other hand, closed (non-convertible) virtual currencies are not treated as property for tax purposes due to their lack of conversion beyond their highly restricted use such as for games, frequent flyer miles, in-store gift cards, and the like.

A taxpayer who "mines" virtual currency, according to the IRS, must include the fair market value of the virtual currency in gross income as of the date of receipt of the currency. If the mining constitutes a trade or business and the activity is not undertaken as an employee, the net earnings from self-employment resulting from the activities is considered self-employment income and is subject to self-employment tax. Virtual currency paid by an employer as remuneration for services constitutes wages for employment tax purposes. Payments made using the currency are subject to information reporting and backup withholding, as are any other payments in property required by law and regulation.[54] No further update by the IRS to its 2014 Guidance has been issued, notwithstanding the critical comments made below.

The Guidance has caused considerable controversy as addressed by the American Institute of Certified Public Accountants (AICPA) discussed below. Commentators are also generally critical concerning the determination of the "basis" of a Bitcoin or other virtual currency. Repeatedly, the troubling aspect is how a taxpayer who purchases virtual currencies at different prices, from different sources, and at different times is to arrive at a basis for tax purposes. An example of the difficulty, as posed by one commentator, is the miner who mines 10 bitcoins one day at one price, another 10 bitcoins the following day, and another a third day, all at different market values and then sells 10 bitcoins thereafter. If the miner cannot determine the tax basis for the transaction, how is the miner to make an accurate filing of a tax return?[55] An additional commentator addresses similar issues and concerns noting that the IRS Guidance failed to address the valuation of bitcoins; the mining of bitcoins; withholdings from bitcoin payments; the use of bitcoins in P2P trading; the use of bitcoins as capital assets; the use of bitcoins as gifts or donations; and the verification of bitcoin transactions.[56]

Another commentator fears that customers of virtual currencies may be unaware of the complexity of tax laws and regulations that apply to their transactions, which are unclear even to tax professionals. He noted that the IRS and state and local governments collect taxes in a variety of ways at different rates and dependent on the nature of the transaction. There are issues of how wages paid in virtual currencies are to be taxed, sales taxes reliant on point-of-sale tax, stocks, and other investments, foreign purchases, and other transactions. Should these be taxed as ordinary income or as capital gains and losses? Inasmuch as Bitcoin and comparable virtual currencies are treated as property the issue then becomes one of whether the assets were held beyond a year and thus be subject to the lower capital gains tax rate or less than a year at the ordinary taxable rate. The determination is based on how the purchases and sales are calculated, which will be an onerous obligation not easily accomplished. The author noted that the IRS decision to treat Bitcoin as property favors investors over daily users who use it as a currency. In so doing, Bitcoin is harmed when used in the marketplace rather than as an investment. Daily transactions would be subject to the applicable sales tax while, at the same time, being subject to capital gains and losses requiring users to determine the fair market value of the currency on the date of use. The end result is the discouragement of the use of virtual currencies, excessive inconvenience to daily users, and the extreme difficulty the IRS faces in trying to enforce its own rulings.[57]

An additional issue concerning the treatment by the IRS of Bitcoin and other virtual currencies as property is the application of §1031 Tax Free Exchange, which provides that a taxable gain on property sold may be deferred if exchanged for like investment property in accordance with certain time constraints. The IRS, as stated, treats Bitcoin and other virtual currencies as property, which would then appear that the §1031 tax deferral treatment would be applicable. Experts, however, are questioning whether the conversion (e.g., euros to dollars or from one type of virtual currency to another) would fall under this section of the regulations. The fear is that possible criminal and/or civil penalties may accrue for failure to properly report taxable gains and losses.[58] The new tax legislation appears to confirm commentators' concerns about the inapplicability of §1031, notwithstanding the IRS's treatment of virtual currencies as property. According to its provisions, only real property will qualify for deferred treatment and not the conversion of bitcoins into ether and other cryptocurrencies. The tax shift comes as the IRS ramps up investigations into individual tax returns for potential unreported gains from virtual currencies, also called cryptocurrencies or digital assets. Any exchange of such currencies will be treated as a taxable event and subject to applicable tax liabilities.[59]

AICPA has expressed considerable alarm for its membership and the clients served by its members. Among the concerns is the alleged IRS contradictory treatment of virtual currency both as not real currency but also as property for tax purposes, which then means that a capital gain or loss should be recorded as if it were an exchange involving property but treated as inventory if held for resale. It would then result in an ordinary gain or loss, but if used as payment, then it should be treated as any other currency that must be converted and its fair market value checked on an exchange. Virtual currency is treated as real currency if, for example, Bitcoin was received by an employee as payment for wages, and if used for payment to an independent contractor would be subject to self-employment tax. When Bitcoin is bought or sold on an exchange then the gain or loss is the difference between its value when received and that when sold. If the taxpayer cannot determine what the basis for the transaction is, he or she will not be able to determine the capital gains tax to be paid.[60]

AICPA addressed its further concern for corporate officers and auditors. For the latter, the complexity of the new technologies, particularly the recording of transactions on a DLT and their application to internal controls, may result in material misstatements. For corporate officers, bitcoins, treated as real currencies, require that their exchange rate at the balance sheet date must be considered and entries adjusted to reflect their conversion to U.S. dollars.[61] In a letter to the IRS dated June 16, 2016, ACIPA asked for additional clarification of the Guidance including the following which to date remain unclear:

- *Acceptable valuation and documentation*—Taxpayers are required to use a reasonable manner to calculate the fair market value of the virtual currency. Questions raised are whether the taxpayers are required to use the market value of one exchange or average of the several exchanges that may be used and which timeframe to use;
- *Expenses of obtaining virtual currency*—Guidance is sought on the treatment of the costs of mining and acquiring virtual currency and when, if ever, any costs of its acquisition is capitalized;
- *Challenges with specific identification for computing gains and losses*— AICPA suggests that an alternative method be permitted for the treatment of convertible virtual currency because taxpayers are required to specifically identify which virtual currency lot was used for each transaction for the purposes of ascertaining the gain or loss of each transaction, but it may be impossible for the taxpayer to track which virtual currency was used for a particular transaction;
- *General guidance regarding property transaction rules*—If the IRS determines that property transaction rules, such as §1031 treatment, should apply differently to virtual currency, then additional guidance is needed as, for example, allowing the treatment of a virtual currency transaction held for investment or business as the same as another virtual currency;

- *Nature of virtual currency held by a merchant*—Guidance is needed whether virtual currency held by a merchant is a capital or ordinary asset; the problem arises when the merchant uses the currency to pay employees and suppliers;
- *Charitable contributions*—Guidance was requested that when virtual currency is donated to a charity in excess of $5000 whether a qualified appraisal will be necessary to substantiate the sum claim as a charitable contribution;
- *Virtual currency as a "commodity"*—Whether virtual currency is considered to be a commodity for the purposes of mark-to-market accounting under IRS regulations;
- *Need for* de minimis *election*—IRS regulations permit up to a $200 deduction per transaction for a foreign exchange rate gain if derived from a personal transaction. For taxpayers with a minimum amount of the currency who use it for small purchases, tracking the fair market value would be excessively burdensome as would calculating the *de minimis* gain or loss. Can the $200 rule be made applicable to these virtual currency transactions?
- *Retirement accounts*—Guidance was requested whether retirement savings accounts are permitted to hold virtual currencies investments; and
- *Foreign reporting requirements for virtual currency*—Guidance was requested concerning reporting of virtual currency accounts and also the application of FATCA to virtual currency.[62]

The Foreign Account Tax Compliance Act (FATCA)[63]

Taxable consequences depend on a number of factors. Thus, an issuer who is located outside the United States may not have U.S. tax consequences unless it has a substantial presence within the United States FATCA may, however, come into play. Under FATCA, certain U.S. taxpayers holding financial assets outside the United States must report those assets to the IRS on an IRS designated form or be subject to serious penalties for not reporting these assets. The taxpayer is also required to report foreign financial accounts on a designated FinCEN form. Foreign financial institutions may also be required to report to the IRS information about financial accounts held by U.S. taxpayers or foreign entities in which U.S. taxpayers hold a substantial ownership interest. They include not only banks but also other financial institutions such as investment entities, brokers, and certain insurance companies. Other non-financial foreign entities will also have to report certain of their U.S. owners.[64] FATCA is part of the Hiring Incentives to Restore Employment (HIRE) Act of 2010.[65]

One commentator, concerned about tax evasion and other malfeasance, stated that FATCA does not require virtual wallet providers to report to the IRS and, thus, the IRS should define cryptocurrencies, virtual wallets, and virtual wallet providers to bring them within the scope of its regulatory oversight. They should be defined as foreign financial assets, foreign financial accounts, and foreign financial institutions.[66]

Internal Revenue Service Enforcement of Regulations

Subpoenas as a Method to Investigate Tax Fraud Cases

The IRS position on taxation of virtual currency transactions has precipitated much confusion and uncertainty. Although there are substantial arguments concerning whether to treat virtual currencies as currencies or property, accounting for such transactions and tracking the basis to be used in reporting has engendered controversy and calls for greater clarification from the IRS. We have noted the difficulty of investigating cryptocurrency transactions because of the anonymity of the parties engaged in purchasing and selling them. Although government investigators may not be able at present to ascertain the identities of users of decentralized virtual currencies, nevertheless, there are a number of proven techniques to circumscribe the roadblock. One of the methods is discussed in a case that made national news, although it pertained to centralized virtual currencies whereby third parties were involved and possessed records of transactions. The issue of privacy was at the forefront when the IRS sought to obtain the records of Coinbase account holders as it arose when the Internet came into global usage. According to its website, the San Francisco Company was founded in 2012 and is a digital wallet and platform whereby merchants and consumers can transact with each other with virtual currencies including Bitcoin, Ethereum, Litecoin, and other similar currencies. It alleges it has over 10 million users who have traded in $50 billion of currency assets.

U.S. v. Coinbase

In *U.S. v. Coinbase*,[67] the IRS served a summons on Coinbase, Inc. whereby it demanded records of nearly all of Coinbase's customers for the period from January 1, 2013 through the end of December, 2015 with respect to transactions in convertible virtual currency. The purpose of the summons was to determine the identity and potential federal income tax liability of persons utilizing Coinbase's transmission services which the IRS believes the capital gains from the transactions were substantially underreported. It requested nine categories of documents including the parties' user profiles, transaction logs, records of payments processed, third-party access, account or invoice statements, records of payments, and other documents. Coinbase refused to comply with the summons which brought about the litigation whereby the IRS sought to enforce the summons. The IRS petitioned and received from the federal court authorization to serve a "John Doe" summons on Coinbase, Inc. for information on the hubsite's users and transactions. The site uses sophisticated tracking software to ascertain unreported gains and losses of parties engaged in Bitcoin and similar transactions.[68] It employs the contractor, Chain analysis, which has a "Reactor" tool for tracking and analyzing Bitcoin transactions. Users of the software include law enforcement agencies, banks, and regulatory agencies.[69] The IRS then modified its request to some 14,355 Coinbase account holders with respect to 8.9 million transactions.

The federal District Court in San Francisco, California, granted the government's request in part. It noted that the modified request concerned transactions that were each at least $20,000 of Bitcoin in a given year. Coinbase argued that the IRS spokesperson's allegations were not supported by personal knowledge, were based on conclusory allegations unsupported by factual knowledge, and other bases. The court disagreed holding that the representative, as senior representative of the IRS virtual currency investigation team, was competent to make the request and refuted other claims of Coinbase, stating that the government had met its minimal obligations for requesting the summons. The court ordered Coinbase to furnish the identities of those persons having transactions in Bitcoin of $20,000 or more including their taxpayer I.D. number, name, birth date, address, records of transactions, and periodic statements and invoices. The court denied the request for all other information including account opening records, copies of passport and drivers' licenses, wallet addresses, and public keys for all wallets/vaults.[70]

The result of the decision enabled the IRS and other government enforcement officials to crack the blockchain shield that had protected both law-abiding and non-law abiding users of virtual currency. Thus, the ability of users of Coinbase, a digital asset broker in San Francisco, California that engages in the purchase and sale of digital as well as fiat currencies worldwide, to maintain the privacy of its customers will be substantially impeded. Customers, believing that their transactions are secret and cannot be compromised, face substantial penalties if disclosures to the IRS are granted in full or in substantial part.[71]

Chainalsis and the IRS

In order to determine the tax obligations of customers who purchase and sell bitcoins, the IRS has contracted with Chainalsis Inc., a Swiss company with offices in New York, to assist in identifying owners of digital wallets.[72] The company alleges that it is able to identify 25 percent of all Bitcoin addresses that account for 50 percent of all transactions. In addition, it has over 4 million tags on Bitcoin addresses from web forums and leaked data sources derived from dark market forums and Mt. Gox deposit and withdrawal information. It appears that the much alleged anonymity of Bitcoin has placed it in the pseudo-anonymity category.[73]

Congressional Proposals to Tax Virtual Currency Transactions

There are a number of Congressional proposals concerning virtual currencies including the taxation of transactions. Among them is a Congressional bill, the Cryptocurrency Tax Fairness Act of 2017,[74] introduced by Representatives Jared Polis, D-Colorado, and David Schweikert, R-Arizona, who are co-chairs of the Congressional Blockchain Caucus. It addresses the IRS classification of digital currency as property that includes the smallest of such transactions thereby de-incentivizing customers from using the currencies to pay for goods and services. The bill would create a structure for taxing purchases made with cryptocurrencies akin to foreign currency transactions by permitting customers to make small purchases with cryptocurrency without having to comply with reporting requirements. The intention of the bill, according to the sponsors, is to permit purchases by digital payments for newspapers and other small purchases, all without concern about the tax implications.[75]

Another proposal is a House bill that concerns the threat to national security. It would direct the Undersecretary of Homeland Security for Intelligence and Analysis to co-ordinate with other federal agencies, state, and local authorities to develop and disseminate a threat assessment regarding the actual and potential threat posed by individuals using virtual currency to carry out terrorist activities or to provide material support for such activities.[76]

Internationally, tax authorities, as in the United States, are requiring electronic filing of tax returns. For example, Mexico requires corporate income tax be filed electronically and the tax authority performs electronic audits. When doing so, the authority sends the taxpayer a pre-assessment and the taxpayer has 15 days to refute with evidence or pay the tax. The trend globally is towards the use of blockchain to expedite filings and accomplish total transparency. The future will see much speedier and efficient use of resources for the calculation and remittance of taxes, adjustments, quality control, and other advantages. The difficulty is the transition period whereby tax professionals will be compelled to learn the new technologies that require a thorough understanding of coding aspects of blockchain technology as modified and altered in future years as well as new tax rules when tax authorities also demand compliance with new procedures. The upside is the immediate feedback concerning additional requirements, payments, and refunds.[77] Universities offering accounting and programs will have to adjust to the new technologies by incorporating information systems and related courses to better train future professionals.

In the chapter on "International Regulation", we note that U.S. government enforcement of wrongdoing is impeded substantially by the internationalization and anonymity of virtual currency transactions. It is incumbent upon governments to work with each other to curtail the criminal, fraudulent, and tax avoidance activities taking place globally. We discuss some of the efforts to date to regulate and call to account the many players involved in the new revolutionary technology.

Notes

1. For a discussion, see Roy J. Girasa, Cyberlaw: National and International Perspectives, Ch. 2, Prentice-Hall, 2010.
2. Dong He, *supra*, note 24, Dong He, Karl Habermeier, Ross Leckow, Vikram Kyriakos-Saad, Hiroko Oura, Tahsin Saadi Sedik, Natalia Stetsenko, Concepcion Verdugo-Yepes, *Virtual Currencies and Beyond: Initial Considerations,* IMF Discussion Note SDN/16/03, Jan. 2016, at 30–31, https://www.researchgate.net/publication/298915094_Virtual_Currencies_and_Beyond_Initial_Considerations
3. The discussion on crowdfunding is, in part, from a paper originally written by this author and published in the North East Journal of Legal Studies 2017 and re-published with permission from Dr. Sharlene McEvoy.
4. Jim Manning, *Vega Fund: Ethereum Venture Capital Crowdfunding Platform,* ETH News, March 12, 2017, https://www.ethnews.com/vega-fund-ethereum-venture-capital-crowdfunding-platform

5. Massolution, *2015CF: The Crowdfunding Industry Report*, http:// *www.crowdso*urcing.org/editorial/global-crowdfunding-market-to-reach-344b-in-2015-predicts-massolutions-2015cf-indus-try-report/45376. See also commentary by Chance Barnett, *Trends Show Crowdfunding to surpass VC in 2016*, Forbes, June 9, 2015, http://www.forbes.com/sites/chancebarnett/2015/06/09/trends-show-crowdfunding-to-surpass-vc-in-2016/#18e99839444b

6. Nav Athwal, *Real Estate Crowdfunding: 3 Trends to Watch in 2017*, Forbes, Feb. 17, 2017, https://www.forbes.com/sites/navathwal/2017/02/17/real-estate-crowdfunding-3-trends-to-watch-in-2017/#40de83b93b4b

7. *Securities and Exchange Commission v. W. J. Howey Co.*, 328 U.S. 293 (1946).

8. Pub.L. 112–106 enacted into law April 5, 2012.

9. Section 301 of the Act states that the full title of Title III is the Capital Raising Online While Deterring Fraud and Unethical Non-Disclosure Act of 2012 or the Crowdfunding Act.

10. 15 U.S.C. §77(d).

11. Securities Act of 1933, 15 U.S.C. §77(d)(a)(6).

12. §4(a)(6) of the Securities Act of 1933.

13. U.S. Securities and Exchange Commission, 17 C.F.R. 200, 227, 239, 240, 249, 269, 274 2016.

14. Rule 17 C.F.R. §230.501.

15. 17 C.F.R. §227.100(a)(2)(ii).

16. Final Rule, §227.201(r).

17. Final Rule, §227.203.

18. Final Rule, §227.204.

19. Final Rule, §227.205.

20. Securities Act of 1934, §3(a)(4)(A).

21. Securities Exchange Act of 1934, §3(a)(80). The final rule, §227.300 (a) (2) defines a *funding portal* as "a broker acting as an intermediary in a transaction involving the offer or sale of securities in reliance on section 4(a)(6) of the Securities Act…that does not: (i) Offer investment advice or recommendations; (ii) solicit purchases, sales or offers to but the securities displayed on its platform; (iii) Compensate employees, agents, or other persons for such solicitation or based on the sale of securities displayed or referenced on its platform; or (iv) Hold, manage, process, or otherwise handle investor funds or securities."

22. A "self-regulatory organization" is defined under the Securities Act of 1934, §3(a)(26) as "any national securities exchange, registered securities association, or register clearing agency."
23. Jobs Act, §302(b) which amends the Securities Act of 1933 (15 U.S.C. 77a *et seq.*) by adding a §4A, Requirements with Respect to Certain Small Transactions.
24. Final Rule, §227.303(b).
25. *Id.*
26. Final Rule, §227.300(b).
27. Final Rules, §227.301.
28. Final Rule, §227.302(b).
29. Final Rule, §227.302(c).
30. Final Rule, §227.302(d).
31. 17 CFR §240.15c2-4.
32. Final Rule, §227.302(e)(f).
33. Final Rule, §227.401.
34. Final Rule, §227.402.
35. Final Rule, §227.304(a)(c).
36. Final Rule, §227.304(b).
37. Final Rule, §227.404.
38. Final Rule, §227.501.
39. Final Rule, §227.503.
40. *Platform* is defined as "a program or application accessible via the Internet or other similar electronic communication medium through which a registered broker or a registered funding portal acts as an intermediary in a transaction involving the offer or sale of securities in reliance on section 4(a)(6) of the Securities Act" (15 U.S.C. 77d(a)(6), Final Rule §227.300 (4)).
41. Martin Zwilling, *Will These 5 Models of Crowdfunding Replace Angel and VC Investors,* Entrepreneur, Feb. 3, 2015, www.entrepreneur.com/article/242767
42. A "public benefit corporation" is a relatively new type of business corporation formed for the purpose of creating a "general public benefit" in addition to business purposes. A general public benefit" is one that has a "material positive impact on society and the environment, taken as a whole, assessed against a third-party standard, from the business and operations of a benefit corporation." "Specific public benefit" purposes include, but are not limited to: "(1) providing low-income or under-

served individuals or communities with beneficial products or services; (2) promoting economic opportunity for individuals or communities beyond the creation of jobs in the normal course of business; (3) preserving the environment; (4) improving human health; (5) promoting the arts, sciences or advancement of knowledge; (6) increasing the flow of capital to entities with a public benefit purpose; and (7) the accomplishment of any other particular benefit for society or the environment." In New York it is governed by Article 17 of the New York Business Corporation Law. The purposes may be found in New York BCL §1702(e). http://www.dos.ny.gov/corps/benefit_corporation_formation.html. Approximately 20 states recognize public benefit corporations including Delaware, California, and New York.

43. https://www.kickstarter.com/about?ref=nav
44. For an excellent review for crowdfunding participants in making their selection of a crowdfunding platform to invest in together with a colorful diagram of possible choices, see Eric Markowitz, *22 Crowdfunding Sites (and How To Choose Yours!)*, http://www.inc.com/magazine/201306/eric-markowitz/how-to-choose-a-crowdfunder.html
45. Pace Crowd Funding, https://crowdfunding.pace.edu/
46. LexShares, https://www.lexshares.com/pages/plaintiffs?gclid=CMG22JCku8sCFRMlgQodwSYG1Q
47. Markowitz, *supra*, note 44.
48. *FTC v. Chevalier*, No. 3:15-cv-01029 (D.C. Or., June 10, 2015).
49. 15 U.S.C. §45(a).
50. U.S. Federal Trade Commission, *Crowdfunding Project Creator Settles FTC Charges of Deception*, https://www.ftc.gov/news-events/press-releases/2015/06/crowdfunding-project-creator-settles-ftc-charges-deception
51. *FTC v. Chevalier, supra,* note 48.
52. U.S. Internal Revenue Service, Letter. No. 2016-0036, March 30, 2016, https://www.irs.gov/pub/irs-wd/16-0036.pdf
53. U.S. Internal Revenue Service, *IRS Virtual Currency Guidance: Virtual Currency is Treated as Property for U.S. Federal Tax Purposes; General Rules for Property Transactions Apply,* March 24, 2014, Notice 2014-21, https://www.irs.gov/newsroom/irs-virtual-currency-guidance
54. *Id.*
55. Jose Andre Roman, *Bitcoin: Assessing the Tax Implications Associated with the IRS's Notice Deeming Virtual Currency Property,* 34 Developments in

Banking Law, 2014–2015, at 451, 454–456, http://www.bu.edu/rbfl/files/2015/07/Roman.pdf

56. Elizabeth E. Lambert, *The Internal Revenue Service and Bitcoin: A Taxing Relationship*, 35 Virginia L Rev., No. 1, Summer, 2015, https://www.jmls.edu/academics/taxeb/pdf/lambert.pdf

57. Scott A. Wiseman, *Property or Currency? The Tax Dilemma Behind Bitcoin*, 2 Utah L Rev. 417–440 at 430–436, https://dc.law.utah.edu/ulr/vol2016/iss2/5/

58. David Klasing, *Virtual Currency and Section 1031- A Retraction and New Position*, Sept. 1, 2017, https://klasing-associates.com/virtual-currency-section-1031-retraction-new-position/

59. Michaela Ross, *Bitcoin, Cryptocurrency Trades Face New Liability in Tax Bill*, Bloomberg Law Big Law Business, Dec. 20, 2017, https://biglawbusiness.com/bitcoin-cryptocurrency-trades-face-new-liability-in-tax-bill/

60. Rick Barlin, *Bitcoin: Rise of Virtual Currency and its Downfalls: IRS Regulations and Other Drawbacks For Bitcoin*, The CPA Journal, Oct. 2, 2017, https://www.cpajournal.com/

61. *Id.*

62. Troy K. Lewis, *Comments on Notice 2014–21: Virtual Currency Guidance*, AICPA Letter, June 10, 2016, https://www.scribd.com/doc/315796895/AICPA-Comments-on-Notice-2014-21-Virtual-Currency-Guidance

63. Some of the tax issues discussed herein relied on Elena Eyber, *The Rise and Regulation of Virtual Currency* (Jan. 23, 2017), CCH Group, http://news.cchgroup.com/2017/01/23/rise-regulation-virtual-currency/

64. U.S. Internal Revenue Service, *Summary of FATCA Reporting for U.S. Taxpayers*, https://www.irs.gov/businesses/corporations/summary-of-fatca-reporting-for-us-taxpayers

65. Pub.L. 111–147, 124 Stat. 71, enacted March 18, 2010, H.R. 2847.

66. Elizabeth M. Valentine, *IRS, Will You Spare Some Change? Defining Virtual Currency for the FATCA.* 50 Valparaiso U. L. Rev. 863–911 at 865, Sp. 2016.

67. *U.S. v. Coinbase*, No. 17-cv-01431-JSC (D.C.N.D.Ca. Nov. 28, 2017).

68. *John Doe*, No. 3:a16-CV-06658-JSC (N.D. Ca. Nov. 17, 2016). For a commentary, see Robert W. Wood, *IRS Hunts Bitcoin User Identities With Software In Tax Enforcement Push*, Forbes, Aug. 24, 2017, https://www.forbes.com/sites/robertwood/2017/08/24/irs-hunts-Bitcoin-user-identities-with-software-in-tax-enforcement-push/#534172159cd0

69. Joseph Cox, *IRS Now Has a Tool to Unmask Bitcoin Tax Cheats,* The Daily Beast, Aug. 22, 2017, https://www.thedailybeast.com/irs-now-has-a-tool-to-unmask-Bitcoin-tax-cheats
70. *Id.*
71. Joel Rosenblatt, *Coinbase Likely to Lose Fight to Block IRS Customer Probe,* Bloomberg, Nov. 9, 2017, https://www.bloomberg.com/news/articles/2017-11-10/coinbase-likely-to-lose-bid-to-block-irs-probe-of-customer-gains
72. A copy of the contract may be found at https://assets.documentcloud.org/documents/3935924/IRS-Chainalysis-Contract.pdf
73. Jeff John Roberts, *The IRS Has Special Software to Find Bitcoin Tax Cheats,* Fortune, Aug. 22, 2017, http://fortune.com/2017/08/22/irs-tax-cheats-bitcoin-chainalysis/
74. H.R. 59 and H.R. 3210.
75. Jaren Polis, *Creating tax parity for cryptocurrencies,* Press Releases, Sept. 7, 2017, https://polis.house.gov/news/documentsingle.aspx?DocumentID=398438
76. *Homeland Security Assessment of Terrorist Use of Virtual currency Act (An Act to direct the Under Secretary of Homeland Security for Intelligence and Analysis to develop and disseminate a threat assessment regarding terrorist use of virtual currency),* H.R. 2433, https://www.comgress.gov/bill/115th-congress/house-bill/2433/text
77. Simon Jenner, *Blockchain: The Digital Tax Function's Leading-Edge Technology?,* Tax Notes International, at 1087–1089, Dec. 11, 2017, https://www.taxnotes.com/document-list/tax-topics/tax-policy

.

International Regulation

The advent and speed of financial innovations brought about initially by the Internet that serves as a basis for the transformation of global payment systems inevitably has raised significant concerns among law enforcement agencies about criminal activity. Among the issues are concerns voiced by national central banks about the incorporation of new currencies into the global financial network and governmental apprehensions in their endeavor to protect their citizens from harmful investments. We discuss some of the ongoing efforts by nations and by international agencies to understand and promulgate measures to encourage innovative financial endeavors and thwart inevitable harmful activities.

International Organizations And Entities

The Bank for International Settlements

The Bank for International Settlements (BIS),[1] through its Committee on Payments and Market Infrastructures, issued a report on digital currencies in November, 2015. In the report, BIS set forth the supply-side

© The Author(s) 2018
R. Girasa, *Regulation of Cryptocurrencies and Blockchain Technologies*, Palgrave Studies in Financial Services Technology, https://doi.org/10.1007/978-3-319-78509-7_8

factors that may influence the currencies' future development which primarily are *fragmentation* due to the numerous digital currencies in circulation; *scalability and efficiency,* which at the time of this report, was smaller than traditional payment systems; *pseudonymity* (not anonymity) inasmuch as the distributed ledger is usually publicly available; *technical* and *security concerns* by malicious actors using falsified ledgers; and *business model sustainability* that will be difficult to achieve. It also noted the demand-side issues of security, cost, usability, volatility, risk of loss, irrevocability, processing speed, cross-border reach, data privacy, and marketing and reputational effects.

The regulatory issue BIS addresses is the degree of regulation that should occur both on a global and national level. It recommends five categories of actions to be addressed, namely: (1) information/moral suasion whereby users are made aware of the risks of partaking in the currencies; (2) regulation of specific entities such as exchanges, merchant acceptance facilities, and digital wallet applications; (3) interpretation of existing regulations to ascertain whether they need updating due to the rise of the new technologies; (4) broader regulation to enlarge regulations applicable to traditional payment methods and intermediaries to cover the new currencies; and (5) prohibition by the various national states.[2]

BIS also addressed the implications of virtual currencies for central banks and their role in acclimating to virtual currencies. BIS' emphasis is on consumer protection and the basis for its value predicated on the user's perception of value. With the decentralized nature of virtual currencies, it will be difficult for central banks to anticipate possible disruptions. There are legal risks due to the lack of a legal structure to govern their use. There are implications for financial stability and monetary policy owing to their impact on retail payment systems, liquidity for central banks, and the degree of interconnection between users of traditional and non-traditional currencies. A future course of action may include banks' own investigations of the distributed ledgers in payment systems.[3]

European Union

European Central Bank (ECB)

The ECB, as early as October, 2012, was concerned about virtual currencies shortly after their issuance. It referred to them as "virtual currency schemes," because of the two aspects of resembling money and possessing their own retail payment systems. After reciting the characteristics of the currencies, it noted the business reasons for their creation and growth, namely, for virtual community users to participate in them; to generate revenue for their owners; to have control over them in accordance with their business model and strategy; and to compete with traditional currencies such as the euro and the dollar.[4]

After reciting case studies, risks to central banks, and other considerations, the ECB's conclusion was that at the time of the report (October, 2012), virtual currencies did not pose a risk to price stability provided they remained at a relatively low level; they tend to be inherently unstable and low risk because of their low volume and lack of wide acceptance; are not currently regulated when the report was issued; could pose a challenge to public authorities due to use by criminal elements, money launderers, and persons committing fraud; could impact central banks if the public perceives their abuses as due to a lack of central bank intervention; and do come within central banks' authority to the extent that they become part of the payment system.[5]

In a later report in 2015, the ECB noted the dramatic increase in the number of decentralized virtual currencies and the increased dangers to the payment system and, perhaps, more importantly, to the users who are exposed to risks of exchange rate, volatility, counterparty relating to the anonymity of the payee, investment fraud, and other risks. It expressed concern over the lack of co-ordinated governmental efforts from national authorities to mitigate these risks which range from warnings, statements, and clarification of the legal status of the currencies, to licensing, and supervision of their activities. It thus recommended a co-ordinated response by the legislative, regulatory, and supervisory frameworks to the various schemes discussed in its earlier report.[6]

EU Directive on Money Laundering

The EU enacted the Fourth Anti-Money Laundering Directive on May 20, 2015—its mission is twofold, (1) to counter money laundering used for criminal purposes and (2) to combat the financing of terrorist activities.[7] Member states were required to bring the requirements of the Directive into force at the end of December, 2016. The European Union Commission thereafter proposed, among other changes, amendments that virtual currency exchange platforms be incorporated into the Directive. It distinguished *virtual currency exchange platforms*, which are currency exchange offices that trade virtual currencies for real (fiat) currencies, from *virtual currency custodian wallets* in which providers hold virtual currency accounts on behalf of customers wherein payments can be made or received.

Virtual currency exchange platforms can be considered as "electronic" currency exchange offices that trade virtual currencies for real currencies (or so-called "fiat" currencies, such as the euro). On the other hand, virtual currency custodian wallet providers hold virtual currency accounts on behalf of their customers by providing virtual wallets from which payments in virtual currencies can be made or received. In the "virtual currency" world, they are the equivalent of a bank or payment institution offering a payment account.[8] "Member states are to ensure that providers of exchange services between virtual currencies and fiat currencies, custodian wallet providers, currency exchange and check cashing offices, and trust or company service providers, are licensed or registered...."[9]

Interestingly, a report of the European Commission appears to conclude that virtual currencies seem rarely to be used by criminal organizations, even with the characteristics of anonymity, due mainly to the lack of sophistication in their use.[10] Other initiatives, especially after the ransomware attack on May 12, 2017, include the project TITANIUM (Tools for the Investigation of Transactions in Underground Markets) whereby researchers from four law enforcement agencies have gathered together to develop and implement tools to combat money laundering schemes and other criminal activities while safeguarding individual privacy and other fundamental rights. It aims to analyze legal and ethical requirements and put in place guidelines for storing and processing data, information, and knowledge required for criminal investigations.[11]

The European Parliament in a resolution of May 26, 2016 on virtual currencies called for a proportionate regulatory approach that does not stifle the innovation or add to costs in setting forth the regulatory challenges created by the widespread use of virtual currencies and Distributed Ledger Technology (DLT). It calls for the creation of a Dynamic Coalition on Blockchain Technologies at the Internet Governance Forum, and requests the EU Commission to promote a shared and inclusive governance of DLT so as to avoid the problems that the EU had in regulating the Internet. It suggests that the major EU legislation, including EMIR (European Market Infrastructure Regulation), CSDR (Central Securities Depositories Regulation), SFD (Social Fund for Development), MiFID/MiFIR (Markets in Financial Instruments Directive and Regulation), UCITs (Undertakings for Collective Investments Securities), and AIFMD (Alternative Investment Fund Managers Directive), could provide a regulatory framework for the governance of virtual currencies and DLTs in line with the activities carried out, irrespective of the underlying technology. Even as virtual currencies and DLT-based applications expand into new markets and extend their activities, more tailor-made legislation might be needed. With respect to the Anti-Money Laundering Directive that seeks to end the anonymity associated with such platforms, the European Parliament expects that any proposal in this regard will be targeted, justified by means of a full analysis of the risks associated with virtual currencies, and based on a thorough impact assessment.[12]

European Securities and Markets Authority (ESMA)

"ESMA is an independent EU authority that contributes to safeguarding the stability of the EU's financial system by enhancing the protection of investors and promoting stable and orderly financial markets."[13] It had undertaken in 2015 a study of virtual currency entitled "Call for Evidence." It noted that virtual currency investment products consist of two different types, namely, collective investment schemes (CISs), and exchange platforms that offer different types of virtual currency derivatives. It identified 12 collective investment schemes, two regulated companies based in Europe that offer financial contracts for difference (CFDs) in bitcoins and litecoins; 17 active platforms that offer CFDs or binary options for bitcoins or litecoins; and a number of exchange platforms that offer futures and other derivatives that are unregulated and their locations unknown.

ESMA's focus was on three issues: (1) investment products which have virtual currency as an underlying funding platform; (2) investment in virtual currency-based assets/securities, and the transfer of those assets/securities; and (3) other uses of the distributed ledger in relation to investment. The document, while raising the issues, asked for comments from investors and other participants. Specifically, ESMA noted that with respect to the first issue, there are traditional investments that may have exposure to virtual currencies such as collective investment schemes or potentially non-registered derivatives such as options and contracts for difference. For the second issue, wherein traditional assets are exchanged for virtual currencies, and the third issue concerning other uses beyond virtual currency that may be applicable to investors, ESMA asked for comments and responses to a series of questions illustrating its concern about the size and volume of DLT-based uses; the profile of investors; and other related issues.[14]

A number of months thereafter, in June, 2016, ESMA published the responses to the questions raised in April, 2015. It described the benefits and risks of DLT to securities markets within the EU. The benefits noted were:

• Clearing and settlement—increased speed, efficiency, elimination of multiple third parties, and possible one-step process for clearing and settlement;
• Record of ownership and safekeeping of assets—promote a unique database, remove contractual ambiguities through smart contracts, increased automation, directly issue digital securities, track ownership, and act as a trusted source;
• Reporting and oversight—facilitate collection, consolidation, and sharing of data by use of a singular source;

- Counterparty risk—shorten the settlement cycle of the transaction and possibly remove the need for a central clearing facility because of the immediacy of the settlement;
- Efficient collateral management—reduce and/or remove counterparty risk for cash/spot transactions, and improve processing or reduce the need for collateral movements;
- Availability—permit transactions on a seven-day, 24-hour basis;
- Security and reliance—DLT is highly secure and resistant to cyberattacks;
- Costs—major benefit of significant reduction of costs by reducing the need for individual ledgers and business continuity plans; and
- Additional benefits—enhanced pre-trade information, ease of advertising, matching of buyers and sellers, and verification of ownership.[15]

The key challenges, according to the 2016 discussion paper are:

- Technological issues—interoperability with existing systems and between different networks; the need to settle in central bank money and a recourse mechanism; position netting; and margin finance and short selling;
- Governance and privacy issues—the need for rules for the non-permissioned and the permissioned systems to validate transactions, minimum capital requirements, focus on the prevention of fraud or error, correction mechanisms and penalties, and possible intellectual property violations; privacy invasion may occur with Know Your Customer requirements, and storage of private data;
- Regulatory and legal issues—fitting the DLT into the existing regulatory framework, legality and enforceability of the records kept on DLT, and supervision of the DLT network;
- Key risks—cyber risk, fraud, and money laundering; operational risks; market volatility, interconnectedness, and new pockets of risks; fair competition and orderly markets;
- Other risks—complexity of encryption techniques, and uncertainty that may arise with the migration of the DLT to a new environment.[16]

European Union's New Blockchain Initiative

The EU Commission with support from the EU Parliament launched the E.U. Blockchain Observatory and Forum whose purpose is to "highlight key developments of the blockchain technology, promote European actors and reinforce engagement with multiple stakeholders involved in blockchain activities."[17] Having recognized the technology as a "major breakthrough" that will inevitably transform how business models in the numerous areas of financial activity will be transformed, it noted that the benefits accruing will reduce costs while increasing trust, traceability, and security. The Observatory and Forum will monitor blockchain developments, fund projects, cooperate with existing EU states' and businesses' initiatives, ensure transnational co-operation, consolidate expertise, and address challenges arising from the use of blockchain. It will partner with ConsenSys,[18] which has established itself as a global leader in the blockchain ecosystem.

European Court of Justice Ruling

Does the exchange of fiat currencies for comparable value Bitcoin virtual currency and vice versa constitute a transaction subject to VAT (Value Added Tax) under Article 2 of the VAT Directive which imposes the tax on the supply of goods and/or services for a consideration within the territory of a member state of the EU? The European Court of Justice rendered a judgment on October 22, 2015 in response to a request for a preliminary ruling from the Supreme Administrative Court of Sweden. The Court noted that Article 14(1) of the Directive states that *supply of goods* shall mean the transfer of the right to dispose of tangible personal property as owner and Article 24(1) defines *supply of services* to mean any transaction that does not constitute a supply of goods.[19]

The Court stated: "first, that the 'bitcoin' virtual currency with bidirectional flow, which shall be exchanged for traditional currencies in the context of exchange transactions, cannot be characterized as 'tangible property' within the meaning of Article 14(1) of the Directive, given that virtual currency has no purpose other than as a means of payment" comparable to traditional currencies inasmuch as it is money which is legal tender. Therefore, transactions which involves the exchange of the currencies do not constitute a "supply of goods" under Article 14(1). With respect to "supply of services" to be subject to VAT, there must be a direct link between the services supplied and the consideration received by the taxable person. The court further determined that the transaction is a supply of services within Article 24(1); however, the said exchange of currencies falls within the exemptions stated in Article 135(1)e of the Directive which exempts means of payment from VAT. Bitcoin is neither a security conferring a property right nor a security of comparable nature, nor is it a current account or a deposit account that would have caused it to come within the ambit of the tax.[20]

The implications of the decision are that services that provide exchange services for bitcoins are exempt from VAT as are other exchange services that exchange foreign currencies. One commentator suggested that the exemption may be open to examination due to the anonymity afforded Bitcoin users and persons participating in the exchange of Bitcoin.[21]

Organisation for Economic Co-operation and Development (OECD)[22]

The OECD does not appear to have taken an official or recommended position regarding virtual currencies but its views have been expressed in several authorized articles by OECD staff. In a Working Paper, the OECD Chief of Staff discussed the nature and valuing of cryptocurrencies, their risk events, market volatility, fraud, substitutes for Bitcoin, and the diverse regulatory measures being taken by governmental entities. He noted a paradox in that the more unlawful and wrongful the anonymous use of cryptocurrencies, the more likely government are incentivized to intervene. In concluding remarks, he observed that the generic policy issues to be addressed include a discussion of whether to ban cryptocurrencies; grant recognition of the technology; best practices of registration for consumer protection; a level playing field for all players in the financial field; governmental backing for the currencies; and remedies for non-compliance of regulations.[23]

United Nations (UN)

The UN expressed its concern about virtual currency in the context of terrorism. In addition to resolutions condemning terrorism, it has commenced a joint project between the UN Counter-Terrorism Committee Executive Directorate and the Swiss non-governmental organization ICT4Peace entitled "Tech against Terrorism." The public-private endeavor is directed towards the prevention of the spread of terrorism through the use of the Internet. Included is the restraint of use of virtual currencies by the groups.[24]

G20

It appears that virtual currency, in particular, Bitcoin, will be on the agenda for the next G20[25] to take place on November 30–December 1, 2018 in Buenos Aires, Argentina. The French Finance Minister, Bruno Le Maire, proposed that the regulation of Bitcoin, and presumably other virtual currencies, will be on the agenda indicating international concern about the effect the new technology and currencies have on national and international economies.[26]

IOSCO

The International Organization of Securities Commissions (IOSCO) has commenced a study on the effects and consequences of the technologies underlying virtual currencies. In international meetings of the heads of national securities commissions, the benefits and risks of DLT and FinTech were discussed together with the challenges and regulatory efforts that national governments should consider and undertake.[27] On January 18, 2018, the IOSCO Board issued a communication warning wherein it stated that there are clear risks posed by Initial Coin Offerings (ICOs), generally in exchange for Bitcoin or Ether and even for fiat currency. The concern is that the offerings are often outside the legal jurisdiction of the customers thereby raising investor apprehensions. It made reference to a meeting of the IOSCO Board on October 17–19, 2017 that discussed the growing usage of Icos to raise capital as an area of concern.[28]

Many other international organizations are beginning to discuss and offer possible suggestions and commentaries on the development of virtual currencies and their effect upon the relevant spheres of concern. It appears that only effective co-operation among the various governmental and non-governmental entities will diminish Icos' and virtual currency exchanges' wrongdoings in the foreseeable future.

Selected Countries Permitting and/or Regulating Virtual Currencies[29]

Argentina

Argentina does permit trade in virtual currencies but also recognizes the difficulty of enforcing anti-money laundering regulations in their use. The country's Unidad de Informacion Financiera announced on July 4, 2014, that all financial services companies had to commence reporting all virtual currency transactions because of the perceived threat by criminal elements to conceal their financial dealing using cover provided by P2P transactions. The country is treating Bitcoin and other virtual currencies as currencies that are subject to its regulatory framework.[30]

Australia

Australia has issued a series of regulations concerning virtual currencies commencing in 2014.

On August 20, 2014, the Australian Taxation Office issued a series of rulings concerning the tax treatment of virtual currencies that was finalized on December 17, 2014. It determined that Bitcoin is not deemed to be money or a foreign currency but rather is treated as a barter arrangement for tax purposes and as an asset for capital gains tax purposes. Individuals who purchase digital currency are subject to the country's goods and services tax while businesses engaged in the exchange services of buying and selling digital currency, including Bitcoin, are required to pay income tax on the derived profits.

The Reserve Bank of Australia, which is the principal regulator of the country's payment system, maintains the view that digital currencies had not raised major concerns because of their limited use but, nevertheless, it is assessing whether the current regulatory framework could accommodate the new alternative mediums of exchange. The Australian Securities and Investments Commission has issued warnings about the risks of engaging in virtual currency transactions but had not issued regulations because it did not deem such engagements as providing financial services, although firms providing advice and arrangements for other persons may be subject to its regulatory authority over financial products.[31]

Austria

The Financial Market Authority of Austria has not issued any regulations concerning Bitcoin and other virtual currencies but has issued a warning, similar to other national central banks, of possible cryptofraud and urged extreme caution by investors because of the lack of governmental intervention and supervision for which reimbursement may not be available. It noted, for example, the Ponzi-like scheme of Sergei Mavrodi. Austria's prosecutors are investigating fraudulent activity with the Authority in an attempt to mitigate fraudulent activity.[32]

Belgium

Belgium, albeit issuing warnings of the dangers of engaging in virtual currency transactions, has not promulgated any regulations barring or regulating their use. The Belgian National Bank warns of the currencies' lack of legality as a means of payment and that any losses are not covered under the country's deposit guarantee scheme. It will await further development before acting further in this regard.[33]

Belarus

The government of Belarus in a decree, On Digital Economy Development, signed by President Alexander Lukashenko, on December 22, 2017, and an earlier announcement by the National Bank of Belarus, formally recognized cryptocurrencies, particularly Bitcoin and ICOs, permitting their exchange for the government's fiat currencies. The decree makes Belarus the first European country to grant recognition of the virtual currencies as legal currencies. All such exchanges will be tax free for five years.[34]

Brazil

Brazil's Central Bank, as most other national central banks, has issued a warning concerning digital currency again reciting the lack of guarantees; that they are brokered by non-financial entities; are volatile; are subject to illegal activities; and other standards warnings. It noted that the currencies did not pose a threat to Brazil's financial system but is following developments which may lead to regulatory enactments.[35] In a recent development, Brazil's Securities and Exchange Commission regulator (CVM) issued a prohibition against the purchase of cryptocurrencies by local investment funds alleging they are not considered to be financial assets. In a joint statement with the central bank in December, 2017, it warned of risks, albeit to date there has not been any regulation enacted by the country's legislature.[36]

Bulgaria

Bulgaria's regulation deals with the tax treatment of virtual currency. It appears that Bitcoin and other virtual currencies are treated as currencies for tax purposes requiring that income derived from such transactions be taxed as income from the sale and exchange thereof. Such income is reportable on the taxpayer's annual tax return.[37]

Canada

The Canadian Securities Administrators (CSA), in Staff Notice 46-307,[38] gave recognition to the increase in cryptocurrency offerings such as ICOs, ITOs, and sales of cryptocurrency funds. While acknowledging their impact in the provision of new opportunities to raise capital for businesses, nevertheless the CSA is concerned about their volatility, transparency, valuation, custody and liquidity, and the use of unregulated cryptocurrency exchanges. Accordingly, it advises that regulations require approval by the regulatory authority and a prospectus be given to the investor unless exempted. It specially provides, concerning cryptocurrency, that a platform that facilitates trade in coins/tokens may be securities that require compliance with governmental regulations unless exempted therefrom. A cryptocurrency exchange that offers cryptocurrencies that are securities must determine whether it is a marketplace and, if so, must comply with the rules governing exchanges or alternative trading systems.

It further noted that ICOs and ITOs used by businesses to raise capital from investors through the Internet by the exchange of fiat currency or a cryptocurrency such as Bitcoin, are similar to traditional company offerings because their value may increase or decrease dependent on how the business plan has been administered. Although businesses may believe that the exchange is exempt from governmental compliance measures, a coin or token may be deemed a security when examined in the totality of the transaction based on the economic realities of the transaction and a purposive interpretation of the objectives of the offerings. Therefore, in determining whether an investment contract exists, the government applies a test akin to the U.S. *Howey* case, to wit: (1) an investment of money; (2) in a common enterprise; (3) with the expectation of profit; and (4) to come significantly from the efforts of others.[39]

Unless exempt, such as exclusive dealings with accredited investors or if the issuer is relying on the use of the Offering Memorandum (OM) to non-accredited investors, certain prescribed details have to be furnished to investors including the nature of the business, the type of ecosystem utilized, the minimum and maximum offering amounts, intended use, time of expiration, and other important details. Factors that indicate the requirement for registration for determining whether a legal person is trading in securities for a business purpose are: (1) soliciting a broad base of investors, including retail investors; (2) using the Internet, including public websites and discussion boards, to reach a large number of potential investors; (3) attending public events, including conferences and meetups, to actively advertise the sale of the coins/tokens; and (4) raising a significant amount of capital from a large number of investors. Persons who are deemed to fall within the purview of the registration requirements will be subject to strict compliance standards.[40]

Columbia

Columbia's Central Bank (Banco de la Republica de Columbia) issued an Opinion in which it stated that only the Columbian peso may be used as a medium of exchange, effectively banning cryptocurrencies within the country. It does permit inhabitants to purchase them abroad as investments but warns of the attendant risks.[41]

Croatia

The Croatian National Bank, after noting that several transactions in Bitcoin had already taken place within the country. Croatia is following EU recommendations and regards the use of virtual currency as legal but it is not considered to be legal tender. It awaits further developments from its central bank, if any, in the future.[42]

Cyprus

Cyprus, after its Securities and Exchange Commission gave standard warnings of risks,[43] appears to welcome Bitcoin and other virtual currencies. In Limassol, Cyprus' second largest city, Bitcoin Cash was launched by Coinbase and Gdax in January, 2018 to act as a community center for discussions about Bitcoin hosted by alleged experts from the FinTech company, Hello Group. The city was also noted for the launch of its first

Bitcoin ATM in December, 2017.[44] As a financial center and alleged tax haven it should come as no surprise to the global community that virtual currency should flourish therein.

Czech Republic

Bitcoin, as well as other virtual currencies such as Litecoin, are not only legal within the Czech Republic but are being accepted for a variety of goods and services, from restaurants to taxi services. This has been described as Bitcoinmania.[45]

Denmark

Denmark's Financial Supervisory Authority had early on indicated that although the cryptocurrencies are unsafe, it did not intend to regulate them or their exchanges.[46] The Authority noted, however, that the Consumer Ombudsman is to be notified of payment substitutes to the extent that they are used to acquire goods and services before they are put into operation. Providers of payments services and e-money must be authorized by the Authority. Payment substitutes, which appear to include use of virtual currencies, are to comply with the provisions of the Payment Services Act that includes requirements for information to be provided to users, and liability regulations, charges, and redemption of any remaining balance.[47]

Estonia

Observing the remarkable rise of Bitcoin and other cryptocurrencies, Estonia decided to launch its own version of a virtual currency in late 2017. It was considering three models for the currency to be named "estcoin" which would be pegged to the euro. The managing director of Estonia's e-residency program stated that Estonia did not intend to conflict with the pronouncements of the European Central Bank but rather to permit its residents to become part of and facilitate in engagement with the global business community.[48] On the other hand, Mario Draghi, the president of the ECB, stated definitively, when posed with Estonia's initiative, that: "The currency of the euro zone is the euro."[49]

Finland

As with many other nations, Finland views virtual currency as a commodity rather than as a currency inasmuch as it is not in accord with its definition, according to the head of oversight at the Bank of Finland. Residents are free to engage in the purchase and trade of Bitcoin but have been advised of the attendant risks.[50]

France

The French Ministry for the Economy and Finance, in its Communique of July 11, 2014, instituted four measures to counteract the risks of illegal and fraudulent use of Bitcoin and other virtual currencies. To counteract the anonymity of the currencies, distributors of the bitcoins are required to identify and verify users subject to a capital gains tax with a threshold of margin tax of €5000, and institute a possible spending cap to protects users of and investors in the currency.[51]

The Ministry issued a report, after noting the risks among the multifunctionality of virtual currencies, in which it made a number of recommendations to prevent fraud and money laundering. Among the recommendations are three possible strategies, namely: (1) limiting the use of virtual currencies; (2) regulation and co-operation; and (3) knowledge and co-operation. For limiting the use, it suggests mandatory proof of identity when opening a virtual currency account; an obligation to declare such accounts; strictly capping the sums that can be paid by their use; and that the identity of a party to a transaction be checked using reliable means. For regulation and co-operation, it recommends harmonizing regulations concerning virtual currency exchanges at the EU and international level; preventing virtual exchanges located abroad, and who have French users, from circumventing French law; and setting a minimum requirement when the account is opened by a service provider. For the last recommendation of knowledge and investigations, it recommends an adaptation of the legal framework and investigative methods and the improvement of sector knowledge and risk monitoring.[52]

Germany

Germany treats virtual currencies, and specifically bitcoins, as units of account, i.e., as financial instruments comparable to foreign exchange but which are not legal tender under the German Payment Services Supervision Act. They may be used privately as a means of payment in barter transactions and as a substitute currency contractually under private law. They differ from digital currencies such as e-money, which does have a central authority and is considered as legal tender. When used privately as a substitute for cash or deposit money in exchange transactions, for sale or acquisition of the currencies, or by self-mining, they do not require government authorization. When, however, the transactions are performed commercially via platforms as exchanges, then the panoply of government authorizations would be required including being subject to taxation and other governmental applications.[53]

Greece

Greece has not enacted any legislation or regulation regarding virtual currencies other than to warn potential users of the attendant risks. It does have anti-money laundering laws and regulations that may be applicable but for the foreseeable future users may transact virtual currencies without regulatory concern unless fraud and other malfeasance occurs.[54]

Hong Kong SAR

Although part of China, this is an autonomous region and appears to have taken advantage of China's prohibition of virtual currency. The Hong Kong-based exchange, Tidebit, launched in 2015, is handling a sizeable quantum of Bitcoin as investors fled mainland China for the welcoming atmosphere in the region.[55] The government, through its Financial Services and Treasury Bureau and the Securities and Futures Commission (SFC), has launched a campaign to educate the public about the risks and dangers of investing in ICOs and virtual currency. The Commission also noted that digital tokens may be subject to its jurisdiction as securities.[56]

The SFC again warned about the potential risks of dealing in cryptocurrency exchanges in or connected to Hong Kong on February 9, 2018. It issued warning letters to seven cryptocurrency exchanges within the island city region stating that they should not trade on exchanges in Hong Kong or those with connections to Hong Kong warning them that they should not trade cryptocurrencies which are "securities" as defined in the Securities and Futures Ordinance (SFO) without a license. Most of the exchanges indicated that they had either not engaged in cryptocurrency exchanges or had ceased doing so by removing them from their platforms. The SFC's CEO, Ashley Alder, urged the exchanges and market professionals to act as gatekeepers to prevent fraud and dubious fundraising that often occur through crowdfunding.

The Hong Kong SFC had received numerous complaints from investors who indicated that they were unable to withdraw fiat currencies or cryptocurrencies from their accounts that were opened by cryptocurrency exchanges. They complained of misappropriation of assets, manipulation of the market, or technical breakdowns that resulted in substantial losses. The SFC's Executive Director of Intermediaries, Julia Leung, stated: "If investors cannot fully understand the risks of cryptocurrencies and ICOs or they are not prepared for a significant loss, they should not invest,… Investors who store their fiat currencies and cryptocurrencies with unregulated cryptocurrency exchanges should be aware of the risks of hacking and misappropriation of assets." The Commission further warned of extreme price volatility, hacking, and its inability to prosecute fraud because of the extraterritorial nature of the exchanges.[57]

Hungary

Hungary initiated legislation in 2018, namely the Blockchain and Virtual Currency Regulation.[58] The regulation covers the whole range of legal issues affecting the technology and currency in considerable detail. Previously, the Central Bank of Hungary issued the typical warnings of risks associated with the new technologies. It cautioned about the currency's susceptibility to theft, volatility, and lack of government backing.[59]

Iceland

Iceland had experienced a serious financial crisis whereby its banking system was in jeopardy. Capital controls that had been in place under the Foreign Exchange Act No. 87/1992 were amended in late 2016 (No. 826/2017) to permit almost unrestricted investments using Icelandic currency to make purchases. Presumably, this will include the purchase of virtual currencies likely viewed as commodities.[60]

India

There is much confusion in India concerning whether to permit the exchange of cryptocurrencies and, if so, the regulatory requirements to be imposed. Although banking officials have voiced concern, nevertheless the purchase, sale, and exchange of bitcoins and other cryptocurrencies appear to be flourishing. India's Central Bank has warned speculators on a number of occasions not to purchase bitcoins due to the likelihood of significant losses caused by the bubble created in trading and which has cost investors a premium of 20 percent above purchases outside of India.[61] A new type of cryptocurrency, Laxmicoin, appears to be the latest speculative entre in digital currency. It operates like Bitcoin, is also based on blockchain technology, and a total coin supply of 30 million is awaiting approval and consent from the Reserve Bank of India.[62]

Indonesia

The Bank Indonesia has stated that virtual currencies, including Bitcoin, are not recognized as lawful currency and are forbidden for use as payment in Indonesia. Its Act No. 7/2011 on the Currency states that currency shall be money issued by the Republic of Indonesia and every transaction that has the purpose of payment, or other obligations which need to be satisfied with money, or other financial transactions conducted within the territory of the Republic of Indonesia, has to be fulfilled with Rupiah. After noting the risks thereof, it affirms the prohibition of all payment systems and financial technology operators in Indonesia, both bank and non-bank institutions, from processing transactions using virtual currency, as stated in Bank Indonesia Regulation No. 18/40/PBI/2016 on Implementation of Payment Transaction Processing and Bank Indonesia Regulation No. 19/12/PBI/2017 on Implementation of Financial Technology.[63] It appears that Bitcoin and other such currencies may be purchased and sold as such but may not be used as payment for goods or services.

Iran

Iran, which had banned cryptocurrencies, is conducting a review and appears to be more permissive in permitting the use of virtual currencies. The Deputy Director of the Central Bank of Iran, Naser Hakimi, while warning of the risks and uncertainty of their use, nevertheless, envisioned a positive side by offering traders unable to gain credit alternative means of attaining investment capital.[64] Iran has been the target of international sanctions and continues to be under such threat especially from the current U.S. administration.

Ireland

The Central Bank of Ireland has been quoted in the Dáil Éireann, which is the Assembly of Ireland and the principal chamber of the Oireachtas, the Irish Parliament, that it does not regulate bitcoins, and they are not considered to be legal tender within the EU. The Revenue Commissioners have expressed concern about tax evasion with respect to any gains from their use and VAT charges. It determined that tax evasion for the present is not extensive but will continue to monitor their use.[65]

Israel

Israel has not enacted legislation regulating virtual currencies although it cautions its citizens to be cautious in their investments in the new currencies. A likely reason for a more hand-off approach may be due to Israel's high-tech leadership. In a joint statement by the Bank of Israel, the Capital Market, Israel Securities Authority, and the Israel Money Laundering and Terror Financing Prohibition Authority, the state is monitoring the use and trade in virtual currencies and their macro-effects, risks, terror financing, and taxation.[66]

Italy

Italy's Central Bank has issued a series of pronouncements concerning virtual currency following closely the recommendations of the ECB. Its *Warnings on the use of virtual currencies*, and its *Notice About the use of virtual currencies*, both of January 30, 2015, apparently echo that of the European Banking Authority (EBA) and the Financial Action Task Force, and the bank also states that it recognizes the legality of the use of virtual currency and its exchange for non-legal tender amounts while advising financial institutions not to buy or invest in the currencies pending the creation of a formal legal framework for their exchange. The bank's *Notice of Central Authority for Reporting on virtual currencies* of February 2, 2015, differs from other regulatory regimes in that, although financial institutions are to comply with existing AML/KYC (Anti-Money Laundering/ Know Your Customer) requirements, businesses that engage in virtual currencies are not required to follow the said requirements.[67]

Japan

Effective April 1, 2017, the Japanese government gave recognition to virtual currency by amending its Banking Act by adding §3 known as "The Virtual Currency Act." It recognizes virtual currency as "asset-like values" that are electronically recorded, excluding Japanese currency, foreign currency, and currency-denominated assets, that are usable as payment for goods or services to "indefinite parties" and which can be transmitted by electronic data processing systems.[68] Although not considered legally as a currency, virtual currency is recognized as a method of payment and as an asset that has taxable consequences comparable to the exchange of other assets. The Act distinguishes virtual currency from digital currency which is defined as a currency-denominated asset exchangeable for monetary obligations or repayment.[69] Virtual currency exchanges that provide services for the conversion of virtual currencies and real currencies are also given recognition and made subject to regulations that require extensive registration requirements under the Amended Settlement Act.[70]

Jordan

The Central Bank of Jordan, as many other national banks, warned that Bitcoin and other virtual currencies are not legal tender and pose significant non-reimbursable risks to users. A circular was issued to banks from the executive director of the payment services at the Central Bank, Maha Bahu, that all banks, exchange services, financial companies, and payment service companies are prohibited from dealing with the said virtual currencies. There was evidence of hacking at two exchanges that has created anxiety concerning their use.[71]

Lebanon

The Governor of the central bank of Lebanon, Governor Riad Salameh of Banque du Liban, similarly warned of the risks of virtual currencies, banned their use, and made reference to the Central Bank of Jordan's position. He noted, however, that electronic currency will play a prominent role in the future and thus announced a plan to introduce the bank's own digital currency based on blockchain technology.[72]

Lithuania

The (central) Bank of Lithuania issued a somewhat comprehensive review and position referencing virtual currencies. Its conclusions were as follows: (1) financial market participants (FMPs) providing financial services should not participate in activities or provide services associated with virtual currencies; (2) the FMPs should ensure actual separation of the financial services provision activity from activities associated with virtual currencies, as well as ensure appropriate and non-misleading communication about the nature of services provided by FMPs; and (3) in providing financial services to customers who are engaged in activities associated with virtual currencies, FMPs should ensure compliance with the requirements of money laundering and terrorist financing prevention legislation, and take appropriate measures to manage the risk of money laundering and/or terrorist financing. Referencing ICOs, the bank noted that when the ICOs have the characteristics of securities, they are subject to the country's laws concerning securities. When they have the characteristics of crowdfunding, collective investment undertakings, investment services, or financial instruments, they also are subject to applicable laws regulating them.[73]

Luxembourg

The Grand Duchy of Luxembourg, through its financial regulatory authority (CSSF), takes the position that no one may undertake activity within the financial sector without permission from the Minister of Finance in accordance with Article 14 of the Law of April 5, 1993. Accordingly, persons transacting virtual currencies as means of payment, creation, or exchange are required to receive ministerial authorization. Its press release does indicate that the CSSF is willing to regulate the new currencies which, unlike other nation-states, treats Bitcoin as scriptural money and not as a commodity.[74] Thus, it appears that the use of virtual currencies is not unwelcome and some commentators believed that the Grand Duchy could act as a hub for the new currencies.[75]

Malaysia

The Malaysian Central Bank, Bank Negara Malaysia, is undertaking a proposed cryptocurrency regulation that will regulate use. Its Governor indicated concern over possible criminal and other unlawful use of the currency which will be made subject to the country's Anti-Money Laundering, Anti-Terrorism Financing and Proceeds of Unlawful Activities Act of 2001. The use of cryptocurrency is apparently not banned but will be made subject to significant governmental oversight.[76]

Mexico

Mexico does not recognize virtual currencies, particularly Bitcoin, as currency because of its lack of central bank standing. Nevertheless, the country has been permissive to date in permitting the purchase and trade of cryptocurrencies. There are currently a number of proposed legislative actions that recognize the value of digital assets in transforming and updating the technological financial sector of the economy.[77] In its most recent pronouncement, Mexico's finance ministry and central bank have warned investors and users of the risks of cryptocurrencies and that ICOs and attempts to raise funds for them may violate the country's markets and securities laws, although there have not been any ICOs to date.[78]

Netherlands

The Bank of the Netherlands, on May 8, 2014, issued a statement "Virtual Currencies Are Not a Viable Alternative" in which it cautioned that they are unlikely to replace the current financial system and fiat money (the euro) and are innately risk-laden. It did state that "neither the central bank nor any other official body has required any Bitcoin-related businesses to obtain a license or face any type of official scrutiny." Dutch banks have been willing to engage in business with the new forms of currencies and regulators are not exercising authority over Bitcoin startups, thereby allowing the technological development to occur and expand. It appears that the government is acting as a pioneer in the development of the new technologies.[79]

New Zealand

New Zealand is taking a hands-off policy toward cryptocurrencies. The New Zealand Reserve Bank representative, Toby Fiennes, stated in early 2018 that the bank will not issue regulations targeting malfeasance in connection with the currencies even in the light of ransomware and other threats posed by their use. He was quoted as stating: "The dynamic cyber environment means that organizations have to be nimble in their approach to cyber security – focused on outcomes, rather than prescriptive compliance exercises….Looking forward, the Reserve Bank and other regulators will need to make sure the regulatory regime in New Zealand is adaptive should any new business models become systemic, while not unduly harming innovation."[80]

Norway

It appears that Norway has a receptive attitude toward Bitcoin and likely other virtual currencies. At least one bank in Norway, Norwegian Skandianbanken, is permitting customers to integrate their Bitcoin wallet holdings with fiat deposits, enabling them to examine the value of their holdings simultaneously.[81] In 2013, the Norwegian Tax Administration stated that as a capital property, profits made from such sales are taxable.[82]

Philippines

The Bangko Sentral Ng Pilipinas issued a circular in 2017, setting forth the guidelines for virtual currency exchanges within the Philippines. It states that the policy of the central bank is to provide an environment that encourages innovation while at the same time ensuring that it is not used for money laundering or terrorist financing but also that customers are adequately protected. It specifically recognizes that virtual currencies have the potential to revolutionize the delivery of financial services with a faster, economical transfer of funds both domestically and internationally. The central bank thus intends to regulate them to ensure the said policy goals are met. Exchanges are required to procure a certificate of registration from the bank in order to engage in transfer of the currency.[83]

Poland

Poland's central bank, the National Bank of Poland and the Polish Financial Supervision Authority, while not banning the use of cryptocurrencies, has expressed significant concern about their risks and has engaged in a campaign to discourage inhabitants from transacting in them.[84] The bank has a website called "watch out for cryptocurrencies" that contains warnings about the dangers of investing in the currencies as well as the standard comments about lack of governmental protection and guarantees, and several other risks.[85]

Portugal

The Bank of Portugal (Banco de Portugal) issued the standard warnings about the risks attendant to virtual currencies and presumably they comply with EU Council and Parliament directives. A director of the bank stated its concerns noting that virtual currencies, specifically Bitcoin, is a convention, a computerized solution based on a very powerful technological base, a fantastic network, the blockchain, which allows payments without intermediation. He suggested the bank is reviewing measures to evaluate the new reality in order to regulate their unlawful use.[86]

Saudi Arabia

Saudi Arabia has taken a hands-off approach to ICOs, Bitcoin, and other virtual currencies believing that the market for these currencies is too immature within the kingdom for regulatory purposes. The Saudi Arabia

Monetary Authority is monitoring virtual currencies and may take steps in future years to regulate them when they become more relevant.[87]

Serbia

The National Bank of Serbia made reference to the views of the European Banking Authority issuing the standard warnings and advising that the dinar is the currency of Serbia and that all payments are settled in dinar-denominated means of payment. Virtual currencies are subject to the Law on Payment Transactions and the Law on Foreign Exchange Operations. Pursuant to the Decision on Types of Foreign Exchange and Foreign Cash to be Purchased and Sold in the Foreign Exchange Market, banks and licensed exchange dealers may buy and sell foreign cash only in currencies stipulated by the Decision. It appears that Bitcoin and other virtual currencies may be privately purchased but exchange into Serbia's fiat money may violate its statutory and regulatory provisions.[88]

Singapore

The Monetary Authority of Singapore (MAS) stated that the offer or issuance of digital tokens will be regulated by MAS if the tokens are deemed to constitute "products" under the Securities and Futures Act. As in all other national entities, the concern is money laundering and terrorist financing. Referencing its first pronouncement on March 13, 2014, wherein it stated that virtual currencies were not per se regulated, the clarification of August 1, 2017 details the government's concern about the rise and risks of the currencies and the degree of regulation required. The communique stated its observation that the function of digital tokens has evolved beyond that of a virtual currency and may, for example, represent ownership or a security interest over an issuer's assets or property. Therefore, they may be considered as an offer of shares or units in a collective investment scheme which would make them subject to Singapore's Securities and Futures Act. They may also constitute a debt and thus a debenture under the Act. If so, then the digital token issuance would

have to comply with licensing and other statutory and regulatory requirements. Issuers are warned to seek appropriate legal advice as to whether
registration requirements are applicable.[89]

Slovenia

Slovenia also has issued extensive warnings of the risks of virtual currencies. A concern that arose is the taxation of transactions involving bitcoins
and other such currencies. In essence, its Tax Administration's position is
that they are not monetary assets under its laws and thus individuals selling bitcoins are not subject to capital gains or income tax. Miners accruing
rewards and the like, however, may be taxed like any other income from
profits generated from trading and mining bitcoins.[90]

South Africa

The South African Reserve Bank issued a Position Paper on Virtual
Currencies.[91] It states that under the South African Reserve Bank Act,
only the bank may issue banknotes and coins. It reiterates the risks attendant to virtual currencies, their lack of status as legal tender, and government backing. It also notes that currently they do not pose a substantial
risk to the national currency, although monitoring will be required to
ascertain their interconnection. The Paper does emphasize potential positive aspects of the new technologies and currencies. Although reserving
the right to change its stance, the bank is withholding any regulations
impeding the exchange of virtual currencies.

South Korea

Like the People's Republic of China, South Korea has taken a dim view
of virtual currency, weighing up whether to ban it entirely or heavily
enforce restrictions. In September, 2017, the Suwon district court held
against the government in a police seizure of bitcoins with respect to an
individual who had operated an illegal pornography website for four

years. The court stated that it was not legally proper for authorities to seize bitcoins because they are in the form of electronic files and have no physical status like cash, so cannot assume to have any objective standard value.[92] The government's Justice, Park Sang-ki, stated that a bill was being prepared to ban cryptocurrency trading after a series of raids on banks trading the virtual currency allegedly for tax evasion. An immediate result was the plummeting of the value of Bitcoin within the country.[93] In addition to the question of tax evasion, the Financial Services Commission and the Financial Supervisory Service jointly inspected six banks to ascertain whether there was money-laundering activity, use of false names for accounts, and to provide guidance to the banks concerning how better to supervise activities.[94]

A constitutional appeal has been lodged immediately after the imposition of the country's anti-virtual currency regulations alleging that cryptocurrencies are not legal tender but rather property or assets that can be exchanged through legitimate currencies for other goods that have economic value.[95]

Spain

The Spanish Government's General Directorate of Taxes issued a binding ruling on March 30, 2015 stating that the purchase and sale of virtual currencies, namely, bitcoins, is exempt from VAT as they constitute financial services. The ruling cited EU Council Directive 2006/112/EC of November 28, 2006 that rendered such transactions as exempt. A discussion is provided in the European Union section above.[96]

Sweden

The Sveriges Riksbank (Swedish central bank) stated that Bitcoin and Ethereum are special forms of currency and are not subject to regulation, and issuers are not under financial supervision. It states that transactions in Bitcoin and other virtual currencies are minor having little impact on Sweden's finances and, thus, require no intervention. It has noted the risks to investors, which are private in nature, and they have been forewarned of the dangers of virtual currencies.[97] With the significant decline in the use of the fiat currency, the krona, Sweden is considering a new national digital currency, e-krona, that would complement the krona offering users a choice for payment transactions.[98]

Switzerland

In a Federal Council report on virtual currencies, it concluded that "the economic importance of virtual currencies as a means of payment is fairly insignificant at the moment and the Federal Council believes that this will not change in the foreseeable future." Therefore, the Swiss National Bank does not intend to issue any regulations restricting such transactions. It will rely on existing statutes to guard against criminal activities and money laundering, which requires verification of the identity of the contracting party and of the beneficial owner. Also, certain business models based on virtual currencies are subject to financial market laws and may require financial market supervision. As in all other discussions, the Council noted the risks to consumers and the need to advise them to take appropriate measures to prevent losses. It will continue to monitor the use of virtual currencies which may later require governmental intervention.[99]

Taiwan

After banning virtual currencies in Taiwan in 2015,[100] the chairman of the Taiwanese Financial Supervisory Commission, Wellington Koo, stated that it need not emulate the actions of China and South Korea in banning ICOs and virtual currencies but rather it should follow Japan's lead in treating "cryptocurrency as a highly regulated, highly monitored industry like securities." There is pending legislation, the Financial Technology Experimentation Act, that would allow ICOs subject to significant government oversight. Taiwan does have active cryptocurrency participation with MaiCoin, a digital assets exchange platform with 25,000 users and AMIS, a blockchain consultancy connected to MaiCoin that has major investors.[101]

Thailand

The Bank of Thailand had initially banned Bitcoin, and presumably other cryptocurrencies, as illegal in 2013. Bitcoin Co. Ltd. had attempted to negotiate its right to trade bitcoins within the country but Thailand's Foreign Exchange Administration and Policy Department stated that such trades may have financial consequences that violate existing regulations.[102] Thereafter, in February, 2014, the bank reversed its position permitting the company to resume operations. In a letter to the company, the bank indicated that the company's exchange operations are not subject to the Finance Ministry's regulations unless foreign currencies are offered in exchange. Cryptocurrencies like Bitcoin are not considered to be currencies or legal tender but rather electronic data that innately have no value.[103]

Turkey

Turkey's Banking Regulation and Supervision Agency (BRSA), in a press release of November 25, 2013, gave the standard warning about Bitcoin and similar virtual currency risks including that of criminal activities, theft of digital wallets, and volatility. It further stated thereafter that inasmuch as virtual currencies are not considered to be electronic money, "its surveillance and audit in scope of the Law [*The* Law on Payment and Securities Settlement Systems, Payment Services and Electronic Fund Institutions] does not seem possible."[104]

United Arab Emirates

The United Arab Emirates (UAE), while also initially appearing to ban virtual currencies, clarified its regulation that went into effect on January 1, 2017 which contained the phrase "all virtual currencies [and transactions thereof] are prohibited." The Central Bank of the UAE stated explicitly that virtual currencies including Bitcoin are not banned but rather their use is under review, which status will be under regulations to be issued in the future. Attorneys for persons using the currencies are told to exercise caution until the regulations are clarified.[105]

United Kingdom

The United Kingdom (UK) and particularly London, as other centers of commercial activity, has become a center for money-laundering through the use of virtual currencies according to Scotland Yard which has called for an overhaul of the regulations concerning their unlawful use.[106] There appears to be no direct legislation that directly regulates virtual currencies that up to now have been outside the scope of the UK payment system that rivals the United States as a global financial center. As in the United States there are anti-money laundering regulations which the government intends to apply to the currencies that would be in compliance with the EU's proposed changes to the EU Fourth Anti-Money Laundering Directive. UK banks, clearly feeling threatened, are opposed to the UK's pragmatic step of providing a regulatory environment for the new currencies and has taken steps to create its own virtual currency which would become part of the Bank of England's review of the Real-Time Settlement system. As in the EU, there is no VAT on virtual currency mining but there may be tax consequences for individuals and corporations that have realized gains or losses when owning and selling virtual currencies which are treated similarly to gains and losses on fiat currency transactions.[107]

The 2015 UK Treasury report, in response to a call for information, outlined the benefits and risks of virtual currencies.[108] The benefits repeated those of others cited (speed, security, wider use of DLT for transfer and recording of securities, and the like), which need not be elaborated upon again. Noteworthy are the risks posed: anonymity of criminal behavior; cross-border transfers that make illicit activity difficult to control; ransomware that allows criminals to extort payments for computer disruptions; money laundering; evasion of tax and penalties; and risks to the financial and monetary stability of the UK and EU. Notwithstanding the risks posed by DLT, the UK concluded that it was committed to the encouragement of new and innovative payments and technological development; to enforce anti-money laundering regulations; give law enforcement tools and support to combat criminal use of DLT; work with the British Standards Institution and the digital industry to develop pioneering voluntary standards for consumer protection; offer innovative payment options in competition with existing DLT;

coordinate with scientific and engineering firms to address the challenges brought about by the new technologies; and undertake central bank-issued digital currencies.[109]

Vietnam

Vietnam has also issued the standard warning to its inhabitants about investing in virtual currencies. The Ministry of Public Security warned about Ponzi-like schemes that have caused major financial losses globally and has been monitoring trading platforms and investment schemes that have resulted in a number of arrests and shutdowns of firms that have acted unlawfully. Nevertheless, Vietnam has Bitcoin community banks and exchanges, such as Airbitclub and BitKingdom, that have been allowed to operate openly without governmental intervention.[110] Regulations are being considered that may have a substantial impact on virtual currencies.[111]

Countries Banning Bitcoin and Other Virtual Currencies

Bangladesh

Bangladesh Bank declared that the bank and other government institutions do not recognize the legality of virtual currency and it is not approved for payments or other purposes within the country. Traders face possible imprisonment of up to 12 years for engaging in the exchange of bitcoins.[112]

Bolivia

Bolivia's Central Bank (BCB) has banned the circulation and use of virtual currencies. Pursuant to Resolution No. 044/2014, regulations were issued on May 6, 2014 making such usage unlawful. The Bolivian Supervisory Authority of the Financial System detained some 60 crypto-currency promoters who had been arrested by police authorities. The promoters allegedly were training others to engage in the forbidden trade.[113]

China

The People's Republic of China (PRC) caused a tumble in Bitcoin value when its central bank declared ICOs for digital token sales to be illegal. Conversions of coins to digital tokens are forbidden. Companies that had engaged in such offerings were to refund all moneys received from sales and faced fines for the offerings.[114] The PRC did so by the release of two notices: (1) Notice of Seven Ministries Including the People's Bank of China on Guard against Risks of Token Offering and Financing (Joint Notice) and (2) Notice on the Rectification of Token Offering and Financing Activities.[115] The Notice of Seven Ministries stated that the financing activity through the use of virtual currencies involves unlawful sales of token, securities, and fund-raising and is not legal tender. Thus, all types of token offerings are declared illegal; entities and individuals participating in them are to withdraw the offerings and financing; and governmental authorities are to investigate and prosecute violations thereof. All trading on exchanges is to cease forthwith and provide no services in connection thereto. Financial institutions and non-financial payment institutions are forbidden from providing accounts, or underwriting and insuring, and shall report all transactions concerning virtual currencies.[116]

In the Notice on the Rectification of Token Offering and Financing Activities, local offices of the Internet Financial Risks Rectification Working Group are to investigate ICO offerings and activities and report them to the local offices in their jurisdiction and a copy be sent to the China Banking Regulatory Commission, the China Insurance Regulatory Commission, and the China Securities Regulatory Commission by September 4, 2017. Local offices are to investigate and prosecute infractions including interviewing, monitoring accounts, and freezing assets of platform executives if violations are discovered. As a result of the prohibition of sales of virtual currencies,[117] Chinese investors, prohibited from engaging in virtual currency exchanges in China are looking to Japan and other nations that give recognition to the transfer of digital assets.[118]

Ecuador

The National Assembly of Ecuador banned Bitcoin and other decentralized virtual currencies and created a new state-run electronic currency in its place. The goal, according to the government, is to assist the underserved segments of the population but may also be an effort to undermine its fiat currency tie to the US dollar. The electronic money to be developed by the central bank will be backed by the assets of Banco Central del Ecuador.[119]

Kyrgyzstan

The National Bank of the Kyrgyz Republic declared that the Republic's sole legal tender is its own national currency and that the use of virtual currency, particularly Bitcoin, as a means of payment is a violation of its laws. Persons engaged in the use of the virtual currency are subject to "all of the possible negative consequences of the possible violation of the legislation of the Krygyz Republic."[120]

Morocco

Morocco, although stating it is interested in the technology underlying virtual currencies, nevertheless declared that virtual currencies are a violation of its foreign exchange regulations, which would cause users to be subject to penalties and fines. The Bank Al-Maghrib and the Morocco Office des Changes (Foreign Exchange Office) in co-operation with the Professional Group of Banks of Morocco stated that any such use in connection with foreign countries that do not utilize the country's authorized intermediaries are subject to criminal penalties.[121]

Nepal

The Nepal Rastra Bank issued a Bitcoin Ban Notice causing the shutdown of the country's Bitsewa digital currency exchange. A number of people were previously arrested for engaging in Bitcoin trades which subjected them to fines and up to three years' imprisonment.[122]

Alternative National Virtual Currency

Russia and Venezuela

Russia and Venezuela, faced with sanctions, are exploring alternative possibilities for virtual currencies. Rather than an outright ban, they are exploring the possibility of creating their own state-sponsored form of cryptocurrency emulating the success to date of Bitcoin and its underlying technology. The concept is to create a new currency that could ignore the power of the U.S. dollar and the central control of the U.S. central bank as well as the central banks of the major Western European countries that have participated in the ban. Russia and Venezuela suggest that the new currency, Petro, backed by the countries' oil and other resources, and Russia's crypto-ruble, would avoid Western central banks' control over dominant currencies, thereby circumscribing the bans imposed upon the nations.[123] Although other nations are favorable to the idea of digital currencies, it appears that trust and acceptance are fundamental to virtual currencies having value, which may hinder acceptance of these national attempts.

Russia has gone further and the First Deputy Governor of the Central Bank of Russia, Olga Skorobogatova, has suggested that the BRIC countries (Brazil, Russia, India, and China) and the Eurasian Economic Union (EEU)[124] create their own joint digital currency rather than individual state virtual currencies. Official discussions of the concept are slated for some time in 2018 by the BRIC countries and the EEU member states. Earlier, in September, 2017, a similar suggestion was proposed by the head of the Russian Direct Investment Fund, Kirill Dmitriev, whereby the BRIC countries plus South Africa would have a joint virtual currency through the New Development Bank using the BRICS Interbank Cooperation Mechanism that would enable them to replace the U.S. dollar and other current currencies with the Chinese yuan as the lead currency to be used for the settlement of debts.[125]

Notes

1. The Bank for International Settlements, headquartered in Basel, Switzerland, was established on May 17, 1930 and is an international financial organization owned by 60 member national central banks and Hong Kong SAR, that make up about 95 percent of global GDP. Its mission is to serve central banks in their pursuit of monetary and financial stability, to foster international co-operation in those areas, and to act as a bank for central banks. https://www.bis/org/cpmi/publ/d137.htm
2. Committee On Payments and Market Infrastructures, *Digital currencies,* Bank for International Settlements, Nov., 2015, https://www.bis.org.cpmi/publ/d137.htm
3. Id.
4. European Central Bank, *Virtual Currency Schemes*, Oct. 2012, http://www.ecb.europa.eu/pub/pdf/other/virtualcurrencyschemes201210en.pdf
5. *Id.* For a discussion of the ECB's report and the EU's concern and regulation of virtual currencies, see Aneta Vondrackova, *Regulation of Virtual Currency in the European Union,* Prague Law Working Papers Series 2016/III/3, 2016, http://prf.cuni.cz/en/workingpapers-1404048982.html
6. *Virtual currency schemes – a further analysis,* European Central Bank, Feb. 2015, http://www.ecb.europa.eu/pub/pdf/other/virtualcurrencyschemesen.pdf
7. Directive (EU) 2015/849 of the European Parliament and of the Council of 20 May 2015 on the prevention of the use of the financial system for the purposes of money laundering or terrorist financing, amending Regulation (EU) No 648/2012 of the European Parliament and of the Council, and repealing Directive 2005/60/EC of the European Parliament and of the Council and Commission Directive 2006/70/EC, http://eur-lex.europa.eu/legal-content/EN/TXT/?uri=ce lex%3A32015L0849
8. European Commission, *Fact Sheet,* Memo 16/2381, http://europa.eu/rapid/press-release_MEMO-16-2381_en.htm
9. Proposed amendments to the Fourth Anti-Money Laundering Directive, http://www.europarl.europa.eu/RegData/etudes/BRIE/2017/607260/EPRS_BRI(2017)607260_EN.pdf. The text of the proposal for an amendment to (EU) 2015/849 is Eur. Parl. Doc. (COD) 2016/0208,

http://ec.europa.eu/justice/criminal/document/files/aml-directive_
en.pdf

10. Stan Higgins, *EU Report: Digital Currency Use by Organized Criminals is Rare*, CoinDesk, July 18, 2017, https://www.coindesk.com/eu-report-digital-currency-use-by-organized-criminals-is-rare/

11. European Commission, *Project to prevent criminal use of the dark web and virtual currencies launched by international consortium*, Cordis News and Events, http://cordia.europa.eu/news/ren/141335-html

12. Eur. Parl. Doc. (2016/2007(INI)) (May 26, 2016).

13. European Securities and Markets Authority, *About ESMA*, https://www.esma.europa.eu/about-esma/who-we-are

14. European Securities and Markets Authority, *Call for Evidence: Investment using virtual currency or distributed ledger technology*, April 22, 2015, ESMA/2015/532, https://www.esma.europa.eu/sites/default/files/library/2015/11/2015-532_call_for_evidence_on_virtual_currency_investment.pdf

15. European Securities and Markets Authority, *Discussion Paper: The Distributed Ledger Technology Applied to Securities Markets*, Feb. 6, 2016, ESMA 2016/773, https://www.esma.europa.eu/press-news/esma-news/esma-assesses-usefulness-distributed-ledger-technologies

16. *Id.*

17. European Commission, *European Commission launches the EU Blockchain Observatory and Forum*, Press Release, Feb. 1, 2018, http://europa.eu/rapid/press-release_IP-18-521_en.htm

18. ConsenSys, https://new.consensys.net/

19. European Court of Justice, Judgment, October 22, 2015, ECLI: EU:C:205:718, http://curia.eu/juris/document/document.jct?docid=1 70305&doclang=EN

20. *Id.*

21. Mirko L. Marinc, Koert Bruins, Roger van de Berg, and Esteban van Goor, *European Court of Justice decides on landmark case regarding the VAT treatment of bitcoin*, Lexology, Oct. 28, 2015, https://www.lexology.com/library/detail.aspx?g=f67931b0-9136-4a53-8b7c-47b762fe12f6

22. The OECD is composed of 35 countries, almost all from the developed world, the United States, Canada, Japan, South Korea, countries that are also members of the EU, Mexico, Chile, and other economic powers, *OECD About*, http://www.oecd.org/about/

23. Adrian Blundell-Wignall (2014), *The Bitcoin Question: Currency* versus *Trust-less Transfer Technology*, OECD Working Papers on Finance,

Insurance and Private Pensions, No. 37, (2014), https://doi.org/10.1787/5jz2pwjd9t20-en

24. United Nations Security Council Counter-Terrorism Committee, *Official Launch of Knowledge-sharing platform in support of the global tech industry tackling terrorist exploitation of the Internet,* (2017), https://www.un.org/sc/ctc/blog/event/official-launch-of-knowledge-sharing-platform-in-support-of-the-global-tech-industry-tackling-terrorist-exploitation-of-the-internet/

25. The G20 (Group of Twenty) consists of central bank governors of the leading industrial nations plus the EU. The nations represented are Argentina, Australia, Brazil, Canada, China, France, Germany, India, Indonesia, Italy, Japan, South Korea, Mexico, Russia, Saudi Arabia, South Africa, Turkey, the UK, the United States, and the EU.

26. *French finance minister calls for bitcoin debate at G20,* Reuters, Dec. 17, 2017, https://www.reuters.com/article/uk-markets-bitcoin-g20/french-finance-minister-calls-for-bitcoin-regulation-debate-at-g20-idUSKBN1EB0SZ

27. *IOSCO Plans to Research Blockchain Technology,* News BTC, Feb. 22, 2016, http://www.newsbtc.com/2016/02/22/iosco-plans-to-research-robo-advisors-and-the-blockchain-technology/

28. OICU-IOSCO, *IOSCO Board Communication on Concerns Related to Initial Coin Offerings (ICOs),* Media Release, Jan. 18, 2018, http://www.iosco.org/news/pdf/IOSCONEWS485.pdf

29. For an excellent guide, see Robin Arnfield, *Regulation of Virtual Currencies: A Global Overview* (2015), Virtual Currency Today, http://www.nfcidea.pl/wp-content/uploads/2015/02/Regulation-if-Virtual-Currancies-by-Jumio.pdf

30. La Unidad de Informacion Financiera, https://www.argentina.gob.ar/uif

31. Chapter 2, *Overview and recent developments: What is digital currency?,* Parliament of Australia, https://www.aph.gov.au/Parliamentary_Business/Committees/Senate/Economics/Digital_currency/Report/c02

32. *FMA in Austria Issues Warning against Fraudulent Virtual Currency Schemes,* News BTC, Nov. 15, 2016, http://www.newsbtc.com/2016/11/15/fma-in-austria-issues-a-warning-against-fradulent-virtual-currency-schemes/

33. Simont Braun, *Virtual Currency in Belgium,* http://www.simontbraun.eu/fr/news/1954-virtual-currency-in-belgium

34. *E-Money and virtual currencies,* Digitalwatch, Dec. 22, 2017, https://dig.watch/issues/e-money-and-virtual-currencies. For an untranslated

copy of the press release from the National Bank of Belarus, see decree, see https://www.nbrb.by/Press/?id=6534, cited in Coinformer, *State Bank in Belarus Builds on Blockchain,* Coinfirmation, July 19, 2017, http://coinfirmation.com/state-bank-of-belarus-builds-on-blockchain/

35. Nermin Hajdarbegovic, *Brazilian Central Bank Outline Digital Currency Risks,* CoinDesk, Feb. 20, 2014, https://www.coindesk.com/brazilian-central-bank-outlines-digital-currency-risks/

36. *Brazil regulator bans funds from buying cryptocurrencies,* Reuters, Jan. 12, 2018, https://uk.reuters.com/article/brazil-bitcoin/brazil-regulator-bans-funds-from-buying-cryptocurrencies-idUSL1N1P71DV

37. r/bitcoin, *Tax authorities in Bulgaria say bitcoin is "virtual currency",* Reddit, April 2, 2014, https://www.reddit.com/r/Bitcoin/comments/220ek1/tax_authorities_in_bulgaria_say_bitcoin_is/

38. Canadian Securities Adminsitrators, *Cryptocurrency Offerings,* Staff Notice 46-307, Aug. 24, 2017, http://www.osc.gov.on.ca/en/SecuritiesLaw_csa_20170824_cryptocurrency-offerings.htm

39. *Id.*

40. *Id.*

41. Opinion No. JDS 14696, July 12, 2016, cited in Carlos Fradique-Mendez and Sebastian Boada Morales, *Columbia: Virtual currency regulation,* Intn'l Financial L. Rev., Sept. 26, 2016, http://www.iflr.com/Article/3588434/Colombia-Virtual-currency-regulation.html

42. Maria Santos, *Croatia considers Bitcoin legal: 45 members of the Swiss parliament want the same,* Bitcoins, March 17, 2015, https://99bitcoins.com/croatia-considers-bitcoin-legal-45-members-of-the-swiss-parliament-want-the-same/

43. *CYSEC Announcement on Virtual Currency,* Global Banking and Finance Review, Nov. 21, 2017, https://globalbankingandfinance.com/cysec-announcement-on-virtual-currencies/

44. *Bitcoin Cash Embassy to Open in Limassol, Cyprus,* Bitcoin.Com, Dec. 20, 2017, https://news.bitcoin.com/bitcoin-cash-embassy-open-limassol-cyprus/

45. tom93, The Czech Republic is a Paradise for virtual currencies. You will pay Bitcoin in the village, Steemit, 2017, https://steemit.com/bitcoin/@tom93/the-czech-republic-is-a-paradise-for-virtual-currencies-you-will-pay-bitcoin-in-the-village

46. *'We Don't do Bitcoin': Denmark's finance director exempts crypto-currencies from its function,* RT, Dec. 17, 2013, https://www.rt.com/news/bitcoin-denmark-regulator-unsafe-395/

47. Denmark's National Bank, *Virtual Currencies*, http://www.national-banken.dk/en/publications/Documents/2014/03/Virtual_MON1_2014.pdf
48. Peter Teffer, *Estonia to launch own virtual currency*, EUobserver, Dec. 19, 2017, https://euobserver.com/economic/140344
49. Francesco Canepa, *ECB'sDraghi rejects Estonia's virtual currency idea*, Reuters, Sept. 7, 2017, https://www.reuters.com/article/us-ecb-bitcoin-estonia/ecbs-draghi-rejects-estonias-virtual-currency-idea-idUSKCN1BI2BI
50. Kati Pohjanpalo, *Finland Central Bank Rules Bitcoin Is Not A Currency*, Bloomberg, Jan. 20, 2014, https://mashable.com/2014/01/20/bitcoin-commodity-finland/#9wUWMiSqYPqp
51. Tanaya Macheel, *French Government Outlines New Regulations for Bitcoin Market Transparency*, Coindesk, July 11, 2014, https://www.coindesk.com/french-government-outlines-new-regulations-bitcoin-market-transparency/
52. Virtual Currencies Working Group, *Regulating Virtual Currencies*, Ministry for the Economy and Finance, June, 2014, https://www.economie.gouv.fr/files/regulatingvirtualcurrencies.pdf
53. BaFin, *Virtual Currencies (VCs)*, Federal Financial Supervisory Authority, https://www.bafin.de/EN/Aufsicht/FinTech/VirtualCurrency/virtual_currency_node_en.html
54. *The Legal Framework of Currency Exchange Licensing and Operation in Greece*, Law and Tech, Nov. 29, 2017, http://lawandtech.eu/en/2017/11/29/virtual-currency-exchange-licensing-in-greece/
55. Samuel Haig, *Hong Kong Exchange Tidebit Seeks to Capitalize Upon Chinese Cryptocurrency Crackdown*, Bitcoin.Com, Oct. 4, 2017, https://news.bitcoin.com/hong-kong-exchange-tidebit-seeks-to-capitalize-upon-chinese-cryptocurrency-crackdown/
56. *Jong Kong launches public education campaign on cryptocurrency and ICO risks*, Ecotimes, Feb. 2, 2018, https://www.econotimes.com/Hong-Kong-launches-public-education-campaign-on-cryptocurrency-and-ICO-risks-1130103
57. Hong Kong Securities and Futures Commission, *SFC warns of cryptocurrency risks*, Feb. 9, 2018, https://www.iosco.org/library/ico-statements/Hong%20Kong%20-%20SFC%20-%20Warning%20of%20Cryptocurrency%20Risks.pdf
58. *Hungary: Blockchain and Virtual Currency Regulation 2018*, Global Legal Insights, https://www.globallegalinsights.com/practice-areas/blockchain-laws-and-regulations/hungary

59. Jonathan Millet, *Hungarian National Bank Considers Virtual Currency Like Bitcoin Risky,* NEWSBTC, Feb. 19, 2014, http://www.newsbtc.com/2014/02/19/hungarian-national-bank-considers-virtual-currency-like-bitcoin-risky/

60. Ernst & Young, *Iceland Amends Foreign Exchange Act,* Global Tax Alert, http://www.ey.com/gl/en/services/tax/international-tax/alert--iceland-amends-foreign-exchange-act

61. Dan Falvey, *'DON'T invest in Bitcoin' warns Indian central bank despite surge in cryptocurrency value,* Express, Dec. 9, 2017, https://www.express.co.uk/finance/city/890101/bitcoin-cryptocurrency-investment-india-bank

62. Tarun Mittal, *What is Laxmicoin, possibly the first legal Indian cryptocurrency?* Yourstory, Nov. 22, 2017, https://yourstory.com/2017/11/what-is-laxmicoin-indian-cryptocurrency/

63. Bank Indonesia, Bank Indonesia Warns All Parties Not To Sell, Buy, or Trade Virtual Currency, Press Release, Jan. 18, 2018, http://www.bi.go.id/en/ruang-media/siaran-pers/Pages/sp_200418.aspx

64. Joshua Althauser, *Central Bank of Iran Plans Comprehensive Review of Cryptocurrency Policy,* Cointelegraph, Nov. 15, 2017, https://cointelegraph.com/news/central-bank-of-iran-plans-comprehensive-review-of-cryptocurrency-policy

65. *Regulation of Bitcoin in Selected Jurisdiction,* Library of Congress Law Library, https://www.loc.gov/law/help/bitcoin-survey/

66. Moti Bassok, Shelly Appleberg, and Reuters, *Bitcoin Is Risky, Israel Warns Amid Talk of Regulating Virtual Currency,* Haaretz, Feb. 20, 2014, https://www.haaretz.com/israel-news/business/1.575233

67. Stefano Capaccioli, *Central Bank of Italy Declares Virtual Currency Exchanges Are Not Subject to AML Requirements,* Bitcoinmagazine, Feb. 4, 2015, https://bitcoinmagazine.com/articles/central-bank-italy-declares-virtual-currency-exchanges-not-subject-aml-requirements-1423096093/

68. Article 2, §5 of Act on Financial Transactions that is part of the Virtual Currency Act. *The Virtual Currency Act explained,* Bitflyer, https://bitflyer.jp/en/virtual-currency-act

69. *Id.*

70. Act on Settlement of Funds as amended (Act No. 59 of 2009 as amended) cited by Makoto Koinuma, Koichiro Ohashi, and Yukari Sakamoto, *New Law & Regulations on Virtual Currencies in Japan,* Lexology, Jan. 24, 2017, https://www.lexology.com/library/detail.aspx?g=b32af680-1772-4983-8022-a2826878bcd5

71. Omar Obeidat, *Central bank warns against using bitcoin,* The Jordan Times, Feb. 22, 2014, http://www.jordantimes.com/news/local/central-bank-warns-against-using-bitcoin

72. Lisa Froelings, *Lebanese Central Bank Criticizes Bitcoin as "Unregulated" Commodities,* Cointelegraph, Oct. 29, 2017, https://cointelegraph.com/news/lebanese-central-bank-governor-criticizes-bitcoin-as-unregulated-commodities

73. Board of Bank of Lithuania, *Position of Bank of Lithuania On Virtual Currencies and Initial Coin Offering,* Oct. 10, 2017, https://www.lb.lt/uploads/documents/files/Pozicijos%20del%20virtualiu%20valiutu%20ir%20VV%20zetonu%20platinimo%20EN.pdf

74. Josee Weydert, Jad Nader, Vincent Wellens, and Nicolas Rase, *Luxembourg and European Developments on Bitcoins,* Lexology, June 26, 2014, https://www.lexology.com/library/detail.aspx?g=78bd56d2-bf6b-4823-a23f-332d13f827ba

75. Patrick Murck, *Luxembourg To Become European Virtual Currency Hub,* LuxembourgForFinance, Sept. 7, 2014, http://www.luxembourgforfinance.com/en/luxembourg-become-european-virtual-currency-hub

76. Joshua Althauser, *Malaysian Central Bank To Issue Cryptocurrency Regulation in Early 2018,* Cointelegraph, Nov. 24, 2017, https://cointelegraph.com/news/malaysian-central-bank-to-issue-cryptocurrency-regulation-in-early-2018

77. *Bank of Mexico Rejects 'Virtual Currency' as Legal Classification for Bitcoin,* News Bitcoin.Com, Jan. 6, 2018, Bitcoin.com, https://news.bitcoin.com/bank-of-mexico-rejects-virtual-currency-as-legal-classification-for-bitcoin/

78. *Mexican authorities warn cryptocurrency offerings could be a crime,* Reuters, Dec. 13, 2017, https://www.reuters.com/article/us-markets-bitcoin-mexico/mexican-authorities-warn-cryptocurrency-offerings-could-be-a-crime-idUSKBN1E72GV

79. Wendy Zeldin, *Netherlands: Central Bank Statement on Virtual Currencies,* Library of Congress Global Legal Monitor, June 4, 2014, http://www.loc.gov/law/foreign-news/article/netherlands-central-bank-statement-on-virtual-currencies/

80. Samuel Haig, *New Zealand Reserve Bank Lax on Cyber and Crypto Regulations,* Bitcoin.Com, July 23, 2017, https://news.bitcoin.com/new-zealand-reserve-bank-rejects-need-for-expansive-cryptocurrency-cyber-crime-regulations/

81. *Norway's Largest Online Bank Adopts Direct Bitcoin Integration,* CCN, May 16, 2017, https://www.ccn.com/banking-bitcoins-age-norway-bank-adopts-direct-bitcoin-integration/

82. Elin Hofberberg, *Bitcoins Are Capital Property, Not Currency, Says Norwegian Tax Authority,* Library of Congress Global Legal Monitor, Dec. 11, 2013, http://www.loc.gov/law/foreign-news/article/norway-bitcoins-are-capital-property-not-currency-says-norwegian-tax-authority/

83. Bangko Sentral NG Pilipinas, *Guidelines for Virtual Currency Exchanges,* Circular No. 944, Jan. 17, 2017, http://www.bsp.gov.ph/downloads/regulations/attachments/2017/c944.pdf

84. Alan, *The Central Bank of Poland Starts Campaign Against Virtual Currencies,* bitGuru, Jan. 2, 2018, http://bitguru.co.uk/polish-central-bank-starts-campaign-against-virtual-currencies/

85. Maryam Manzoor, *Polish Central Bank Creates Website Warning Investors Against Cryptocurrencies,* Cryptovest, Jan. 2, 2018, https://cryptovest.com/news/polish-central-bank-creates-website-warning-investors-against-cryptocurrencies/

86. Francisco Memoria, *Portugal's Central Bank Director: Bitcoin Isn't A Currency,* CCN, Nov. 9, 2017, https://www.ccn.com/portugals-central-bank-director-bitcoin-isnt-currency/

87. Gola Yashu, *Saudi Arabia's Regulators Not Looking to Regulate Bitcoin,* News BTC, Oct. 23, 2017, http://www.newsbtc.com/2017/10/23/saudi-arabia-not-looking-regulate-bitcoin/

88. *NBA Warns That Bitcoin is Not Legal Tender in Serbia,* National Bank of Serbia, Oct. 10, 2015, http://www.nbs.rs/internet/english/scripts/showContent.html?id=7607&konverzija=no

89. Monitory Authority of Singapore, MAS clarifies regulatory position on the offer of digital tokens in Singapore, Media Release, Aug. 1, 2017, http://www.mas.gov.sg/News-and-Publications/Media-Releases/2017/MAS-clarifies-regulatory-position-on-the-offer-of-digital-tokens-in-Singapore.aspx

90. Nermin Hajdarbegovic, *Slovenia Clarifies Position on Cryptocurrency Tax,* CoinDesk, Dec. 24, 2013, https://www.coindesk.com/slovenia-clarifies-position-cryptocurrency-tax/

91. South African Reserve Bank, *Position Paper on Virtual Currencies,* Position Paper No. 02/2014, Dec. 3, 2014, https://www.resbank.co.za/RegulationAndSupervision/NationalPaymentSystem(NPS)/Legal/Documents/Position%20Paper/Virtual%20Currencies%20Position%20Paper%20%20Final_02of2014.pdf

92. *Korean Court Rules Bitcoin Seizure as Illegal Confiscation,* Bitcoin Law, Sept. 11, 2017, https://www.ccn.com/korean-court-rules-bitcoin-seizure-illegal-confiscation/

93. *Why The Government Plans To Ban Cryptocurrency Trading, And What It Mean For Bitcoin,* Reuters quoted in Newsweek, Jan, 11, 2018, http://www.newsweek.com/why-south-korea-plans-ban-cryptocurrency-trading-and-what-it-means-bitcoin-777782

94. Christine Kim, *South Korea inspects six banks over virtual currency services to clients,* Reuters, Jan. 8, 2018, https://www.reuters.com/article/us-southkorea-bitcoin/south-korea-inspects-six-banks-over-virtual-currency-services-to-clients-idUSKBN1EX0BG

95. Nam Hyun-woo, *Constitutional Court to decide on digital token,* The Korea Times, Jan. 1, 2018, http://www.koreatimes.co.kr/www/biz/2018/01/488_241850.html

96. Alajandro Gomez de la Cruz, *Bitcoin is exempt from VAT in Spain,* Law & Bitcoin, April 16, 2015, http://lawandbitcoin.com/en/bitcoin-is-vat-exempt-in-spain/

97. *Virtual Currencies,* Sveriges Riksbank, https://www.riksbank.se/en-gb/financial-stability/the-financial-system/payments/virtual-currencies/

98. *Sweden could be first with national digital currency,* RT, Nov. 16, 2016, https://www.rt.com/business/367141-sweden-digital-currency-launch/

99. Swiss Confederation, *Federal Council report on virtual currencies in response to the Schwaab (13.3687) and Weibel (13.4070) postulates,* June 25, 2014, http://www.news.admin.ch/NSBSubscriber/message/attachments/35355.pdf

100. Leyva Guillermo Beltran, *Taiwan Declares Bitcoin an Illegal Asset,* Nov. 2, 2015, http://www.newsbtc.com/2015/11/02/taiwan-declares-bitcoin-illegal-asset/

101. David Green, *UPDATE: Taiwan Must Be Brave on Cryptocurrency Stance,* The News Lens, Oct. 7, 2017, https://international.thenewslens.com/article/80463

102. Kavitha A. Davidson, *Bank of Thailand Bans Bitcoins,* TheWorldPost, July 31, 2012, https://www.huffingtonpost.com/2013/07/31/thailand-bans-bitcoins_n_3682553.html

103. Cristoph Marckx, *Bank of Thailand issues another statement on Bitcoin,* CCN, March 18, 2014, https://www.ccn.com/bank-of-thailand-issues-another-statement-on-bitcoin/

104. Gonenc Gurkaynak, Ceren Yildez, and Ecem Elver, *Banking Regulation And Supervision Agency's Guidance: How To Deal With Global Players*

And Bitcoin In Turkey?, Elig, Oct. 6, 2015, http://www.mondaq.com/turkey/x/432212/Financial+Services/Banking+Regulation+And+Supervision+Agencys+Guidance+How+To+Deal+With+Global+Players+And+Bitcoin+In+Turkey

105. Ed Clowes, *UAE Central Bank clarifies virtual currency ban*, Gulf News, Feb. 1, 2017, http://gulfnews.com/business/sectors/banking/uae-central-bank-clarifies-virtual-currency-ban-1.1971802

106. *Bitcoin and other virtual currencies on Scotland Yard's radar because of money laundering*, MercoPress, Dec. 5, 2017, http://en.mercopress.com/2017/12/05/bitcoin-and-other-virtual-currencies-on-scotland-yard-radar-because-of-money-laundering

107. Peter Howitt, David Borge, John Pauley, and Subherwal Patel, *Virtual Currencies in the UK*, Ramparts Lexology, Oct. 16, 2017, https://www.lexology.com/library/detail.aspx?g=20736649-246a-4526-8ad0-3b4f309fc88d

108. HM Treasury, *Digital currencies: response to the call for information*, March, 2015, https://www.gov.uk/government/uploads/system/uploads/attachment_data/file/414040/digital_currencies_response_to_call_for_information_final_changes.pdf

109. *Id.*

110. *Virtual Currencies and Ponzi Schemes in Vietnam*, News BTC, Oct. 7, 2016, https://www.newsbtc.com/2016/10/07/virtual-currencies-ponzi-schemes-vietnam/

111. Jamie Redman, *Vietnam May See Virtual Regulation Soon*, Bitcoin.Com, Dec. 6, 2016, https://news.bitcoin.com/vietnam-virtual-currency-regulation-soon/

112. *Why Bangladesh will jail Bitcoin traders*, The Telegraph, Sept. 14, 2017, http://www.telegraph.co.uk/finance/currency/11097208/Why-Bangladesh-will-jail-Bitcoin-traders.html

113. Dan Cummings, *Bolivian Officials Detain Users of Virtual Currency*, ETHNews, May 31, 2017, https://www.ethnews.com/bolivian-officials-detain-users-of-virtual-currency

114. Yulu Yilun Chen and Justina Lee, *Bitcoin Tumbles as PBOC Declares Initial Coin Offerings Illegal*, Bloomberg, Sept. 4, 2017, https://www.bloomberg.com/news/articles/2017-09-04/china-central-bank-says-initial-coin-offerings-are-illegal

115. *Notice of Seven Ministries Including the People's Bank of China on Guard against Risks of Token Offering and Finance* (Joint Notice) (Sept. 2, 2017). *Notice on the Rectification of Token Offering and Financing Activities* (Zheng Zhi Ban Han (Sept. 4, 2017), No. 99. The notices in

Chinese may be found in Michael House, Geoffrey Vance, and Huijie Shao, *China Halts ICOs and Token Sales and China-Based Trading Platforms Suspend Trading Amid Reports*, Perkins Coie Virtual Currency Report, Sept. 18, 2017, https://www.virtualcurrencyreport.com/ 2017/09/china-halts-icos-and-token-sales-and-china-based-trading-platforms-suspend-trading-amid-reports-of-additional-government-restrictions/ of Additional Government Restrictions.

116. *Id.*
117. *Id.*
118. Lulu Yilun Chen and Yuji Nakamura, *China's bitcoin barons seek new life in Japan and Hong Kong*, Bloomberg, Oct. 29, 2017, https://www. japantimes.co.jp/news/2017/10/29/business/chinas-bitcoin-barons-seek-new-life-japan-hong-kong/#.Whq-Kk2WzIU
119. Stan Higgins, *Ecuador Bans Bitcoin, Plans Own Digital Money*, CoinDesk, July 25, 2014, https://www.coindesk.com/ecuador-bans-bitcoin-legislative-vote/
120. Kyrgyz Bank, *Warning of the National Bank of the Kyrgyz Republic on the spread and use of the 'virtual currency', in particular, bitcoins (bitcoin)*, July 18, 2014, http://www.nbkr.kg/searchout.jsp?item=31&material=5 0718&lang=ENG
121. Jon Southurst, *Using Bitcoin and Virtual Currencies Is Illegal, Says Morocco Central Bank*, Bitsonline, Nov. 20, 2017, https://t.me/ bitsonline
122. *Bitsewa Exchange Closes as Nepal Takes Hard Line on Bitcoin*, DCEBrief, Oct. 9, 2017, https://dcebrief.com/bitsewa-exchange-closes-as-nepal-takes-hard-line-on-bitcoin/
123. Nathaniel Popper, *Russia and Venezuela's Plan to Sidestep Sanctions: Virtual Currencies* New York Times, Jan. 3, 2018, https://www.nytimes. com/2018/01/03/technology/russia-venezuela-virtual-currencies. html?_r=0
124. Eurasian Economic Union (EEU) is composed of member countries comprising Belarus, Kazakhstan, and Russia pursuant to a treaty that was signed on May 29, 2014, which became effective as of January 1, 2015 and to which Armenia and Kyrgyzstan acceded in late 2014.
125. *Russia suggest creating single virtual currency for BRICS and EEU*, Reuters, Dec. 28, 2017, https://www.rt.com/business/414444-brics-eeu-joint-cryptocurrency/

Conclusion: The Future of Cryptocurrencies

As the technological universe becomes increasingly complex, there appears to be little doubt that the use of paper and metallic money may encounter the transition seen in the communications sector as evidenced by the decline of paper news offerings and bricks-and-mortar shopping. Banks and other financial institutions, while bemoaning and disparaging Bitcoin and other upstarts—as Jamie Dimon the famed CEO of JP Morgan Chase characterized Bitcoin as a fraud and doomed to failure[1]— nevertheless, have begun to join forces to pool resources to identify and evaluate the technology and its potential uses to improve efficiency and security. The CEO of Morgan Stanley, James Gorman, takes a more cautionary position, stating that Bitcoin is more than a fad, citing its attributes of anonymity and privacy.[2]

As identified by the recently appointed Federal Reserve Chairperson, Jerome H. Powell, the latest technological innovation should enable payment systems to address significant legal, operational, and financial risks as well as information security and privacy. The streamlined system using Distributed Ledger Technology (DLT) will lead to faster processing, reduced reconciliation, and a reduction in the capital and liquidity costs of operations. As with all innovative advances, Powell noted that digital currency is a prime target as a potential vehicle for global criminal

© The Author(s) 2018
R. Girasa, *Regulation of Cryptocurrencies and Blockchain Technologies*, Palgrave Studies in Financial Services Technology, https://doi.org/10.1007/978-3-319-78509-7_9

activities such as money laundering, raises privacy concerns, and puts bank in competition with private sector products and systems.[3] Jamie Dimon's claim may in part be attributable to a fear that banks will be substantially less needed for monetary transactions due to DLT's avoidance of third-party mechanisms to transact payments coupled with significantly greater protection by making hacking almost impossible. Thus, rather than inveighing against the new technologies, banks and other financial institutions will have to adapt to and gain from them.[4]

There are suggestions that central banks should adopt the innovations and issue their own digital currencies as the current century's analogue to paper currency. Fed Governor Randal K. Quarles cautions that: central banks, particularly in the United States, which have highly developed banking systems and robust demands for physical cash, should proceed slowly, instituting extensive reviews and consultations about legal issues; the inherent risks attendant thereto; the deployment of unproven technology; privacy matters; money laundering; and a host of other difficulties. There is a grave danger that such issuance would be subject to cyberattacks, terrorist financing, and be disruptive to other global banking sectors. Potentially, deposits could shrink considerably thereby preventing banks from making loans and providing liquidity to the financial sector. Rather than issue its own virtual currency, banks should become increasingly more innovative and competitive by providing around-the-clock internet-based access to accounts, mobile banking, and other payment capabilities.[5]

The practice of law will undergo major innovative changes that are already on the horizon. Courts have adapted to internet technologies by filing court documents online rather than by hard copies with the clerk's offices; and trials are being transformed with electronic introduction of evidence rather than the slow methodology previously used in most court. Smart contracts are now replacing older modes as exemplified by Barclays Bank's adoption of R3 technology with its introduction of Corda, a new DLT platform that creates templates for smart contracts that will expedite their formation at a minimal cost. Barclays is also experimenting with expedited banking services using Ethereum blockchain with 11 R3 member banks.[6] The Pentagon is exploring blockchain technology to create a secure and impenetrable messaging service.[7] Christine Lagarde, the managing director of the International Monetary

Fund (IMF), stated that a priority of the IMF is to combat terrorism that will require "harnessing the power of financial technology…" which has been used to conceal the identity of virtual currencies but also may be used to make the financial system less vulnerable to attack and able to identify terrorist financial flows.[8]

It is understandable that innovation creates new opportunities for industry and employment of personnel but also leaves in its place losses to both, requiring retraining and reorientation of the sectors of the economy most affected. Even the most brilliant managers, such as Dimon, who may initially be correct about the Bitcoin bubble, will have to adapt to the technological revolution that is growing exponentially, causing significant disruptions but also affording positive benefits as do new strategies. Among the problems that regulators will continue to encounter is the ability to keep up with technological changes that are occurring at an exponential pace and which will have disastrous consequences if unchecked.[9] Predicting what will occur in the future is almost a useless endeavor given the changes wrought over the past two decades. A likely scenario, as posited by one commentator, is the transformation of blockchain technology from exploration and development in 2015, early adoption in 2016–17, growth in 2018–24, and maturity thereafter.[10]

Governments will have to determine to what degree they will permit the blockchain digital transformation process and the use of cryptocurrency. As one author notes, there are a number of ways for governments to impede the growth of the new technology. Among them is the extreme view of banning cryptocurrency, as in China today; taxing it so as to make it financially not viable; attack it with other technologies to be developed; cast doubt as to its usefulness such as by propagating the view that it is primarily used to commit unlawful acts; or use its financial power to buy and sell cryptocurrencies causing major disruptions in its price structures.[11] It appears, however, that governments, rather than impeding, are acclimating and encouraging its use, finding it beneficial particularly in the creation of greater transparency in reporting and taxation of transactions. With respect to the North American Free Trade Agreement, President Donald Trump has expressed serious reservations concerning its renewal and wishes to renegotiate many of its terms. Mexico, as part of the renegotiations through its undersecretary Vanessa

Rubio of the Finance Ministry, stated that the focus should be on new FinTech companies and the new services emanating from them.[12]

Will the new technologies lead to a greater democratization of the global political landscape as posited by one commentator citing the decentralization and more egalitarian features of cryptocurrencies?[13] There is little doubt that former closed societies, such as China and Russia when part of the Soviet Union, have been radically transformed by the Internet. It can only be speculated as to what will occur with respect to the future development of the global economies that will either remain on the sidelines while the rest of the world advances in technological breakthroughs or join in the spread of new forms of currencies and methodologies for the transfer of assets.

A more interesting, possible futuristic, trend is whether quantum computing will replace Bitcoin and other comparable cryptocurrencies. As one observer noted, while the chance of randomly guessing the private key of a user of the SHA-265 algorithm (e.g. Bitcoin) is one in 115 quattuorvigintillion (i.e., 115×10^{75}), quantum computing may reduce the odds to 1 in 14.[14] There are estimates that Bitcoin as well as all encryption could be compromised within 10 years. Quantum computing may then be able to calculate the private key using the public key, which currently cannot be accomplished.[15] Bitcoin's response is that creating a quantum computer will be a massive scientific and engineering undertaking. At present, quantum computers have less than 10 qubits whereas to attack Bitcoin, would require 1500 qubits. It is unlikely that such a computer can be created before 2030–40 at which time current research into failproof algorithms will have made the system unbreakable.[16]

Notes

1. Hugh Son, Hannah Levitt, and Brian Louis, *Jamie Dimon Slams Bitcoin as a 'Fraud'*, Bloomberg, Sept. 12, 2017, https://www.bloomberg.com/news/articles/2017-09-12/jpmorgan-s-ceo-says-he-d-fire-traders-who-bet-on-fraud-Bitcoin
2. Hugh Son, *Bitcoin 'More Than Just a Fad', Morgan Stanley CEO Says*, Bloomberg, Sept. 27, 2017, https://www.bloomberg.com/news/articles/2017-09-27/bitcoin-more-than-just-a-fad-morgan-stanley-ceo-gorman-says

3. Governor Jerome H. Powell, *Innovation, Technology*, and the Payments System, Mar. 3, 2017, https://www.federalreserve.gov/newsevents/speech/powell20170303a.htm
4. Nick Bolton, *Should Jamie Dimon Be Terrified About Bitcoin?*, Hive, Vanity Fair, Sept. 13, 2017, https://www.vanityfair.com/news/2017/09/should-jamie-dimon-be-terrified-about-Bitcoin
5. Randal K. Quarles, *supra* at c. 4, note 92.
6. Pete Rizzo, *How Barclays Used R3's Tech to Build a Smart Contracts Prototype*, Coindesk, Apr. 26, 2016, https://www.coindesk.com/barclays-smart-contracts-templates-demo-r3-corda/
7. Joshua Althauser, *Pentagon Thinks Blockchain Technology Can Be Used as Cybersecurity Shield*, Cointelegraph, Aug. 20, 2017, https://cointelegraph.com/news/pentagon-thinks-blockchain-technology-can-be-used-as-cybersecurity-shield
8. Christine Lagarde, *Working Together to Fight Money Laundering & Terrorist Financing* Speech at FATF Plenary Meeting, June 22, 2017, http://www.fatf-gafi.org/media/fatf/documents/speeches/Speech-IMF-MD-Christine-Lagarde-22June2017.pdf
9. See, for example, comments by Gary Coleman citing World Economic Forum agenda, *How we can regulate the digital revolution?* Reuters, Mar. 29, 2017, https://www.weforum.org/agenda/2017/03/how-can-we-regulate-the-digital-revolution/
10. Divya Joshi, *How the laws & regulation affecting blockchain technology can affect its adoption*, Business Insider, Oct. 20, 2017, http://www.businessinsider.com/blockchain-cryptocurrency-regulations-us-global-2017-10
11. Tim Lea. Tim Lea, *Could quantum computing make crypto currencies valueless?* Quora, https://www.quora.com/Could-quantum-computing-make-crypto-currencies-valueless
12. Emerging Technology, *Quantum Computers Pose an Imminent Threat to Bitcoin Security*, MIT Technology Review, Nov. 8, 2017, https://www.technologyreview.com/s/609408/quantum-computers-pose-imminent-threat-to-bitcoin-security/
13. *Quantum computing and Bitcoin*, Bitcoinwiki, https://en.bitcoin.it/wiki/Quantum_computing_and_Bitcoin
14. Steemit, *10 Ways Government Could Stop Cryptocurrencies*, https://steemit.com/cryptocurrencies/@thehutchreport/10-ways-governments-could-stop-cryptocurrencies

15. Anthony Esposito, NAFTA talks must include discussion on fintech: Mexican negotiator, Reuters, Aug. 16, 2017, https://www.reuters.com/article/us-trade-nafta-mexico/nafta-talks-must-include-discussion-on-fintech-mexican-negotiator-idUSKCN1AX03Z?il=0

16. Steven Johnson, *Beyond the Bitcoin Bubble*, New York Times Magazine, Jan. 21, 2018, 37–41, 52

Appendix 1: How Bitcoins Enter into Circulation and Are Used in Transactions

© The Author(s) 2018
R. Girasa, *Regulation of Cryptocurrencies and Blockchain Technologies*, Palgrave Studies
in Financial Services Technology, https://doi.org/10.1007/978-3-319-78509-7

Bitcoin Miners

Bitcoin miners essentially serve two purposes: 1) generating new bitcoins to enter into circulation and 2) verifying transactions by ensuring that they occurred and did not involve double spending of a bitcoin. Over time, the computer processing power needed to mine new bitcoins has increased to the point where mining requires specialized computer hardware and has become increasingly consolidated into large mining pools.

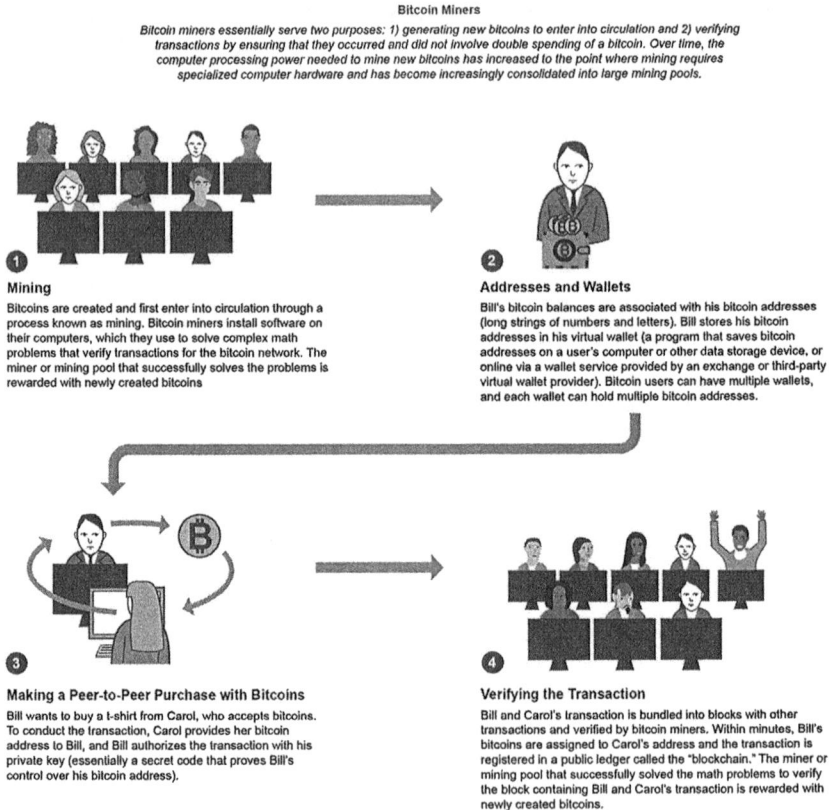

① Mining

Bitcoins are created and first enter into circulation through a process known as mining. Bitcoin miners install software on their computers, which they use to solve complex math problems that verify transactions for the bitcoin network. The miner or mining pool that successfully solves the problems is rewarded with newly created bitcoins

② Addresses and Wallets

Bill's bitcoin balances are associated with his bitcoin addresses (long strings of numbers and letters). Bill stores his bitcoin addresses in his virtual wallet (a program that saves bitcoin addresses on a user's computer or other data storage device, or online via a wallet service provided by an exchange or third-party virtual wallet provider). Bitcoin users can have multiple wallets, and each wallet can hold multiple bitcoin addresses.

③ Making a Peer-to-Peer Purchase with Bitcoins

Bill wants to buy a t-shirt from Carol, who accepts bitcoins. To conduct the transaction, Carol provides her bitcoin address to Bill, and Bill authorizes the transaction with his private key (essentially a secret code that proves Bill's control over his bitcoin address).

④ Verifying the Transaction

Bill and Carol's transaction is bundled into blocks with other transactions and verified by bitcoin miners. Within minutes, Bill's bitcoins are assigned to Carol's address and the transaction is registered in a public ledger called the "blockchain." The miner or mining pool that successfully solved the math problems to verify the block containing Bill and Carol's transaction is rewarded with newly created bitcoins.

*Government Accountability Office, *Virtual Currencies: Emerging Regulatory, Law Enforcement, and Consumer Protection Challenges,* Report to the Committee on Homeland Security and Governmental Affairs, U.S. Senate, GAO-14-496 (May, 2014), at 42, https://www.gao.gov/assets/670/663678.pdf

Appendix 2: SEC Commissioner Jay Clayton's List of Questions Investors Should Ask Before Engaging in Cryptocurrencies[1]

Who exactly am I contracting with?

- Who is issuing and sponsoring the product, what are their backgrounds, and have they provided a full and complete description of the product? Do they have a clear written business plan that I understand?
- Who is promoting or marketing the product, what are their backgrounds, and are they licensed to sell the product? Have they been paid to promote the product?
- Where is the enterprise located?

Where is my money going and what will be it be used for? Is my money going to be used to "cash out" others?
What specific rights come with my investment?
Are there financial statements? If so, are they audited, and by whom?
Is there trading data? If so, is there some way to verify it?
How, when, and at what cost can I sell my investment? For example, do I have a right to give the token or coin back to the company or to receive a refund? Can I resell the coin or token, and if so, are there any limitations on my ability to resell?

© The Author(s) 2018
R. Girasa, *Regulation of Cryptocurrencies and Blockchain Technologies*, Palgrave Studies in Financial Services Technology, https://doi.org/10.1007/978-3-319-78509-7

If a digital wallet is involved, what happens if I lose the key? Will I still have access to my investment?

If a blockchain is used, is the blockchain open and public? Has the code been published, and has there been an independent cybersecurity audit?

Has the offering been structured to comply with the securities laws and, if not, what implications will that have for the stability of the enterprise and the value of my investment?

What legal protections may or may not be available in the event of fraud, a hack, malware, or a downturn in business prospects? Who will be responsible for refunding my investment if something goes wrong?

If I do have legal rights, can I effectively enforce them and will there be adequate funds to compensate me if my rights are violated?

Note

1. Jay Clayton, Statement on Cryptocurrencies and Initial Coin Offerings (Dec. 11, 2017), SEC Public Statement, https://www.sec.gov/news/public-statement/statement-clayton-2017-12-11

Index[1]

---

[1] Note: Page numbers followed by 'n' refer to notes.

© The Author(s) 2018   **257**
R. Girasa, *Regulation of Cryptocurrencies and Blockchain Technologies*, Palgrave Studies
in Financial Services Technology, https://doi.org/10.1007/978-3-319-78509-7